AN INDOMITABLE SPIRIT

AN INDOMITABLE SPIRIT

STORIES ABOUT LIFE BY SIDNEY D. LOWE
Son of the Mountains, Marine and Navy Vet

Edited by LINDA LOWE

Published by
Linda Lowe
PROSPECT, KENTUCKY
Laldegraaff@gmail.com

ISBN-13: 979-8-218-63695-1

Copyright © 2025 by Linda Lowe

All rights reserved. This book or any portion thereof may not be reproduced or used in any manner whatsoever without the express written permission of the publisher, except for the use of brief quotations embodied in critical articles or book reviews.

For Myrtle Mae Boggs Lowe
(1886–1938)

"The indomitable human spirit" refers to the quality of unwavering perseverance and resilience in the face of adversity, essentially the unbreakable strength within a person that allows them to overcome challenges and never give up, no matter how difficult the situation.

Contents

Preface..xi

PART 1. WEST VIRGINIA MEMORIES 1925–1942

Goose for Christmas Dinner.................................3

A Family-Values System 5

Samantha...8

Maintaining Neighborly Relations......................10

Where Have All the Bedbugs Gone? 12

First Crush...14

Living in the Shadow..16

The Mill 18

Night Terrors..22

George, the Stunt Man.......................................24

Gigging Johnson Creek......................................26

Going Around the Gin Pole 28

George Drives a Hard Bargain...........................30

Target Practice 32

The Watermelon...33

A Chance Encounter 35

The Swimming Lesson 38

A Lesson in Larceny...40

Reaching for Immortality 43

For Love of Huckleberry Finn 45

Emergency Rations 52

Ancil's Baptism 54

Uncle Mart..57

Houston...64

I Become a Fireman 69

Coffin Nails..71

"Uncle" Dick...74

"If Ye Ain't, Hanner, Don't!" 78

The Fish That Caught Me 80

The Summersville Courthouse Incident.............................85

PART 2. **SEMPER FI 1942–1945**

"Do Ye Know Where Looneyville's Ay-ut?" 101

The Pot Walloper.. 102

Fire in the Hole!... 106

Doing The Laundry, Marine Corps Style 109

The Battle of Tarawa 113

From Innocence to Reality................................... 123

It's My Party 127

A Moment of Sheer Terror.................................... 129

Love Battery 134

Fox Battery... 144

Dangerous Dan McGrew.. 161

Shelter Buddies 163

The Laziest Man Alive 168

A Good Night to Die 171

Farewell to Arms.. 176

War's End 182

PART 3. A SAILOR'S LIFE AND BEYOND 1945–2013

Stumbling Toward Paradise, Part 1 187
Stumbling Towards Paradise, Part 2 192
The Case of the Elusive Exhortation 195
I Baptize Thee . . . For Sure! 199
Travels with Tiger 202
Out of the Mouths of Babes 204
The Prosecution of Mary Randolph 205
The Proper Baptism of the Padre 211
A California Interlude 215
On the Way to Okinawa 217
Ships I Have Known and . . . Loved? 227
Transition: Hills to Sea to Desert 252
The Wedding Fee 254
The Honeymoon That Wasn't 256
Stroke! 259

❋

Afterword: Homeward Bound 277
Acknowledgments 297
Photo Credits 299

Preface

"I was born at Gandeeville, Roane County, West Virginia, on March 28, 1925, the seventh child of Thomas Hoyt and Myrtle (Boggs) Lowe. My brother Darrell lobbied mightily for me to be given his name, but the consensus among those present was that two Darrells would be entirely too many; Dale was a compromise. My eldest sister had studied in school about Sydney, Australia, and thought it a most romantic and exotic name. My poor mother, perhaps jaded by the naming of too many children, had no overriding concern in the matter. Thus, Sidney Dale Lowe I became."*

So began the life of my father, a man who was born just before the Great Depression, lost his mother at thirteen, and survived a fire that destroyed his family home at fifteen. He then lived with a succession of family members, lastly with his sister Maudie, who took in the three surviving children of their sister Evelyn when she was killed in a house fire with two of her other children.

Already sensing it was time to move on, he was given a push by Fate when unfairly expelled from school. Unable to bear this humiliation, he walked off the school grounds, straight into the U.S. Marine Corps recruiting center—and adulthood. Only seventeen, he was shipped from boot camp directly to American Samoa then to one of the most gruesome battles of World War II, the Battle of Tarawa.

We know of these things because my father was a prolific writer and storyteller, who captured his life experiences on the page in a way that reveals not only important events of his life, but the kind of man he was.

---

*From the early writings of Sydney Dale Lowe.

In *An Indomitable Spirit,* we read about the mountain boy growing up in rural West Virginia during the Depression, the marine who learned firsthand the realities of war, the coal miner, the family man, and the adventures of a navy chaplain. We learn that ships can be "happy" or "unhappy"—from a man who served aboard twenty-eight vessels in twenty-six years at sea. And we get to witness the profound struggle of a man struck down by a stroke late in life, whose indomitable spirit gave my family and me the chance to spend twelve precious years with him, in New Mexico and Kentucky, both as caretakers and recipients of his grace and inspiration.

Before he died, I promised my dad that I would put his writings into a book. I hope I have done his work and his life justice. May all who read this feel the greatness of this man and the blessing of his heart.

Linda Lowe
Louisville, Kentucky
March 2025

PART 1

West Virginia Memories 1925–1942

Goose for Christmas Dinner

Ours was a very primitive farmstead by today's standards, as were most rural homes of that time. We did have central heat—a huge old wood-fueled Burnside stove located in the center of the living room. There was no running water closer than the creek, which meant that there were no indoor plumbing facilities. Fresh water for drinking and cooking purposes came from a nearby spring.

Outdoor privies served their intended purpose for our family and for the other homes in the area. Typically located on and extending over the creek bank, these amenities depended on the rising waters, after the frequent rains, for their cleansing and flushing effect. Each year saw predictable outbreaks of typhoid fever and diphtheria, though there was limited understanding of the cause-and-effect relationship between the sanitary facilities and those devastating waterborne diseases.

One of my earliest memories has to do with hurried wintertime trips to the outdoor toilet. At that time, at least in our area, most little boys wore a short-waisted blouse and short pants that buttoned to the blouse. When the call of nature was felt, my mother would unbutton and remove my pants, then send me racing bare bottomed for the toilet, all pennants and appendages flying in the brisk wind.

Enter the goose—a very large and ill-tempered gander that regularly mistook my exposed physical parts for a wiggling caterpillar or a small white grub worm. Given a good running start, I was usually able to reach the safety of the outhouse before he reached the worm!

One cold December day, the frozen ground was covered by a few inches of new-fallen snow—enough to significantly retard my progress toward my intended goal. I can still see that goose—half running, half flying across the winter landscape like a runaway freight train, intent on making a meal of the gift Nature had supplied. I lay in the snow, screaming and struggling, until Mom came to my rescue. I suppose no real damage was done, but I have always felt that I might have grown into a decent-size man had it not been for that darned goose!

That evening Mom said to my father, "Tommy, we always have ham or turkey for Christmas dinner. This year, why don't we cook a goose instead?"

Ahh, the sweetness of revenge—to eat him who would have eaten me. It was the best Christmas dinner I ever had.

A Family-Values System

The term *family values* has, in the 1990s, become something of a social and political buzzword, to the detriment of *genuine* family values. Politicians, religionists, sociologists, and others at the cutting edge of social change speak much of family values.

Unfortunately, they seem obliged to define those values and to determine how they should be taught and promoted, as though their actions and beliefs should become universal law. In doing so, they negate the very thing they seek to promote.

At best, the term means a code of conduct, defined and taught by precept and example at the grassroots level—within the actual family unit. Then, and perhaps only then, does a child assimilate and internalize those values under the guidance of parents who practice the same.

Such values cannot be codified and imposed by decree. In fact, they cannot be imposed at all. They can only be accepted or rejected on the basis of one's personal experience within that family as its members act and interact.

Growing up in the late 1920s and '30s in our rural West Virginia community, we were exposed to a rigidly defined and strictly practiced family-value system. Its effectiveness was enhanced by being shared by most of the families in the community, since most shared a common ethnic, social, and economic background and status. I suppose there must have been some minor differences in how those values were taught, especially in how the various elements were ranked in importance, but by and large, it was a very uniform assessment of the eternal fitness of things.

In our family, the primary values upheld were:

1. Strict obedience to parental demands, characterized by instant compliance. Disagreement was sometimes tolerated; disobedience, never.

2. *Family loyalty, extending beyond the nuclear family to include aunts, uncles, and even distant cousins.* Since one's support system came from the family, few things were more important to the survival and well-being of all.

3. *Respect for one's elders.* Adults were addressed as "Sir" and "Ma'am"; elderly acquaintances were called "Uncle" and "Aunt," blood relationships notwithstanding.

4. *Honesty, dependability, and keeping one's promises.* Deals were concluded with a handshake; the highest of commendations was "his word is as good as his bond." Contracts were for situations in which mutual trust did not exist—for banks, lawyers, and others one did not trust. Since one would be a fool to do business with an untrustworthy person, contracts were superfluous. A request for a written agreement between friends amounted to a personal insult and was sufficient reason to terminate the friendship.

5. *Children are to be seen, not heard.* Comments and opinions were welcomed only from those mature enough to have something worth saying. All others were expected to keep their silence.

Further down the list, perhaps, but not to be minimized, were the following:

6. *Be stoic and self-contained.* Do not permit your actions to produce trouble for yourself or others. Never burden others with your problems or get yourself in difficulty so deeply that you can't get out. Don't whimper, don't complain, and even if you're hurting, don't *ever* let them see you sweat!

7. *Don't try to "rise above your raisin'."* This *meant* don't feel that you are better than others, but it was often *perceived* as an injunction against trying to improve one's situation. This is the only maxim cited here with which I disagree.

8. *Don't tell lies about your neighbor.* Don't engage in malicious gossip, which only hurts others. If you can't say something good, say nothing.

This last, while often violated, was an important lubricant to smoothly operating community relationships. It must have assumed a very high place on my mother's view of the "eternal fitness of things," for I rarely remember her sounding off about a neighbor, and then only on extreme provocation.

I am compelled to inject a word of appreciation and admiration for my mother, Myrtle, whose foresight, management skills, and sheer grit and tenacity prevailed against nearly impossible odds. Through the most discouraging times and in the emotionally depressing circumstances of her situation, she seemed to know that we could endure, and it was largely due to her survival skills that we were able to do so.

I wish that I could acquit myself half as well.

Thomas and Myrtle on their wedding day, 1907

Samantha

After Sunday services in our community church, most families practiced the old custom of "visiting around"; one family would invite another home for dinner, followed by an afternoon of pleasant talk for the adults and quiet play for the children.

A neighboring family who often attended services yet was rarely extended social invitations was that of a woman believed by some to be of questionable morals, whom we shall call Samantha.

Samantha's husband had become disabled, and the family subsisted on a small state pension of a few dollars a month, which Samantha allegedly augmented as she had opportunity. The community's shunning of one of its members troubled my mother. She believed that "if you give a dog a bad name, he'll justify it."

Always a champion of the underdog, and ready to give the benefit of any doubt, Mom, one memorable Sunday, invited Samantha and her family to come home with us for dinner.

We children knew all about Samantha's reputation, and we were sure that Mom had taken leave of her senses; still, we quickly became engrossed in play with the visiting children until called for dinner. We had stewed chicken with dumplings, an all-time favorite dish, with mashed potatoes and gravy, green beans, and an assortment of cakes and pies.

As we began hungrily devouring the delicious meal, Mom asked casually, "Aren't the chicken and dumplings good? Samantha fixed them while I did the potatoes and beans." Instant shock registered on the faces of "our" children and, without asking permission, we all rushed outside, gagging and retching in an attempt to purge our stomachs of the food tainted by Samantha's touch.

Of course, Samantha was embarrassed, but Mom was scandalized and outraged by our shockingly rude behavior toward a guest. She quickly interrupted the purging party, marched us all back into the dining room, and demanded that we apologize to our guest, insisting that we do so instantly, abjectly, and individually.

After the visitors went home, we were lined up and thoroughly whipped. Although decried today, physical punishment was not only permitted but often encouraged by the family values of the time, in the belief that the shortest route to a child's heart and mind was *via* the backside. We were duly instructed in the error of our ways.

We were also advised of a few facts of life of which we were lamentably unaware. Mom acknowledged that not everyone in the community approved of Samantha's alleged manner of making a living by selling her most personal commodity. But even if the rumors were true, she was only doing what she must to support her family in the only way open to her, and she cared for her family better than some of those who felt that they were above associating with her. If others had trouble with that, then those people had a bigger problem than Samantha who, after all, was basically a good person and a good neighbor, always willing to aid those who needed a helping hand.

The bottom line: Whatever Samantha's behavior, it did not justify ours. We were never to repeat our disgraceful and unforgivable behavior. Neither were we ever to forget the lessons of Samantha's sacrifices.

Rocky Branch Church, where we went to church with Samantha and her family. Women entered the left door; men, the right door.

Maintaining Neighborly Relations

Most of our neighbors were good, honest, and caring people. They did not intrude unduly on others, no doubt feeling that their own troubles were sufficient, though they were always happy to help where help was needed. One's reputation was built, in large part, on neighborliness; that is, if a neighbor fell ill or if a disaster struck, one's own concerns were put aside while the neighbor's crisis was dealt with. Most were good neighbors to one another but, unfortunately, not all.

One man in the community seemed to believe that his own existence was validated only to the degree that he could make life more difficult for others. He was a peeping Tom, a child molester, and an opportunistic thief, often stealing garden produce, stock feed, and even things that had no value to him. Living close by, we were frequent victims of his avarice. He has been dead for many years, so I will not identify him here. Those who knew him will know of whom I speak.

My mother always raised a generous supply of popcorn in her garden. It was an old type of "rice" corn, much inferior to the hybrids grown today. When harvested, it had to be thoroughly dried for several days to prevent spoilage, usually on newspapers spread under the kitchen range.

In the winter of 1931, a friend sent Mom a few grains of a new and superior type of popcorn. That spring, the precious grains were planted and tended with the greatest of care. The vigorous stalks grew taller and bore larger ears than any we had ever grown. They would mature until the first frost, when they would be harvested and dried, becoming the seed supply for a much larger crop the following season. They were her pride and joy, and several friends had already been promised a "start" of the new seed as she anticipated the pleasure of sharing with them.

The first frost came. Mom hastened to her garden to harvest the precious new seed, only to discover that someone had been there in the night and not an ear of corn remained. She was a gentle and soft-spoken woman, yet those who considered her a pushover were badly mistaken.

Later that day she received a request from our neighbor's wife. She was sick, and would my mother please come and help her with her housework? Of course she would, without question.

Leaving her own chores, she hastened to do what she could to help. She washed the breakfast dishes and prepared to sweep and mop the kitchen floor. She glanced under the kitchen range and there, carefully spread out on newspapers to dry, was her hoard of popcorn! It was hers without doubt, for she had the only seed of its type in the community.

This was a delicate matter, requiring very careful thought.

She said not a word as she finished cleaning the neighbor's house. Not wishing to provoke a quarrel, yet being unwilling to leave matters as they were, she prepared to leave. She gathered the ears of corn in her apron and walked into the sickroom to say good-bye.

Then, as she turned to go, she said calmly, "Oh, I appreciate your husband's taking in my popcorn and drying it for me. Please give him my thanks. I'll just take it on home with me now."

Where Have All the Bedbugs Gone?

Goodnight, sleep tight;
don't let the bedbugs bite.

—Ancient bedtime greeting/prayer

Gone to Glory, every one, I hope! Modern housing, better bedding, and higher standards of sanitation have gone far toward ridding our homes of that ancient scourge, the bedbug. Not that anyone misses them, of course. However, in earlier times, the lowly bedbug was a formidable foe and one to be reckoned with.

Frontier circuit-riding preachers have written volumes about harrowing, sleepless nights passed in vermin-infested beds in backwoods cabins. The tiny insect, not even 1/8-inch long, makes its living by biting into human skin and feasting on fresh blood. When crushed, it leaves behind a blood stain and a most unpleasant odor. It lives in upholstered furniture, in the walls and floors of older homes, and especially in beds.

In my childhood, my parents had a felt mattress on their bed. We children slept on pads, or ticks, filled with straw or corn husks—a perfect habitat for the bedbug. In search of a material less hospitable to *Cimex lectularius,* some people gathered field balsam, an aromatic herb indigenous to the area. Though it may have worked to repel the nocturnal pest to some extent, and certainly made for a sweeter smelling bed, it took nearly a lifetime to gather enough to stuff a bed tick.

My mother was death on bedbugs. She maintained that it was no sin to have them, for that was nearly inevitable. The sin lay in keeping them. One of my more vivid memories has to do with her ordering the beds stripped and their ticking mattresses emptied of straw, which was then burned. The ticking cover was boiled and sun-dried before being refilled with fresh straw.

The felt mattress of my parents' bed was pulled out into the sun, where every tuft and seam was thoroughly drenched with full strength Lysol, a drill repeated both spring and fall—or more often if needed. The floors were scrubbed with Lysol-treated water and lye soap. But still, still they came. It seemed impossible to completely eradicate them.

The story was often told of a bedbug hitching an early morning ride on the clothing of a sleepy-eyed steel mill worker. During the course of the work shift at the mill, our subject was brushed off the worker's clothing and fell into a vat of molten iron. The mill was engaged that day in making a run of cast-iron skillets.

Of course, the insect was encased in one of those utensils, which was sent to the company store, where it was eventually purchased by that same mill worker's wife. Over the next several years, that skillet was heated smoking hot hundreds of times, and an equal number of times was hung on a nail in the wall of the cabin home, where it was exposed to freezing cold.

Thirty years passed. One night the worker came home drunk and in a foul mood. His wife, to impress on him the error of his ways, gave him a sharp rap on the skull with her trusty iron skillet, shattering it into a hundred pieces. And there on the floor, amidst the wreckage of this tender domestic scene, crawled the lowly bedbug, a little pale and somewhat shaky on his feet, but still quite healthy, thank you.

I don't know where all the bedbugs have gone, yet I will wager that some are still around. When mankind succeeds in making a bomb powerful enough to annihilate the world, I'll bet that if you look closely enough, you will find, crawling somewhere in the radioactive debris, a bedbug. He may be a bit pale and slightly off his feed for a few days, but he will recover quite nicely.

First Crush

After years of suffering from Black Lung disease, my brother Virgil's heart stopped beating in August of 1983. Although it should have been no surprise, his death was sudden and unexpected. It was as if, after living for so many years under the threat of catastrophe, we had become inured to the reality of his situation. And so, we were gathered around yet another family grave in Rocky Branch Cemetery.

As we turned to accept the condolences and polite chatter of friends, I saw her approaching with a half-smile on her lips. I recognized her immediately. Even fifty-plus years later she was lovely—a beautiful woman, secure in her comeliness. It was my first teacher, my first romantic attachment. I had loved her as only a child can love, with an adoration unsullied by even a hint of carnality, for this was a love that was spiritual and pure. Had she asked me to bleed for her, I would have asked simply, "How much?"

However, I must tell you of her earnest, despite misguided, attempt to correct my left-handedness. In my worship of her, it was as if I were Job and God had set His face against me. I was bereft and inconsolable, afflicted as with a plague of boils. My very soul ached within me, but God had made me as I was and nothing could repair the misrouted circuitry between the right brain and the left, which had created such confusion in handedness.

It is inconceivable, and I do not believe, that her actions had any malignant intent or purpose. She was simply and purely attempting to rectify what she believed to be willfulness on my part at worst, or at best, an easily correctable mistake of Nature.

At the gravesite, she smiled as she extended her hand. "Are you Dale?" she inquired.

"Yes, I am," I responded. And I have never been able to understand what prompted me to add, "And I'm still left-handed."

One-room schoolhouse (active 1910–1953),
Heritage Park, Spencer, West Virginia

My eldest sister, Maude, seventeen years my senior, taught in this one-room school about the same time I was in Rocky Branch School on Johnson Creek. The school was later moved to Heritage Park, where it can be visited today.

Living in the Shadow

There is a sense in which we all live in the shadow of something or someone. In my case, it was the large, beneficent shadow of my older brother Darrell. Five years my senior, he was my mentor, my protector, and my hero.

I am not sure what I was to him. There must have been times when I was his tormentor, his burden, and a millstone about his neck, for he was often charged with my care. Few limits were placed on our activities; however, he always knew that if things went wrong, he was the responsible party and any consequences were sure to fall on his shoulders.

Ours was a time and a culture in which a person's competence was judged heavily on his willingness to put his body at risk in defense of his reputation, his possessions, or his point of view. A rite of passage for many young men involved the courage and toughness to challenge his father's authority and control by demanding to be dealt with as a man and an equal, not as a child. Meanwhile, against the day of accounting in his father's court, a young man practiced by challenging his peers.

Darrell was a fierce and capable fist fighter who found frequent opportunity to advance his skills. Though he appeared to love a good fight, he was not a bully, for I never knew him to deliberately provoke a challenge; nor did I know him ever to shrink from one.

Typically, it was I who guarded our things—coats, groceries, etc.—whenever Darrell was challenged by someone physically. In one well-remembered scenario, while we lived in Spencer, my mother sent us to the store to purchase a few grocery items, which we carried home in a gunnysack. A gang of three or four young toughs, who often lay in wait for us, demanded our money or our goods. Darrell had anticipated them and instructed me ahead of time to sit on the sack of groceries while he fought off our attackers. "They can't steal our stuff if you're sitting on it," he reasoned. So I sat on the sack and wailed while he fought.

This was our plan going forward. Against such odds, I am sure he did not always win the fight; still, in no case do I remember ever losing the sack of groceries. The attacks ended only when our father began to shadow us on our trips, staying well behind us but near enough to intervene if trouble threatened.

Although there must have been times when he resented my interference with his liberty and the necessity of his guardianship, Darrell was a good brother whom I remember with gratitude and affection.

The stairs in Spencer, on which I sat guarding the gunny sack containing our groceries.

The Mill

In my childhood, parents were much more casual about the supervision of children and their activities than is the case at present. We were routinely expected to assume responsibility for chores and were permitted freedoms that would be unthinkable today.

For example, at the age of eight years, I was allowed the use of a .22 caliber rifle and regularly went hunting alone. And after school on Fridays, I was often encouraged to walk several miles, across country and through the woods, to visit my bachelor uncle, Martin Boggs, on his farm at Looneyville. After a weekend with him, I returned directly to classes at Rocky Branch Grade School on Monday morning. We were taught to act responsibly and, for the most part, tried to live up to expectations.

In defense of parental attitudes, we lived in a homogeneous community in which all residents knew one another and did not hesitate to take corrective action if a child was seen misbehaving. We could hardly travel far enough to achieve anonymity, and we could not hope to escape the watchful eyes of those who knew us and would report any errant behavior to our parents.

As a second grader, I was often allowed to accompany one of two elderly neighbors on their infrequent trips to Walton. "Uncle" Jeff Schoolcraft traveled by hack (horse and buggy) and sometimes took me along for company. "Uncle" Will Walker was nearly blind with cataracts and drove a huge old 1919 Willys/Overland touring sedan. Because of his limited vision, I was sometimes delegated to riding shotgun with him and was expected to point out such things as bridge abutments, rocks in the road, and other such obstacles. Although it was never put in those terms, I suspect that I was there to go for help if the unexpected happened. On those 10-mile journeys, we rarely met another vehicle.

One hot and sultry day in my seventh summer, both we and our neighbors "Uncle" Will and "Aunt" Lizzie Walker were in need of having corn ground into meal for kitchen use. None of the adults felt that they could spare the half-day required for a trip to the grist mill in Walton, nor were they willing to excuse the older children from their work in the fields. Since I could contribute little at the end of a grubbing hoe, I was designated to make the trip. A horse was soon loaded with a gunny sack containing a bushel of shelled corn, and I was boosted up on top of it and started on my journey. I remember the incident not because of anything unusual in its nature, but because of an unexpected and traumatic turn of events.

Though I was no doubt proud to be entrusted with such an important task, I was in no sense blind to the reality of the situation; I was simply aboard as an interpreter. Had the horse been able to speak English, he would doubtless have been sent without me. It was less that such enormous trust and confidence was placed in me than that the horse was trusted implicitly. The horse knew the way to the mill and the miller knew his job. The entire transaction could be completed without outside assistance or intervention. Then once I turned the horse around, the miller would complete the transaction and send us on our way home. It was difficult to imagine that anything could go wrong.

The first leg of the journey was completed without incident. The horse plodded slowly along while I sat on top like a tiny Turkish pasha, pretending that events were unfolding at my command. I turned the horse at the Pocatalico River bridge and stopped him in front of the mill structure. The miller, who was sitting on the porch of the mill, lifted me to the ground and unloaded our cargo. He poured the shelled grain into a hopper and set the ponderous machinery in motion. The building shook and the burrs rumbled ominously as the corn was transformed from whole grain into finely ground meal. Soon a thin stream of cornmeal was flowing from the burrs into a strategically placed measuring box. I watched as the miller constantly sifted the pulverized grain through his fingers, intently observing the quality of the finished product. As the box filled, the miller's "tithe" or "toll" was removed and the remainder of the "grist" was returned to the gunnysack.

When the grinding was completed, the miller casually tossed the sack of meal across the horse's back and returned me to my place atop it. He slapped the horse's rump with a broad hand and started us back down the road from whence we had come.

Just past the Jim Gandee place, about three-quarters of a mile out of Walton, the "foolproof" scenario began to come apart. A small trickle of water passed from the roadside ditch and through a culvert under the highway. The horse, thirsty from his morning's walk in the hot sun, decided to reward himself with a refreshing drink. With his front feet in the ditch and his head lowered toward the water, the sack of meal began to slide slowly and inexorably toward the ground. Frantically, I attempted to avert the impending disaster by shifting my slight weight on the sack, but to no avail. In an instant, both the sack and I were unceremoniously deposited on the shoulder of the road. Relieved of his burden, the horse calmly stepped into the ditch, cooling his hooves in the water and cropping hungrily at the succulent grass of the ditch bank.

I was in deep, deep trouble and I knew it. It was a panic situation in the worst of all possible worlds. To abandon the cargo on the ditch bank was unthinkable. To reload it aboard the horse was impossible, for the sack and its contents weighed more than I. It was now past noon, and I was hungry and thirsty. Though I should have known better, I had no confidence that anyone would come looking for me, ever. I was hopelessly, totally, and perhaps terminally lost.

In the face of my helpless condition, I did what perhaps most seven-year-olds would do. I gave way to my fears, vented my emotions, and sat wailing by the roadside.

After some time had passed (it seemed forever), a single motorist approached. He must have read the situation instantly and accurately. He stopped, calmed my fears, and reloaded the sack on the horse's back. Leading the horse back onto the roadway, he restored me to my place and, after checking the load for stability, sent us on our way toward home. An hour or so later, we arrived at our destination without further incident. I never knew my savior's identity, but he was without question the most beautiful person I had ever seen.

Twelve years later, as a young marine in the South Pacific, I was able to empathize with the war refugees I observed in their hopelessness and despair. Though our situations were in no sense comparable in terms of their totality and finality, I could remember my own time of weeping inconsolably by a roadside, with my world in shambles, having no ability whatsoever to set things right. I hope, and believe, that it made me a better and more compassionate person.

Night Terrors

I really do not remember exactly when George Boatwright and his family came into our community and into my life. I was probably seven or eight years old. George and I immediately became bosom buddies, and his friendship became one of the truly bright spots of my youth.

We were nearly inseparable, to the dismay of our mothers, who sometimes needed our undivided attention. When chores were to be done, playing with George was forbidden until they were finished; otherwise, we tended to lose track of time and go off task. I was often admonished when leaving the house, "I'll want you to clean the chicken house later, so don't bring George Boatwright home with you or it will never get done." And George once affirmed that his own mother often gave him the same warning, "Don't you dare show up here with Dale Lowe. I have work for you to do."

My father would rarely permit us to share chores to make them go faster. He firmly believed that the time required to complete a job increased exponentially with the number of boys involved and often stated:

One boy is a boy,
Two boys is half a boy,
And three boys is no boy at all.

George lived across the hill from me, and to get home from my place, he had to brave a very dark and dense wooded area at the head of our creek. Both he and I were afraid to go through those woods alone, especially at night, so we tried to remember always to go home before darkness came. If we lost track of time and darkness came upon us, we usually accompanied one another halfway so that neither had to make the entire frightening journey alone. When George got to the top of the hill, he would always signal me with a shrill whistle to let me know that he was "out of the woods" and all right. I would answer with my own whistled signal: "message received."

One evening George stayed late at my house, and I requested permission to go halfway home with him. I promised to bring back a bucket of water from the spring, but it was so black when we reached the darkest area, where the spring was located, that we sat down and talked of our fears, each of us afraid to go on alone. So much time passed that Dad came looking for me with a keen hickory switch in his hand. Suddenly, we each had more to be afraid of than the dark journey home.

As I neared my back door, I heard George's whistled signal from the hilltop. I did not return his signal that night, for while he was safely "out of the woods," I was pretty sure that I was not.

George, the Stunt Man

We did not get to see many movies, George and I. When we did, it was a red-letter occasion and we took full advantage of it, usually sitting twice through the entire double feature, complete with short subjects, coming attractions, and Pathe World News. It was a full day's outing, for we intended to get maximum value from the ten-cent price of admission.

Of course, we believed it all. The actors actually took those falls and did all those death-defying stunts—to us they were not stunts, they were all real. Nothing was staged. As for professional stunt men standing in for the actor, that was unthinkable, and the very suggestion constituted a scurrilous attack on a genuine hero. To us, the wonder was not *that* they did it, but *how*!

Based on what I'm about to tell you, George evidently had given the matter a great deal more thought than I, for one day he directed our ramblings to a sheer cliff overlooking McKown's Creek. It was nearly a hundred feet high, and we could peer over the edge and look down on the tops of eighty-five-foot-tall oil derricks. We had often demonstrated our daring by standing on the cliff's edge, backs to the abyss, hoping to appear more courageous and nonchalant than was actually the case. George pulled it off much better than I, for I could hardly persuade myself to stand within three feet of the edge.

After some posturing and maneuvering on the cliff edge, George took up a position with his back to the chasm and said casually, "Dale, watch this!" Then he launched himself backward off the precipice to what I was sure was sudden death.

I was horror-stricken and, for a moment, paralyzed with shock and fear. When I could make my legs work, I quickly ran to the edge and looked over, expecting to see George's smashed body lying at the base of the cliff. I could see nothing. Then I heard George laugh. I followed the sound close in to the cliff face. There he lay, spread-eagled in the top of a small tree growing out of a ledge some fifteen feet below. He made his way to the narrow ledge out of which the tree grew, and thus around the cliff to safety.

It was all so neatly done that he must have set it up well in advance, with more than one trial run. If his intent was to impress, he succeeded beyond his wildest dreams. I suspect that he may have even impressed himself, enough that for all of his derring-do, he never offered to repeat the stunt.

Gigging Johnson Creek

Due to the severe pollution of the water and the silting of the streambeds, few fish remained in Johnson Creek. Those that did survive were mostly trash fish: silver sides, chub, and suckers. Seldom did we catch a mud cat, a perch, or bass, and then not much above legal size.

However, following the spring rains, an infrequent hardy specimen of game fish would find its way into the shallow riffles and gravel beds of Johnson Creek for spawning. The hope of bagging such a prize made a gigging expedition almost obligatory. Gigging was highly illegal, for it entailed spearing, or *gigging*, fish as they lay in the shallow water of the shoals making nests and depositing eggs. It negated the Game and Fish Department's efforts to encourage game fish to return to the lowland streams.

One dark night in late April, George and I determined to go gigging. We carefully prepared our equipment—sharpened spears, several soccer-ball size wads of rags soaked in crude oil for torches, and a wire basket on the end of a long pole in which to carry the burning torch. The bright light from the blazing torch blinded the illuminated fish as they lay on the gravel bed, rendering them nearly helpless against spearing. It was an easy and popular way to take fish, though definitely not good sportsmanship. Also, there was the

Me, about thirteen years old

added attraction of danger involved, for the game wardens mounted frequent patrols of the streams to capture and arrest poachers during the dark nights of the spawning season.

George and I waded slowly upstream, torch blazing and spear at the ready, alert to the presence of fish and game wardens alike. Soon after passing the house of Carl Sergent, a local resident known for his practical jokes and pranks, we saw the lights of a car coming rapidly up the road beside the creek. When the car drew abreast of us, it suddenly stopped. Two doors slammed as the unknown persons exited the car, and a loud voice shouted, "You go left and I'll go right, and we'll cut 'em off!"

The worst-case scenario had come to pass. We both *knew* that it was Carl Sergent—but what if it wasn't? We simply could not take that chance. Without a word to each other, we dunked the blazing torch in the creek, threw our gigs in the high weeds on the opposite bank, and ran for the woods.

I ran directly for home—a really stupid move. George, always more cunning than I, ran up a mountainside in the opposite direction. I ran until my legs would carry me no farther, stopping to rest and regain my breath in a pawpaw thicket. I lay there in the darkness of the pawpaw patch, listening for the sound of pursuing footsteps, yet none came. After several minutes my heart rate and labored breathing were returning to normal and I began to wonder what had happened to George. Had he, like myself, been able to escape? Or had he fallen into the clutches of *The Law?*

Finally, after what seemed an eternity and a half, I heard a faint, shrill whistle from the wooded mountaintop about a mile away. George was out of the woods and safe. I quickly answered the signal and crept out of the pawpaw patch to await his arrival beside the pathway.

A few minutes later, George found his way out of the woods to where I lay in wait. He was bruised and bleeding from a dozen cuts and abrasions, but we were both safe and relatively sound. We would retrieve our spears another day!

Going Around the Gin Pole

The wooden oil derricks, or rigs, were sixty-five or eighty-five feet high, depending on the depth of the well, and were twenty or twenty-five years old by the time I was old enough to play on them. They were strictly off-limits to us as children but were such an attractive nuisance that we could not resist their appeal.

The purpose of the rig was to support a crown pulley high off the derrick floor. It facilitated drilling and, later, the removal of the tubing and pump from the shaft of the well for cleaning and blasting the oil-bearing sands, which improved the flow of oil.

The derrick was a four-sided structure of perhaps 30' x 30' tapering to a 30" x 30" top into which the crown pulley was set, thus centering the pulley precisely over the well. Because a man was required to work on top of the derrick to rig the pulley, a gin pole was set into one corner of the structure, extending about four feet above the pulley. The workman could then steady himself by holding on to the gin pole as he worked at rigging the crown pulley. The rigger was well paid for his labors, for it was a very precarious and dangerous job.

As children, we often played a thrilling game of tag or follow-the-leader, clambering all over the decaying structures to the accompaniment of the breaking of rotten timbers. We soon learned never to trust our weight to a beam or timber without having a firm hold on another.

In follow-the-leader, one had to follow wherever the leader went. If the leader felt particularly venturesome, he went "around the gin pole," a most daring maneuver, for it demanded that one swing out over empty space while trusting the stability of a 2" x 4" timber of questionable age and doubtful soundness. In time, this particularly foolhardy stunt came to be known as "going around the gin pole."

I still marvel that, to my knowledge, none of the neighborhood children playing these dangerous games on the rigs were ever injured. It makes all the more believable the old adage that God appoints a guardian angel to watch over drunks, damn fools, and little children.

Abandoned oil derrick near Charleston, WV.
The gin pole is located at the top of the derrick.

George Drives a Hard Bargain

As was true of most boys of our time, our toys were few and always of our own making. As has been true of most boys since its invention, the wheel played a large part in our creative fantasizing, for our homes and farms were virtually without wheels of any kind. A favorite toy was a small pulley wheel eight to ten inches in diameter, pushed along by a paddle made from a broomstick and a Prince Albert tobacco can. Automobile tires, if one could be obtained, were fun to roll, but the toy *par excellence* was the wheelbarrow, for if one had a buddy, one could become a passenger, pushing and being pushed in turn. I had no wheelbarrow, although George had made one by sawing a wooden round for the rolling stock. He was such a clever boy!

McKown's Creek had cut a deep and narrow gorge in its path some two miles from George's home. Within its cool depths were many waterfalls and slick moss-covered rocks; it was a favorite place to play. One Saturday, we "drove" to the gorge, where we hid the wheelbarrow in a laurel thicket and methodically went about our business of sliding down each slick mossy rock on the seats of our pants. By the time we worked our way through the gorge, the seat of my overalls had been entirely worn away.

Allow me to digress. During the Depression years, most farm boys did not wear underwear, except for the winter months, when long johns were worn for warmth. I worked on a farm during the summer before I began high school, and this allowed the purchase of my school clothes, including my first undershorts and shirts. I probably would not have invested in them at all had my sister Faye not persuaded me that they made my new clothes look and fit better.

So, we were out of the gorge, George in reasonably good shape and I with no seat in my pants. The problem was that we then had to retrieve the wheelbarrow and travel home on the dusty dirt road. We might have gone cross-country, which entailed crossing several fences, but that meant abandoning the wheelbarrow—unacceptable. Taking the dirt road was the best remaining option, involving passing several houses where my posterior would be exposed for the entire world to see.

Then George, good buddy that he was, proposed an ingenious plan. He would wheel me *past* the houses if I would agree to wheel him *between* the houses. He drove a hard bargain, for while he pushed me perhaps 200 yards, I had to wheel him two miles. It was, however, a deal I was happy, even eager, to accept.

Thanks, George, for sparing me one of life's potentially most embarrassing moments. And I *do* hope that you enjoyed your ride!

Target Practice

An indispensable piece of every country boy's equipment was the slingshot. It bore only the most rudimentary resemblance to the modern store-bought slingshot made of metal tubing and surgical rubber. Ours were made from the crudely formed crotch of a tree branch, rubber bands cut from an old automotive inner tube, and the tongue of an old shoe, from which the pouch was formed. Our ammunition consisted of the rounded gravel found in abundance in the bed of any stream. Anything that moved was fair game, and many of us became quite proficient in the use of our crude weapons.

An oil well stood near the Boatwrights' house. George and I were playing about the derrick floor one day as the well was being pumped, slingshots dangling from our hip pockets. I climbed on top of the belt house and from there got to the walking beam, which pivoted a vertical six or eight feet with each turn of the eccentric shaft of the belt wheel. As I stood on the very end of the moving beam, balancing myself with its movement some fifteen or twenty feet above the derrick floor, George walked up the hillside several yards from the rig. He picked up the broken bottom of a glass bottle and fitted it to the pouch of his slingshot.

"Dale," he shouted, "tell me if you can hear this whistle when it goes by." With that, he extended the slingshot to its full length and released the deadly projectile.

I did indeed hear it whistle as it went by. In fact, it came so near that I felt it tug at my hair as it whizzed ominously past my head.

My guardian angel was still on the job.

The Watermelon

A neighboring farmer on Johnson Creek, Mack Vineyard, had married my father's cousin, in whose home Dad had been partially reared after his mother's death. Mack, though probably undeserving of the reputation, was known by the children of the community to be a mean-spirited man who did not tolerate thievery. Inevitably, an adversarial relationship developed between him and the local children, who operated out of the principle "'Tis no sin to cheat the Devil."

Mack planted watermelons in his cornfield, on the assumption that the growing corn would hide the ripening melons. He let it be known that in midsummer he always slept in his watermelon patch—which also contained pumpkins—with his shotgun by his side.

We children believed that the sweetest melon was a stolen melon, and we boasted loudly—though untruthfully—that we had never bought or grown a watermelon. In fact, every family on the creek had a watermelon patch!

My friend Clyde Schoolcraft and I, as seven- or eight-year-olds, scouted Mack's cornfield regularly, for we *knew* where his melon patch was located. We peered through the fence between the ripening cornstalks until finally, late in the summer, we located a beauty growing well out in the center of the field and decided to claim that baby as our own.

When the season was sufficiently advanced for the melons to be approaching the peak of ripeness, we waited for a dark night. We crept between the strands of barbed wire, tiptoed cautiously to the prize, and seizing it, ran for home as though pursued by demons, fully anticipating the delicious thrill of hearing shotgun pellets whiz sharply past our ears with each step.

We congratulated ourselves lavishly as we took our purloined treasure to our barn loft, where we broke it open with a rock—for we had no knife. We scooped out the pulpy contents with our grubby hands and feasted on what we told each other confidently was the sweetest melon ever stolen. We were pleased, too, that as a bonus, we had pulled something over on the meanest man alive!

The next morning, Dad went to the barn to milk and feed the cow. He returned shortly shaking his head in amazement.

"Myrtle," he said to my mother, "I've just seen something that I can't figure out. There is pumpkin rind scattered all over our barn. Who do you suppose would have done such a crazy thing?"

It seems that we who had set out to cheat the Devil had cheated ourselves. We were left only with the faint yet earnest hope that if Dad ever figured it out, he wouldn't tell Mack Vineyard.

A Chance Encounter

Editor's Note: Please excuse the use of the word "Nigger" in this story. Its use here is a reflection of the time in which this story is set. It is thanks to the compassionate nature of a gentle stranger that a young boy learned the power of words and the price ignorance exacts from others.

In the spring of 1932, our dog was poisoned. She was a German Shepherd named Gyp, a great watchdog and a good mother to her frequent litters of puppies. She was such a good mother that her offspring were always in demand and there was never a problem finding homes for them. Then one morning we called, but she did not respond. We found her in the barn, where she slept, deliberately put to death by a poisoned piece of meat. We all grieved her loss.

A few weeks or months later my father came home leading a beautiful black puppy at the end of a rope. I thought that I had never seen such a marvelous dog, and we quickly became inseparable. For lack of a better choice, and in deference to his color, I called him "Nigger." Inevitably, he began to be called "Nig," but if I wanted to capture his full and immediate attention, I borrowed a page from my mother's book of tactics and ensured his instant obedience by calling him by his full and unabbreviated name: Nigger.

Nig and I, with my friend George Boatwright, were a team. Together we roamed the hills and valleys of the Johnson Creek and McKown's Creek areas. Scarcely a place within a five-mile radius remained unvisited by us, our chief limitation being the distance we could travel and still be home by dinnertime.

One warm summer day, my mother sent ol' Nig and me to Walton to purchase some item from Lonnie Whited's General Store. As we crossed the Pocatalico River, near the mouth of Johnson Creek, we were surprised to be joined by a very large and extremely black man who crawled out from under the bridge as we approached.

Ours was such a poor community, and so far off the beaten path, that transients were rarely encountered. There was only one black couple in the entire county at that time, employed as domestic help by a well-to-do family in Spencer. As a result, black transients were simply never seen.

My newly acquired traveling companion was clean, roughly but neatly dressed, and as we walked and talked, he turned the conversation toward possible employment. He would do any type of work available and asked only to be given a meal in exchange.

Me and my dog, Nig

Though unversed in the finer points of race relations, I was sufficiently aware to know that "Nigger" was a demeaning term and was not to be used as a form of address, so I studiously avoided calling my dog by his name in the presence of my fellow traveler.

As we neared Cold Spring, a natural spring of cool water bubbling out of the hillside, we stopped for a refreshing drink. Of course, Nig flushed a rabbit from a nearby clump of blackberry briers and set off across the highway in hot pursuit. Leaping to my feet, I sternly commanded the dog to return to me immediately, addressing him by his full name: "Nigger, get back here, *now!*"

Knowing that I had inadvertently committed the ultimate faux pas, I furtively glanced at my companion to test his reaction. To my immense relief, he was smiling broadly.

"Why do you call him Nigger?" he asked.

"I dunno," I responded glumly. "'Cause he's black, I guess."

My acute embarrassment was eased when he playfully rumpled my hair with a huge hand. "That's a good name for a good dog," he said, "and don't you forget it."

We chatted amiably as we continued on our way, and I was genuinely sorry to part with him as I turned to enter Whited's store. So I was disturbed and puzzled by the comments of several loafers on the porch.

"Boy, you'd best learn to keep fitter company."

"Don't you know that he might have kilt you and throwed you in the river?"

It would be foolish for me to pretend to be free of prejudices, racial or otherwise. I do not like all of the black people I have met, nor do I like all white people, but I still remember the lesson taught me by my first black acquaintance, who knew all about putting a positive spin on a negative situation and turning away wrath with a soft answer.

My critics, I believe, could have learned something from him, too!

The Swimming Lesson

My last two extended trips to the Johnson Creek area were in 1984 and in 1990. I was quite disappointed to see that many of the hillside farms, which in my boyhood had been kept clear of brush and briars to accommodate larger herds of cattle and sheep, were now largely abandoned and rapidly reverting to forest. The plus side of this situation was that the devastating floods that had occurred in my youth were now more easily kept in check.

In earlier times, lacking vegetation to hold back the water, the slightest rain could cause the creeks to rise, and heavier rains caused terrible flooding. The flood, of course, provided an irresistible attraction for the boys in the community. Those who could swim leaped into the raging, muddy stream with complete abandon, while those who could not were forced to accept the limitation of clinging to a board or log, or wearing that most shameful of all badges of the non-swimmer, an inner tube.

Normally, Johnson Creek could be vaulted with a pole at almost any spot, and would-be swimmers were often hard pressed to find a pool of water deep enough to accommodate them. Still, on one memorable occasion, we neighborhood boys gathered on the Big Rocks at School House Bend, and we tested one another's courage by daring each other to take a swim.

We all knew from our own experiences that a young puppy, dropped into the water, would immediately and instinctively begin to swim. We reasoned that the same instinctive impulse must also operate in the human species.

My brother Darrell, a non-swimmer like myself, wistfully yearned to be gifted with the ability to swim. "By golly," he said, "if I could swim, I would jump in that water and swim all the way to Carl Sergent's place."

One of the boys said, "I can teach you to swim in one lesson."

"Go on now!" Darrell responded. "You can't do that."

"You want me to teach you to swim right now?" his friend persisted.

"Yeah," Darrell challenged. "Teach me!"

The boy immediately grabbed him in a bear hug from behind and forcefully pushed him into the stream. We all watched with great apprehension as Darrell did, indeed, learn to swim—not well, but well enough.

Knowing that I was also a non-swimmer, the boy then turned to me and asked, "Want me to teach you how to swim?"

"N-a-a-h," I alibied hastily, "I've got a sore arm."

A Lesson in Larceny

The one boyhood companion with whom I was most likely to get into trouble was Clyde Schoolcraft. He was a good and loyal friend, but somehow the chemical mix when we got together was not a good one; we dared things that neither would have attempted alone.

Children today—thanks to their personal sets of wheels—may have difficulty comprehending a world in which one could not travel far enough in a single day to achieve anonymity, and certainly not if they were afoot, as we always were.

"Who do you suppose that is walking down the road?"

"Why, I believe that's Tommy Lowe's boy from over on Johnson Creek." At that instant, the citizens phone tree would come alive with inquiries as to why I was so far from home for no apparent reason.

One lazy summer day, Clyde and I decided to walk to Walton, five miles distant, for the purpose of purchasing a "short" pack of Wings cigarettes. A short pack was a package of ten, intended to accommodate Depression Era smokers who might not have the price of ten cents for a full pack of twenty. Many merchants kept an open pack behind their counters from which they sold two cigarettes for a penny. Nevertheless, Clyde and I were going for the full short pack of ten.

We facilitated our crime by stealing one of my mother's fat hens, which we planned to barter to Lon Whited, the storekeeper, in exchange for the smokes. The transaction went well, except that Clyde, while Mr. Whited was occupied with weighing and crating the hen, decided to compound our crime spree by stealing a bottle of warm Nehi orange pop from a crate beside the counter. He failed to account for Mr. Whited, however, who knew nothing if he did not know his inventory. The loss was noted within minutes and the citizen phones up and down Johnson Creek began to ring.

Telephone privacy had not yet come of age, for the citizen system used a coded series of rings to call each individual phone. For example, a long ring followed by two shorts, or two longs and a short, signaled the incoming call, leaving the line open to anyone who cared to pick up their receiver and listen. Since we had no phone, our neighbor was called. People the length of Johnson Creek heard the news.

"Tell Tommy Lowe, when you see him, that his youngest boy just traded me a fat hen for a pack of cigarettes and then stole a bottle of Nehi Orange pop from me. I'll expect payment for the pop."

Meanwhile, Clyde and I had taken to the woods outside of town and were heading cross-country for home. We stopped on top of a hill, broke the neck off the Nehi on a rock, and gulped down the warm, sweet fluid, enjoying our forbidden loot.

Not daring to go home with a cigarette in our pockets, and unwilling to abandon our unused booty, we sat on our hilltop and smoked the entire pack, lighting one off the other. Novice smokers that we were, we failed to account for the effect of the nicotine on lungs and bloodstream until, predictably, our stomachs revolted. Some hours later we managed to stagger home, still sick and fuzzy-headed, to learn that news of our misadventure had gone before us.

For the theft of the hen, one of my mother's best layers, I received a thorough whipping and a stern lecture on the economic consequences to the entire family of taking one of her prime laying hens out of production. For the unauthorized use of tobacco, my father sat me on top of a fence post, handed me his pipe and a handful of his homegrown leaf, saying, "If you want to smoke, then smoke. I'll tell you when you can get down." Within a few minutes I was so sick that I *fell* off my perch and my mother mercifully intervened and put me to bed.

To pay for the stolen hen, I hoed corn for a week. For my labor I was allowed five cents to settle my indebtedness to Lonnie Whited. As I recall, though, my father did have a conversation with him about his knowingly receiving stolen goods and selling cigarettes to a kid. He further advised him of his own culpability in creating an attractive nuisance by leaving highly pilferable goods within the reach of children.

I wish I could say that my lesson was so well learned that I was never again tempted to steal anything and swore off smoking for life. Unfortunately, that would not be true. But I did learn to be more careful when stealing from my mother.

Clyde Schoolcraft and I bought a short pack, 10 cigarettes.

Reaching for Immortality

It was a fine fall day in the Indian summer of 1933. The sky was a clear, bright bowl of cobalt. The sun was pleasantly warm, though the previous night's sharp frost had left a bite in the air that hinted at the changing of the seasons. The new-fallen leaves rustled crisply underfoot. The Master Painter, it seemed, had created a special palette of colors for the occasion, as the forest floor was lavishly splashed with the brilliant red and gold of the maples and the vibrant yellow of the poplars. Even an eight-year-old boy could appreciate that it was a good day to be alive.

My brother Darrell and I had gone into the woods to search for a family of seldom seen black squirrels, which had been in residence in our woodland for as long as either of us could recall. The red and gray squirrels were regularly hunted for the cooking pot, but the blacks were far too rare and precious for that. My father protected them, and we loved to watch them as they chattered and played in the tops of the huge beech trees. The leaves were down, the frost had ripened the beechnuts, and the squirrels were feeding voraciously. We tried to count them as we watched them. Fourteen was the best number we could estimate.

Then Darrell opened his Barlow knife and began to carve his initials in the trunk of the ancient tree. I watched with shining eyes as his strong young hands drove the sharp blade, swiftly and surely forming the letters *RDL*.

"I'll bet this will be here fifty years from now," he said. Then he added, with that fine disdain for time unborn found only in the very young, "I'll bet it will outlive me."

On another crisp fall day, in the Indian summer of 1990, nearly 20 years after Darrell's death, George, Bill Boatwright, and I tramped through that same woodland. The first hard frost of the season had brought down the leaves. The forest floor was a riot of color. A pungent sharpness in the air bespoke the promise of coming winter. I remembered the black squirrels and wondered aloud if any of their descendants remained to eat the sweet meat of the beechnuts. We sat quietly under a huge old beech tree and listened for the sounds of feeding squirrels. The woods were silent. As we arose to continue our ramble, my eye fell on a scar on the trunk of the old tree. Though distorted by fifty years of growth, it was the still decipherable letters of Darrell's initials—*RDL*.

As if by magic, half a century faded away and I was, for a moment, an eight-year-old boy in the company of his fourteen-year-old brother. Again I watched, eyes misted by the poignancy of the memory, as his strong young hands carved his initials in the trunk of the ancient tree—*RDL*.

"You win, Darrell," I said, pensively. "You win the bet."

It was fifty-seven years ago.

It was yesterday.

My brother Darrell

For Love of Huckleberry Finn

It was midsummer of 1934 or '35. George and I were nine or ten years old, and the motion picture *Huckleberry Finn* was scheduled for a showing in Spencer's Robey Theatre. In those days, the announcements of films to be shown were posted on the porch of Lonnie Whited's store in Walton and in other prominent places. We immediately determined that this was the one must-see event of the summer.

Some nearly insurmountable obstacles stood in the way of the realization of our dream. The first was securing parental permission. The second was how to find the price of admission. The third, and somewhat simpler problem, was finding transportation to and from Spencer, a distance of eighteen miles from my house.

We knew the futility of even approaching the first obstacle until we had successfully addressed the second and third. Our game plan was to resolve them in reverse order. We would request permission of our parents only after we had secured the promise of a ride to and from town.

Friday was the day of Spencer's weekly livestock auction. Since several of our neighbors from Johnson Creek always attended that event, we knew we could assist in loading and transporting animals to the stockyard in exchange for a ride.

We were willing to hoe corn, cut weeds and brush, chop wood, or do any number of other chores in order to resolve Problem Number Two. To my surprise, my father, who had secured a short-term summer job painting schoolhouses, offered to hire us to chop the weeds from our cornfield. It was a package deal in which we were to present him with a clean corn field in exchange for the price of admission to the county fair at the end of summer. George agreed to help, and we planned to pull off our own version of the "bait and switch" scam. We would take the bait and hoped to be able to switch the reward later.

Within a week we were ready to approach our parents with The Plan. The cornfield was tidy enough to qualify as "clean." We had the promise of transportation. We had credit with my father in an undisclosed amount, but enough, we expected, to purchase admission to the county fair.

To our surprise, neither set of parents offered any serious opposition. After all, if we had not yet learned how to conduct ourselves in public, we would probably never know. They were entirely cool about any possible danger to ourselves, appearing much more concerned with damage we might inflict on an unsuspecting public.

The Lindbergh kidnapping had occurred only a couple of years before, but that was about money. No one could hope to gain financial benefit by snatching a kid from our poor community. A kidnapper would certainly be toting us back when they learned how much we ate. Most sensible folk concerned themselves with preventing more kids, not with how to get another. If something did happen to one of us, we were easily enough replaced. No, it was useless to worry about something that wasn't likely to happen in any case.

My heart sank a bit when it was suggested that since we would be in town all day with nothing to eat, we would need a few extra cents to purchase food. You can imagine my amazement when we were promised twenty-five cents each—enough for the movie (ten cents), two hot dogs (five cents each), and a Coca-Cola (five cents) at the local Coney Island. We would attend the matinee showing and be out by midafternoon, early enough to catch a ride home with any one of several neighbors who would be in town that day. Our parents were right: honesty and hard work certainly did pay!

On the appointed day, George and I each had a shiny new quarter carefully tied in the corner of a handkerchief and secured to a button hole in our bib overalls to ensure against loss. Proudly, we rode to town in the bed of a pickup truck with a couple of squealing, half-grown hogs and several bleating sheep. We planned to eat in midafternoon, after seeing the movie, which would leave at least an hour to find a ride home.

We bought our tickets the moment the box office opened, for

we wanted to be certain of securing the best seats in the house—in the upper balcony, locally known as Peanut Heaven. The ambiance was marvelously exotic with the darkened room and dramatic music, which seemed to come from all directions.

Many of the movies being shown in our small town were still of the silent variety. A huge pipe organ was located in one of the wings offstage, providing entertainment before and after the screening, during intermission and the changing of reels, and often during silent films to create a mood that matched the action.

We enjoyed the previews of coming attractions, short subjects, and film clips of armed insurrections and other notable happenings gathered from around the world. We endured an interminably long series of advertisements of local merchants, interspersed with announcements that popcorn and soft drinks might be purchased in the lobby. A silent Mickey Mouse cartoon was followed by a serialized cowboy adventure. Finally, already an hour and a half into our afternoon, the magic of *The Adventures of Huckleberry Finn* began to unfold on the silver screen.

Robey Theatre, built in 1907, remodeled in 1926 and still in use today

The film was everything we had hoped for. We, of course, were not the world's best film critics. We barely tolerated the credits that rolled at the beginning or end of the feature. There was no need to inform us of the identity of the actors; we knew they were Nigger Jim and Huckleberry Finn. We laughed at the comical naivete of Jim, while loving him for his loyalty and artlessness. We alternately empathized and fumed as Huck and Jim were victimized by a series of unscrupulous knaves. We howled with glee as Huck, in drag, attempted to clumsily pass as a young girl, only to be unmasked by a spool of thread. We gripped the edges of our seats, white knuckled, as Huck and Jim survived feuds, threats of murder, and worse. We wept unashamedly when Jim was captured and sold down the river. It was total emotional catharsis. It was WONDERFUL—so much so that when it was over we each looked at the other and said, "Let's see it again!"

At last, hungry and emotionally exhausted, we exited the theatre to an empty and darkened street. We sought out the Coney Island to buy our long awaited hot dog; as it turned out, too long awaited, for the restaurant was silent and dark. Our neighbors, all having end-of-day chores to do and cows to milk, had gone home hours ago. We went directly to Plan B. We would walk out of town and ride our thumbs home.

Hitchhiking was not new to us. Whenever we hiked along the dusty road to Walton, we habitually stuck out our thumbs to overtaking traffic. We knew the operative rules for hitchhikers. Those seated alongside the highway with thumbs extended were routinely dismissed as "too lazy to walk" and were, ipso facto, undeserving of a ride.

Only those enterprising enough to hike as they hitched were taken seriously by local drivers. Besides, stationary hitchers were considered to be long distance travelers while walking hitchers were viewed as locals and neighbors. We knew the rules, but we had no experience with nighttime traffic. As we were to learn, there was little to experience.

We hiked in the gathering darkness, trying to ignore our weariness and grumbling stomachs. A mile or so beyond the city limits, after passing Lick Fork Road, we saw the dancing lights of an approaching vehicle. Our spirits lifted. Stepping out into the narrow ribbon of light, we lifted hopeful thumbs. The car slowed and stopped as the driver, obviously a local resident, actually apologized to us that since his car was full, he could not give us a ride. We thanked him politely and walked on, our faith in humanity restored by that single act of kindness and concern.

Had we been sufficiently knowledgeable, we might have heard something in the voice of our would-be benefactor of which we were unaware—that there was no traffic on that road at night and that we were in for a long hike. Nevertheless, our spirits had been revived; essentially, it was a decent and friendly universe. Someone was sure to come along at any moment and give us a ride. We would be home before we knew it.

We trudged past Right Fork, Missouri Run, and Sugar Creek. Through the village of Speed and past Rush Creek Road we doggedly persisted, watching with wistful eyes as house after house grew dark, their occupants turning in into warm and waiting beds. We pressed on up the sharp incline of Bent Hill until, gaining the crest, we began our steep descent toward Gandeeville.

Suddenly, after hours of walking, a second vehicle overtook us. Out came the thumbs, uplifted in that universal symbol of undying hope. The pickup truck stopped and we were invited into the cab.

"Where ya goin?" the driver inquired.

"Johnson Creek," we answered.

"Can't help ya much then," he said, "but I can take ya into Gandeeville, 'bout a mile down the road."

Well, something was better than nothing.

A blister blossomed on my right heel as we limped painfully out of Gandeeville. At Bear Fork, we relieved our swollen feet of the confining shoes to which we were unaccustomed. Tying their laces together and draping them over our necks, we left Wolf Run and Silcott Fork behind.

No cars appeared out of the darkness. None! We endured the hot, sharp pain of strained thigh and calf muscles as we persisted past Givens Hollow. Now we knew that the Pocatalico River and the mouth of Johnson Creek were just ahead. The familiar contours of the hills of home were faintly silhouetted against the starlit sky. Three more miles to go—five for George, unless he could be persuaded to spend what was left of the night at my place. But I was not hopeful for that.

The only frightening part of the entire journey was the Looney Cemetery and the darkly wooded White Hollow just beyond. We had grown up hearing stories of the post–Civil War reconstruction period and the lynching of three renegade bushwhackers there. We knew that each night, their ghosts performed a macabre dance under the sycamore trees from which they had been hanged.

We lifted our aching bodies into an awkward, shambling trot and left White Hollow behind in the darkness. Mercifully, even the ghosts had given up the ghost and retired for the night. A short time later, we were shortcutting through Mack Vineyard's barnyard and picking our way up Dry Fork to my home.

George declined my invitation to stay with me, as I knew he would, for he was sure that his parents must be sick with worry. As I stole quietly through the living room and into my bedroom, a glance at the clock told me that it was after 3:00 a.m. If George sent his customary whistled signal from the hilltop, I was unaware of it. Weariness had silenced the complaints of my empty stomach, and I was asleep long before he had progressed that far.

When I appeared for breakfast the next morning, expecting to be severely reprimanded for my dereliction, my father said, "You sat through the show twice, didn't you?"

"Yeah," I admitted.

"And then you had to walk home, didn't you?"

"Yeah," I admitted again.

"Figured you did," he assured me.

And no further mention of the incident was ever made. I was immensely relieved that no punishment would be meted out, but chagrined by the unseemly lack of concern on the part of my parents. I had no wish to worry them, but common decency demanded that they show *some* small sign of anxiety.

Upon comparing notes later, George assured me that his reception at home was even more bewildering than mine. They had gone to bed early and hadn't even missed him.

"Well," he alibied for them, "they probably thought I was spending the night at your place."

It was such a comforting thought we even half convinced ourselves that it was true.

Emergency Rations

A typical Saturday morning on the farm, especially in winter when chores were less onerous and time-consuming, saw several neighborhood boys meeting at our house for adventure and to explore the woods and streams together. Since boys of our age were always hungry, we scavenged whatever the woods and fields provided—walnuts, hickory nuts, hazelnuts, and beechnuts, as well as paw-paws, persimmons, and the occasional frozen apple overlooked on some farmer's tree.

We almost never went home for lunch out of fear that we might not be able to escape our mothers' clutches and the assignment of some home-related task. To ensure the comfort of our stomachs, and to provide if Nature's bounty failed, the pockets of our overall jackets bulged with emergency rations—a biscuit or two left over from breakfast, an apple from the cellar, or a turnip freshly pulled from the garden. We always carried a generous supply of homegrown peanuts roasted in the shell. Ours was one of the few families in the community to grow peanuts. We were thus assured not only of pleasant winter days afield, but also of cozy winter evenings gathered around the old Burnside heating stove roasting, shelling, and eating goober peas.

My sister Faye could almost always be persuaded to make a few dozen doughnuts, called *sinkers* because they were dropped into sizzling hot pork lard, where they sank to the bottom until done, then floated to the surface. They were then rolled in a mixture of sugar and cinnamon, which melted into a thin glazed coating. They were delicious, though I shudder to think of the cholesterol produced by such quantities of animal fat. I have always been sure that no one else could ever make sinkers like Faye's.

My brother Darrell and I, along with Watson and Edward Sampson, George and Bill Boatwright, Alfred and Faud Batten, and an occasional Schoolcraft, spent many pleasurable days roaming the woods with our pockets full of sinkers and peanuts. It was not such a bad way to grow up, after all. Pass me another of those sinkers, please. And have yourself another handful of those good ol' goober peas!

Ancil's Baptism

Ancil was a solid citizen. Everything about him spoke of what he was: an honest and foursquare man. He was a blacksmith, and the symbol of his life and work was the huge anvil, spiked solidly to the white oak stump that sat at the entrance to his shop, just a step in front of his blackened forge. He was a respected member of the community whose opinion was often sought in matters relating to the life of the country settlement, for it was known that his advice would be thoroughly weighed and well considered.

The tower of cast-off horseshoes beside his shop stood in mute testimony to his industrious nature as he plied his trade. From early morning to near darkness he would be found at work, hammering out on his anvil the implements and appliances required by his farming community.

His father was a traveling preacher and evangelist whose circuit frequently took him away from his home for days at a time. He often said, "Whenever I leave the Creek, the last thing I hear is the sound of Ancil's hammer on the anvil and the first thing I hear when I return is the ring of Ancil's hammer."

Ancil was a fastidious man in an occupation marked by sweat and grime. The uncluttered tidiness of his shop spoke eloquently of his personal habits of order and cleanliness. His tools were kept in good repair, and each lay in its accustomed spot on the worktable, instantly available to his seeking hand. His motions were sure and disciplined, appearing almost effortless as his hammer blows on heated metal formed the tools and equipment needed by his neighbors. If the housewife required a spider for her outdoor kettle, Ancil would provide it. If a wagon wheel lost its steel tire, Ancil would replace it. If a horse or ox required shoeing, Ancil would do the job with efficiency and dispatch.

Ancil was an exceptional man, holding to personal standards that were unsupported by many of his neighbors. Though his face was often smudged by smoke from his forge, and his shirt soaked with sweat, he did not permit these necessary marks of his livelihood to become characteristic of his personal style. Whenever he appeared in public, his attire was unfailingly neat and clean. His language, spare and unstained by crudity, was simple and direct. His credo seemed to be "Work hard while maintaining a clean mind in a clean body."

By this time, early in the twentieth century, the Industrial Revolution had transformed much of the world but had hardly made a mark on his mountain community. Although the automobile was commonly seen on city streets and in more urban environs, rarely did one find its way onto the dirt roads and footpaths of his mountain valley.

Modern water systems and their conveniences, well known to his city contemporaries, remained a novelty to Ancil and his neighbors, most of whom still bathed in a galvanized tub in the kitchen of their homes and did so "once a week, whether they needed it or not." In fact, some refused to bathe at all during the winter months, believing that to do so was to leave the body vulnerable to all manner of disease and infirmity.

As a result, they were often a very scruffy lot, and to spend an evening with them in a crowded room was something Ancil was loathe to do. Although he had no wish to appear prudish, he sometimes wished that his neighbors would wash themselves more frequently. It troubled him greatly, for not only did it set him apart from his neighbors, it prevented his full enjoyment of their company at church, school, and community events.

Although the populace identified itself as having come from a variety of religious disciplines, mostly Methodist, Baptist, and Advent Christian, custom had melded them into a homogeneous whole in terms of religious practices. Almost universally, it was felt that persons baptized by sprinkling or pouring of water were not *properly* baptized at all. Only total immersion was seen as true baptism, preferably in an ice-cold mountain stream. Most parents, therefore, preferred to forego infant baptism, leaving their children to make that decision for themselves as adults.

Since most candidates for baptism were products of midwinter revivals, baptisms commonly were scheduled in late winter or early spring, in order to facilitate their induction into church membership on Easter Sunday. Although this ran counter to their prejudice against midwinter bathing, it was felt that their faith would protect them from any untoward consequences resulting from their frigid immersion.

On an appointed Sunday afternoon, the congregation and supplicants gathered by a previously selected pool of waist-deep water in a local stream. It was important that it be a stream of running water, as opposed to a still pond, to satisfy the biblical reference to the water of baptism as "living" water.

One by one, the candidates were led out into the cold, waist-deep water by the minister, where they were baptized by being lowered backward until submerged, then immediately raised upright. This was to emulate the death of Jesus Christ, his burial in the tomb, and his being raised again to newness of life.

It was on such an occasion that Ancil, having previously announced his desire to submit to the rite of baptism, made his way to the banks of Johnson Creek with his fellow postulants. There he watched as, one after another, each was led out into the icy water and baptized. Most had worn their oldest, and often dirtiest clothing, seeing no reason for changing *before* bathing.

As the ceremony proceeded toward its conclusion, Ancil appeared reluctant to put himself forward to the minister. Finally, the minister approached him and asked, "Ancil, do you wish to be baptized?"

Ancil, with downcast eyes, probing nervously in the dirt with the toe of his shoe, reportedly answered, "Yes. Yes, I do want to be baptized, but just not in the same water with *those* people."

Uncle Mart

One of my earliest memories is of my mother visiting her siblings in the neighboring community of Looneyville with me in tow. In early fall of one of my preschool years, before the late rains had turned the roads into quagmires, the harvesting of garden and fields, and subsequent canning, drying, and pickling were completed. Mom then had time to plan a visit with those members of her family who lived nearby.

Our old horse, Rowdy, was tied to the fence in front of the farmhouse while being saddled and bridled. We were not a two-horse family, but we did have two saddles—a McClellan, a Western saddle also known as a cavalry saddle, with a deep seat for riding astride, and a handsome sidesaddle for use by the ladies.

In that time and place, it was considered little short of scandalous for women to ride astride, so most chose to ride sidesaddle. A heavy saddle blanket was laid across the horse's back and the saddle cinched fore and aft. The sidesaddle was a lighter weight than the McClellan; in appearance, it was more English than the McClellan. A stubby horn protruded from the left side just forward of the seat and a few inches below the center of the saddletree. The rider sat facing the left side, gripping the side-mounted horn with the bend of her right knee. The left leg and foot were supported by a standard riding stirrup. It was a precarious position for any other than a very gentle horse and a practiced rider, but my mother was a lady who would consider no other style of riding.

She was suitably attired in an old pair of calf-length button-up shoes or boots. She wore a very heavy riding habit of stout serge, lined with a lighter matching fabric, which prevented the habit's bunching up and exposing her limbs. A cape of matching material covered her back and shoulders, while leaving the arms and hands free for controlling the horse. Although it was somewhat outdated even at that time, my mother took great pride in being fashionably and suitably dressed for the occasion. Her habit must have been handed down from a sister, as such outfits were custom made and terribly expensive.

Typical Victorian riding habit, similar to my mother's

After she had been assisted into the saddle and had assumed a comfortable riding position, a pair of capacious saddlebags containing a change of clothing for each of us and a few other necessities were laid across the horse's back just behind the seat and secured to the D-rings by leather thongs. With my mother in place, I was then boosted on top between the saddlebags, where I clung to her by encircling her waist with my arms. She was then handed the reins and, with a "Git up, Rowdy" and a nudge in the horse's ribs with the left foot, we were off on our "great adventure"—and for me it *was* a great adventure.

It was a ride of perhaps one-and-a-half to two hours from Johnson Creek to Looneyville, through heavy woods and over-rutted dirt roads and footpaths. Rowdy, on his best behavior as if to disprove his name, plodded patiently along, half asleep, while the miles passed slowly behind us.

A short stop was made at the head of Rocky Branch, where Rowdy was watered and rested before attempting the steep hills ahead. We did not dismount, for remounting might have proven difficult, given the challenges of sitting sidesaddle.

Our next stop was at the simple two-room cabin of Mom's bachelor brother, Martin Boggs (Uncle Mart), on his hillside farm. We could not spend the night there, for he did not have a separate bedroom but slept in a single bed in an alcove off the kitchen. After a brief visit with him and his appropriately, if unimaginatively, named dog, "Dawg," we began the rounds of Mom's other relatives—three brothers and a sister who lived in the Looneyville area—planning to spend the night at whichever house we were invited to or wherever dinnertime overtook us. We would again stop for a short chat with Uncle Mart and Dawg on our return home.

Clarence (Uncle Clair) Boggs lived near Uncle Mart and had several children, some near my own age, and I enjoyed playing with them while Mom visited. Never one to tolerate idleness, Uncle Clair kept the older children fully occupied in the fields.

Aunt Augusta's home was about three miles distant. She had no children at home, and although I liked her well enough, I was always eager to move on to another uncle who had a readymade set of playmates for me.

Cleveland (Uncle Cleve) had several older girls, and one boy two to three years older than I. That was, however, enough difference in our ages to render our interests incompatible.

Milton (Uncle Milt) had many children, among them three boys near my own age and several older girls. His wife, Aunt Bessie, was a careful housekeeper and would not permit the boys access to the house except at mealtime. They even slept in the room above the cellar. This was my favorite stop on our family tour, for these cousins were largely undisciplined and uncontrolled. Though they lived on a large farm, my uncle worked in the oil fields and did little traditional farming. His sons had plenty of free time and were quite imaginative in its use.

An opening to the "Johnny Ferrell" cave was on Uncle Milt's farm, and exploring its reputed five miles of subterranean passages in the company of older cousins was high adventure. It was dry and well ventilated, and Confederate soldiers had allegedly used the cave during the Civil War as a munitions storage place and emergency hideout.

Our primary interest was in finding the deposits of red, yellow, green, and blue clay that it contained. We also enjoyed the delicious thrill of terror experienced in retelling apocryphal tales of people who had become hopelessly lost in the maze of tunnels and now allegedly roamed the cavern as vagabond ghosts.

Uncle Mart was the "odd" member of the family; the one about whom all the others worried, on whom their concerns centered, and who was talked about in secretive, whispered conversation. He was my mother's older brother and a twin to my Aunt Margaret, who lived in another community. He was always neatly and cleanly dressed, and he kept his little house spotless. In appearance, he was slightly built and of less than medium height. His thin-lipped mouth, piercing blue eyes, and snow-white hair were characteristic of the men of the Boggs clan. If he could have kept his teeth clenched while speaking, I'm pretty sure he would have done so.

During the years leading up to World War I, Uncle Mart was engaged to marry a local girl when he was scheduled for conscription into the army. As the date of his induction drew near, his fiancée, not wishing to wait out the war to be married, and unwilling to risk early widowhood, broke off their engagement and eloped with another man. Uncle Mart's grief was more than he could bear, and he was hospitalized with a total nervous breakdown. He spent many months in the hospital before being released. He did eventually return to the community, where he retired to the isolation and consolation of his farm.

Oil had been drilled on his acres, and with that small but assured royalty to supplement the farm income, he was able to support a heavy drinking habit to assuage his broken heart. He retreated into himself, willingly speaking primarily to his faithful canine companion,

Dawg. There must have been a succession of dogs, but if so, each inherited the role and the name of his successor. He, or they, were simply addressed as "Dawg."

A gentle and otherwise hospitable man, Uncle Mart studiously and expertly avoided being drawn into conversation, even with his siblings. Any necessary remarks were channeled through Dawg, just as he preferred being addressed through Dawg, who never left the farm. When Uncle Mart ventured into the community for his occasional trips to the store or post office, he went alone. On those occasions, he hastened to do his business and returned to his farm as quickly as possible. As he passed the home of a brother or sister, they would invite him in for a rest or a drink of cool water. But he would simply shake his head no and continue walking.

That he could carry on a meaningful conversation when necessary was evident, for he was able to care for his farm-related business, the sale of his few head of cattle, negotiating other deals with neighbors, and making purchases from merchants and tradespeople. But he much preferred keeping his own counsel and, at home, allowed Dawg to do his talking for him.

He may have liked children better than adults, perhaps because they made fewer frivolous and intrusive conversational demands. As I grew older, at my mother's urging, I would pay him an occasional weekend visit. Leaving school on Friday afternoon, I walked across the hills to Uncle Mart's, arriving in time for supper and returning to school on Monday morning. With his face nearly vacant of expression, he would meet me at the door.

"Look who is here, Dawg," he would say. "It's Dale, Myrtle's boy. Well, tell him to come in."

With that he would begin to prepare our meal. That was a long discourse for Uncle Mart and, with me, was as close to a two-way conversation as he ever came. As darkness fell, he would spread a pallet on the floor for me, saying, "Bedtime, Dawg," as he retired to his sleeping alcove in the kitchen.

He kept a cow that had to be milked twice daily, and chickens for eggs. His morning and evening chores were simple, since his fuel was the natural gas produced by a well on his farm. As I accompanied him on his twice-daily rounds, he kept up a nearly continuous conversation with himself, though it was muttered and unintelligible.

That he was a lonely man there can be no doubt, although he obviously preferred his own company, and that of Dawg, to the companionship of others. I was a congenial presence for him, though our relationship never went much beyond friendly tolerance. As I left on Monday morning to return to Rocky Branch School, I was always invited, through Dawg, to come back whenever possible.

On rare occasion, he would leave Dawg to superintend the farm while he made his way to Spencer, where he attended the weekly livestock sale and the state-run liquor store. The local police were familiar with him; when he was too deeply in his cups, they would lock him in the jail overnight for his own protection. He never bothered anyone, nor was he in any way violent. As far as I knew, he did not frequent the local bawdy houses. He just drank himself into oblivion. I do not know how he made his way to Spencer, a distance of about fifteen miles, or how he got home. Perhaps he walked both ways or caught a ride with a neighbor. Anyone finding him walking on the highway would have given him a ride.

His favorite nephew was Uncle Milton's oldest son, Virgil, called Houston. Houston had lost an arm in a fall when run over by a freight train during a youthful "hobo" adventure. Unlike Uncle Mart, Houston was married briefly, late in his life, but not before Uncle Mart's and his conjoined descent into a lifetime of alcoholism was an accomplished fact.

Uncle Mart died about 1950, in the back seat of Houston's car, as they were no doubt on some alcohol-related mission. The official cause of death was "heart failure," but there was never a doubt that the primary cause was alcoholism. At some point he had written a simple will, naming Houston as his heir. A few years later, Houston followed Uncle Mart in his own demise and of the same causes. In spite of his "odd" demeanor, Uncle Mart is remembered with sympathy and affection, and is mourned for the tragic circumstances of his life and death.

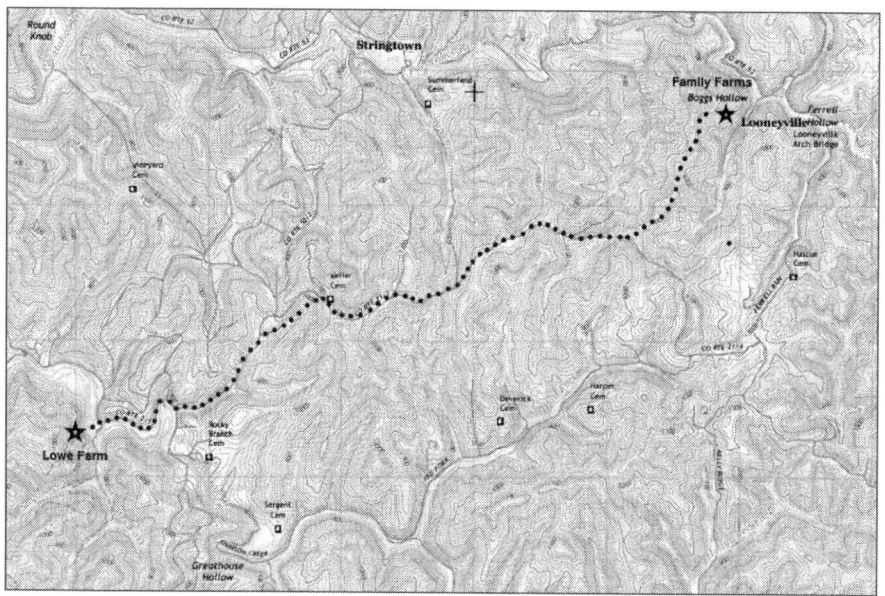

The route we took from our farm to Looneyville

Houston

Not many people bonded with Uncle Mart, except perhaps for his siblings and Dawg, his alter ego . . . and, yes, Houston. Actually, it is unfair to call Dawg his alter ego, for that distinction belonged to Houston. Dawg was merely his constant companion and the vehicle through which Uncle Mart spoke and interacted with his small world. Dawg, on the other hand, neither drank moonshine whiskey nor mourned lost loves.

Houston was my first cousin, the first-born son of my Uncle Milton Boggs and his wife, Bessie. At birth he was given the name Virgil. He was born within days of my older brother, Virgil Lowe. The families were neighbors in the West Virginia community of Looneyville, and the boys grew up together as inseparable companions. To distinguish one Virgil from the other, my brother was nicknamed "Pete" and my cousin, "Houston."

It was inevitable that the boys would learn to drink at an early age, if not from Uncle Milt, then from another uncle, Fred Vineyard, who was married to my Aunt Augusta. Uncle Milt was a steady, daily drinker, keeping several stashes of hidden bottles in various places around the homestead. It was difficult to know when Uncle Milt was drunk, for that was his normal condition.

Uncle Fred was an episodic drinker. His pattern was to go on frequent extended binges, the effect of which was as though he had been a daily drinker, for he hardly sobered up before beginning again.

Uncle Fred was modestly wealthy from oil revenues and had the reputation of raising some of the best shorthorn cattle in the area. Knowing his own habits and limitations, he took Pete and Houston along whenever he left his farm. He was careful to teach each of them to drive his car, so that they could return him to his home whenever he became so inebriated he could not find his own way. The boys grew up mostly—too much—under the influence and tutelage of Uncle Fred.

As a result, the two grew up with a warped view of the world and of manhood. Combined with a lack of encouragement at home, neither Pete nor Houston completed more than the fourth grade in Laurel School.

Pete left home early, probably in his early teens, going to Ohio to make his own way in the world. Houston also left home at about the same time.

Always the adventurer, Houston determined to become a hobo and see the world. At some point early in his vagabond experience, he attempted to hop a moving freight train while inebriated. Losing his footing on the metal bumper, he fell under the wheels of the following boxcar. His left arm was severed just below the elbow.

He returned to Looneyville and home, where he devised a harness for his stump, which allowed him to become adept in the use of hand tools and horse-drawn farm implements. He willingly assisted Aunt Bessie in the home and kitchen, eventually becoming an excellent cook. He also became quite expert in the "cooking" of whiskey, wine, and homebrew, eventually outdoing even his father in finding stashes for his liquid gold.

Aunt Bessie was a very religious woman and an implacable enemy of alcohol. Her eagle eye and unerring nose quickly led her to ferret out the caches of her husband and son. Finding them, she would immediately smash, pour out, or otherwise destroy their potable treasure. The result was an escalating contest in which Uncle Milt and Houston became quite inventive in finding ever more secure hiding places and Aunt Bessie was forced to become increasingly resourceful in spying on her errant husband and son.

One cold January morning, Houston had just finished his last bottle of home-brewed beer. His mother had found and destroyed nearly all of his moonshine. The future did not look good, and he was becoming desperate.

At this time of year, the weather was too cold for the outdoor production of wine or beer. Houston needed a secure location, and a warm one, for running off a new batch, a process of several days or even a couple of weeks. Deep in thought, he wandered out to the barn, where he could consider his options in uninterrupted leisure. Seating himself in the feed room by the horse stalls, looking out upon the frigid scene through a scuttle hole in the wall, he observed a phenomenon of winter: a huge manure pile quietly cooking away in its toasty depths, sending clouds of steam into the frosty air. "That's it," he thought. "I have found the place."

He dared not move too quickly to implement his newfound plan, so he waited until darkness fell. Carrying a 20-gallon crockery jar to the manure pile, he dug down about three feet into the heated depths of the repository. There he placed his heavy container, backfilling around it almost to the top. Mixing the ingredients carefully, he filled the jar three-quarters full and tied a heavy canvas cover over the top. Over that he placed a wooden cover made of boards, before filling the hole completely. Stepping back to observe his handiwork, he was satisfied that if he avoided daytime visits to the manure pile, not even his mother could find his new hiding place; the rich scent of the manure would amply mask the odor of the fermenting mixture as it slowly matured in the perfect hideaway. He was more than pleased with his night's work as he retired to his bed in his room above the cellar.

Allowing the fermentation to progress undisturbed for several days, Houston at last judged that the home brew must be nearing perfection. So one night, lantern in hand, he risked a visit to his miniature brewery. Uncovering the crock, he carefully lifted off the wooden lid and canvas cover. The smell of the rich brew immediately assailed his nostrils. He could not resist a wee taste, and dipped a glass Mason jar into the concoction to draw off a sample. It was wonderful! After refilling his jar, he recovered the crock, meticulously replacing the camouflaging layer of horse manure. Chuckling to himself at his own cleverness, he returned to his room, sure that his mother would never find this hideout.

While he was gleefully congratulating himself on his cunning, he failed to credit his mother with a sagacity and shrewdness of her own. As she finished tidying her kitchen, she stepped out on the back porch for a breath of fresh air. It was then that she saw Houston's lantern lighting his way to the barn.

That's odd, she thought, *that someone would be visiting the barn this late in the evening. I'll just see what he is up to.* Before she had traveled halfway to the barn, she could see Houston digging into the manure pile. Puzzled, she returned silently to the house, determined to await developments.

The next morning, when she knew Houston was occupied elsewhere, she went to the barn. Mounting the odiferous mound with manure fork in hand, she removed the top layer. Then the fork struck wood. She carefully scooped away the remaining manure, lifted off the protecting boards, and removed the canvas cover. She knew instantly what she had found. With her foot, she scraped a generous shovel full of manure into the homemade brew, then covered it exactly as she had found it. She said nothing to anyone about her find, content to let time and Houston's thirst reveal what she had done.

It was not until he had consumed almost the entire fifteen gallons of homebrew, and found several "horse apples" reposing in the bottom of the crock, that he discovered the extent of his mother's craftiness.

Houston spent his life visiting around with friends and relatives, occasionally serving a term as cook in some logging camp or boarding house. One of his favorite stories, which he always retold with great glee, was of the time Aunt Bessie outfoxed him in finding his brewery.

About once a year Houston would show up at Pete's house for a visit that might last for several days. He was always broke, of course, and when he left, he usually did so after appropriating any small sums of money that he might find while wearing Pete's best trousers. Pete, in fondness for Houston, and in honor of their boyhood friendship, never complained about his losses, figuring that Houston deserved whatever he could pilfer because of the loss of his arm and for old time's sake.

The last time I saw Houston was in the late forties. He came to visit in Nicholas County, where Pete and I were living and working in the coal mines. Characteristically, he left after upgrading his wardrobe, wearing Pete's pants.

At some point during that time, Uncle Mart had purchased or built a two-story house on Pocatalico River at Looneyville. Houston moved in with him and became his drinking companion. After Houston married, quite late in life, he became Uncle Mart's designated heir. The property passed to him briefly after Uncle Mart's death and before his own demise a few years later.

He was such a likable and resourceful rascal that anyone victimized by him never held his shortcomings against him.

Rest in peace, Houston.

I Become a Fireman

In September 1942, I moved to Spencer to live with my sister and brother-in-law, Maudie and Herbert Garrett, and entered my senior year at Spencer High School.

Some months earlier, a disastrous fire had destroyed several homes on Alvord Hill, a section of Spencer, because at that time there was no well-organized fire department. There was only an old 1930s vintage Dodge pumper truck housed in a garage near the courthouse. When the fire alarm sounded, anyone who wished to do so responded, but no regular positions were assigned. The first man on the scene was the driver, and others filled in as needed.

That was a problem, for no one was really trained to fill any particular position. The truck also had no starter motor and had to be push-started! This caused a delay until enough men arrived to push the truck to get it running. The *big* problem, however, was that everyone wanted to be chief, and failure to resolve that issue virtually paralyzed the department—to the point that, on occasion, no one deigned to answer the alarm. The city's experience with devastating fires placed an efficient fire department high on its wish list.

A teenage high school student, Melvin Crislip, attended a firefighting course at West Virginia University and became the first regularly appointed chief of the all-teenage Fire Department. Members were all volunteers and were appointed by the city. They were issued badges and were granted limited police powers in the commission of their duties as firemen. I volunteered and was accepted as one of this select group. We were unpaid, held regular drills, and answered all alarms.

Most of the alarms were sounded to extinguish brush fires, but I can remember at least two alarms for *real* house fires. We may have lost both homes, but we did succeed in preventing the fires from spreading, which was our primary goal.

Surprisingly, it was a good and effective fire department; certainly, it was a major improvement over its predecessor. The teenage chief and each of the volunteer firemen tried hard to do a credible job. A major problem was interference from adult wannabe firemen who sometimes tried to take our hoses, insisting on showing us how to *really* fight a fire. More than once, the chief was forced to threaten a citizen with arrest for "interfering with a fireman in the performance of his official duties."

The Spencer Fire Department was recognized as the first and only teenage fire department in the United States at that time. It continued until 1957, when it was converted to an adult department, though still retaining many teenage volunteers.

I served with pride as a member of the Spencer Fire Department. It was with real regret that I turned in my resignation and my badge as I was leaving town to enlist in the Marine Corps in 1942. Though I personally can take little credit for it, we had demonstrated to a skeptical adult community that teenagers were capable of carrying adult responsibilities, and I believe that we performed a valuable service for the city.

A restored 1930s Dodge pumper fire truck

Coffin Nails

During the annual homecoming game between Spencer and Ripley High schools in the early 1930s, fighting was obligatory, both on and off the field. Many who hardly cared about the outcome of the game came primarily to see the fights.

The two towns were seats of government for Roane and its neighboring county, Jackson. Emotions ran high and hot. Frequently, the turmoil got completely out of hand. Supporters of one of the two teams, usually those on the losing side, would begin to shout insulting remarks about the opposition players, coaches, and the crooked officials. They were answered in kind, and the quality of the commentary declined as the level of verbal inventiveness escalated. Soon one group was sure to begin to attack the virtue or question the general attractiveness of the other's women. Physical contact was sure to follow when one side or the other began to sing:

> Oh, the women all use snuff in Jackson (Roane) County,
> Oh, the women all use snuff in Jackson (Roane) County,
> Oh, the women all use snuff
> And they never get enough,
> Oh, the women all use snuff in Jackson (Roane) County.

There were many more verses to the song, all derogatory to the female residents of the two counties, most of which were unrepeatable in polite company. The song rarely progressed beyond the beginning of the second verse before the fans boiled out of the bleachers on either side and met in a melee of flying fists and feet on the playing field.

The players were rarely hurt, but many were the bloody noses and black eyes among the warring fans. Play continued only when a semblance of order was restored. Private contests often continued in the streets and alleys; the visitors usually departed in convoy for their mutual protection and well-being.

All of the foregoing is by way of recognizing that there were, indeed, many women in West Virginia's fifty-five counties who used tobacco in its many forms. Snuff was the preferred form, since it was considered more ladylike than chewing. While the use of ready-made and self-rolled cigarettes was growing rapidly among young males, their use by young ladies was considered quite racy and the sure mark of a woman of easy virtue. Perhaps it was inevitable that the relative cleanliness and convenience of cigarettes, coupled with their heavily promoted glamorous image would, in time, catapult them into acceptability.

In the early years, smoking among women was almost totally limited to elderly family matriarchs. Sitting near the hearth or by a sunny window, they puffed away at their clay pipes from the comfort and security of their rocking chairs. Clay pipes were popular among the older males as well, since they were cheap—often selling for a penny each, without stem, at the community store. A section of elder branch of appropriate size, having a soft pithy center, was easily reamed out and made into a very satisfactory stem. Of course, the clay pipes were quite fragile; a dropped pipe was a shattered pipe. As the old folks often jested, "I smoke clay pipes because if I drop one, I don't have to pick it up."

The use of tobacco was widely considered to be beneficial to one's health and was often recommended to relieve asthma attacks, respiratory illnesses, and to prevent or mitigate the common cold or influenza. Chewed, it was believed to have analgesic as well as antiseptic properties, and everyone knew that smoke blown into an aching ear would bring almost instant relief. A freshly chewed "cud" or "quid," promptly applied to a cut, bee sting, or even snakebite, would draw out the poison and prevent infection. Its potency was thought to be enhanced by applying it over a poultice of cobwebs gathered from a barn corner. Its place was unquestioned in the household emergency supplies where, due to its almost universal availability, it was often the entire first aid kit. I must not neglect to mention that it was widely adjudged a mild aphrodisiac and an enhancer of personal fecundity.

How tragically wrong we were in almost every instance, and what a terrible price we still pay for those errors in belief and practice!

But empirical and pragmatic evidence is difficult to deny. With all of our faith in the old ways as the best ways, the element of doubt inevitably began to creep in. From the assertion that tobacco "never hurt no one," we moved slowly but surely toward the recognition that it was ultimately a health hazard. Cigarettes were referred to, only half in jest, as "coffin nails." To smoke was to "drive another nail in my coffin." The insidious nature of the tobacco habit was addressed in this old song:

> Smoke, smoke, smoke that cigarette;
> Smoke, smoke, smoke it if you puff yourself to death.
> Tell St. Peter at the Golden Gate
> That you hate to make him wait,
> But you gotta have another cigarette.

Graham Lee Hemminger probably describes our late-born ambivalence toward tobacco as well as anyone:

> Tobacco is a dirty weed. I like it.
> It satisfies no normal need. I like it.
> It makes you thin; it makes you lean,
> It takes the hair right off your bean,
> It's the worst darn stuff I've ever seen.
> I like it.

"Uncle" Dick

In the little mountain community of Nettie, in Nicholas County, West Virginia, lived many quaint and colorful characters, but none were the subject of more affection and droll stories than "Uncle" Dick McMillen. He was an honest man who could subsist on his hillside acreage only because his wants and needs were as simple as himself.

Like the original "slow walkin', slow talkin' Jones," Uncle Dick's leisurely pace and measured speech kept the cadence of his uncomplicated thoughts. His notoriety was based on his peculiar manner of speech, fully accentuating the articles "a" and "the" and carefully enunciating verbs ending in "ing." In all other respects, his were the slurred speech patterns of the typical mountain dweller.

Though he could neither read nor write, and had never traveled abroad farther than his two legs could carry him, he affected the persona of the urbane and well-traveled man. To conceal his lack of reading skills, he would often pick up a book or newspaper and pretend to read the meaningless text, interpreting what he "read" by free association.

The story is told, though perhaps apocryphal, of Uncle Dick picking up a newspaper containing a photograph of a New York skyscraper under construction. Since he could not read, the law of averages dictated a fifty percent chance that the paper would be held upside down. Such was the case in this instance. Trying to make sense of the topsy-turvy photo, he announced, to the amusement of all, "Well, I see by the papers that there has been a great shipwreck and many lives were lost."

An avid Republican, he was passionate in his hatred of President Franklin Delano Roosevelt, who had announced a Depression-era farm price-support program that provided for hogs to be slaughtered in their pens, milk to be poured on the ground, and fields left to lie fallow. This infuriated the frugal Uncle Dick, who raised virtually everything he ate on his rocky hillside. Everyone in the community was familiar with his frequent threats to "go to Washington and shoot that worthless SOB."

One day as he trudged along the dusty country road, he hitched a ride with a passing motorist who proved to be an FBI agent passing through the area. It took Uncle Dick only a few moments to bring up his favorite subject—his hatred of FDR. He reportedly said to the lawman, "Somebody ought to take a gun and shoot that worthless SOB, and the next chance I git, I'm a'going to do 'er, too."

He was promptly placed under arrest for threatening the life of the President and taken to the courthouse, where the Sheriff persuaded him that his prisoner was a harmless old man who liked to talk but was incapable of shooting anyone. His release came, however, only after extensive inquiries had been made as to his character and the relative seriousness of his threats.

One of Uncle Dick's choice topics concerned what he called his "Great Journey," in which he detailed the longest trip he had ever attempted. Some matter of business had taken him to Rainelle, a distance of thirty miles from home. Upon concluding his business, he elected to save the bus fare by walking home.

His listeners would urge him on in his description of how he found his way home, on foot, over such a great distance and in unfamiliar territory. His favorite line, to his audience, was when he said, "I jist kep' on a'walkin' on the hard road. Fin'ly, I seed a man a'plowing on a hillside and I knowed I wuz a'getting closter home."

In spite of his virulent hatred of FDR, Uncle Dick was a very religious man. He attended all community events, including services at the three churches in the neighborhood. He was a familiar sight to all as he made his way to or from the house of worship, lantern in hand. His testimony as to his religious experience was assured and anticipated, though his thrifty nature sometimes interfered with his willing participation in the freewill offering.

Standing, he would make a great show of patting down the many pockets of his bib overalls before hauling out his Bull Durham money pouch and dropping a few pennies in the receptacle. "I do love the Lord," he would groan, "and I want to go to heaven when I die, but it does seem like it costs an awful lot."

One of the churches he frequented was Downtain Chapel Methodist Church, which stood at the very top of a windswept hill. Its ancient timbers creaked and groaned under the weight of each wintry blast. The potbellied stove worked overtime and, though red hot, usually failed to bring the one-room structure to a comfortable temperature. The hinge pins on the rusty stove door had long since given way, and it frequently came crashing to the floor, allowing smoke to pour into the room. Someone with gloves would usually succeed in snatching the door off the floor and hastily put it back in place, where it hung precariously until movement and vibration shook it loose again.

Downtain Chapel, Nettie, West Virginia, the site of "Uncle" Dick McMillen's encounter with the red-hot potbelly stove door

Many believers were convinced that the Lord would actively work to protect from harm those whose faith in Him was strong. One night, during an active testimony meeting, the super-heated door came crashing to the floor at Uncle Dick's feet. Someone shouted, "Pick it up, Uncle Dick. The Lord won't let it burn you."

Obediently, Uncle Dick reached down barehanded, picked up the chunk of hot metal, and just as promptly dropped it. Shaking his painfully scorched fingers and hopping on one foot, he admonished the assembled congregation: **"THE *HELL* HE WON'T!"**

"If Ye Ain't, Hanner, Don't!"

One of the major maladies afflicting both children and adults living in our rural area of West Virginia, where weather conditions were severe and personal hygiene difficult to maintain, was scabies, or "the itch." It was highly contagious, being caused by a microscopic mite that burrowed under the skin, causing a reddening, roughness, and thickening of the skin in the affected area.

The mite's entry was facilitated by the cold, damp climate, which chapped and cracked open fissures in the skin of the hands. It was characterized by intense itching and vigorous rubbing and scratching, which only aggravated the situation. Eventually, other areas became infected, as the parasite spread to the feet, the groin, and the trunk of the body. The treatment of choice was a mixture of pork lard and sulfur, which was rubbed into the cracked and roughened skin. This only served to anger the mites and caused them to burrow deeper. The treatment was of dubious value.

The real preventative, of course, was stricter sanitation, washing with a germicidal soap, and staying absolutely dry—none of them viable options in that population and in that climate. In an attempt to stem the tide of wintertime outbreaks of scabies in the schools, the Board of Education and the Board of Health collaborated in periodically issuing Lifebuoy soap to the students, the primary active ingredient in which was Lysol. It was effective and wonderfully soothing and might have gone far to eradicate the itch had it been issued to the entire population, but it was a classic case of too little, too late.

There were few secrets in a community like ours. In one-room schools, the "social equalizer" was the space heater around which the children crowded for warmth. As students' clothing was warmed by the heater, the tattletale odor of sulfur began to permeate the room, revealing unmistakably the identity of those having the itch.

Many cures were offered, but none were really effective and all were more painful than the malady itself. One old-timer in the community and his wife, Hannah, found themselves grievously beset in midwinter by a most troublesome and persistent case of the itch. Advised that a full-body bath of laurel tea would rid them of their torment, they gathered leaves of laurel (*Rhodendron*) and boiled them down into a strong distillation. It was decided that Abe would become the guinea pig and try the concoction first.

Stripping down to the skin beside the kitchen stove, he began to wash himself with the curative. As he washed, he began to experience a burning sensation, which intensified and spread with each application until soon he felt he was being consumed by a raging fire.

Leaping from the kitchen door into the snow, he began to run around and around the dwelling. Wishing to give a warning to his wife, but unable to pause in his tormented circuit, each time he passed the open door he shouted a single phrase of admonishment...

" . . . If ye ain't, . . .

. . . Hanner, . . .

. . . don't!"

The Fish That Caught Me

It was probably in the late 1940s or early 1950s that the West Virginia Game and Fish Department, in an effort to revive the dying sport fishing industry, began to release exotic species into the state's streams. Soon, lowland streams such as those in Roane County began to see significant populations of bass and muskellunge, where such fish had not been known to exist in recent memory.

My father was a fisherman of some renown, though less for the fish he caught than for the stories he told about those fish. One of his favorites, and judging by the enthusiastic response of his audiences as well, was the story of "The Fish That Caught Me." This same story, in some of its many versions, was known as "The Lunker in the Blue Hole." Here is the story as he might have told it.

In its lower regions, Spring Creek (or Pocatalico River, Johnson Creek, Reedy Creek, or the upper reaches of Elk River) runs through some pretty wild and little-explored areas. One beautiful spring day, my friend and I decided on a combined camping/fishing trip to one of those areas, the Blue Hole.

Now I won't tell you where the Blue Hole is, for if I did, you would just go out looking for it—and you might find it. It's a place where a huge subterranean spring comes boiling out from under the bank of the stream. It is a spring so clear and so deep that the water appears to be a deep blue in color, in the same way that the clean, clear air of the atmosphere appears to be blue as we look out into the limitless depths of space.

Anyone with a true fisherman's heart knows that real, soul-satisfying fishing is a solitary occupation—or should I call it a preoccupation? With that special, unspoken consent and agreement that forms the basis of all true friendships, my companion and I split up, and while he wandered off downstream, I headed straight for the Blue Hole.

As I approached the stream bank, I crawled on hands and knees, for I suspected that some big muskie or bass might have taken refuge in the depths of the spring and I had no wish to spook him. Such fish are extremely wary and do not reach their extraordinary size by living carelessly, oblivious to their surroundings, foolishly taking unnecessary risks.

I lay quietly on the stream bank for several minutes, alert to any rippling of the waters or unfamiliar shadows in the depths that might reveal the presence of my prey. Yet the pristine waters betrayed not a hint that any living creature occupied those depths. Then, out on the periphery of my vision, I observed a small frog as it launched itself into its watery element. The frog swam slowly and leisurely toward the center of the Blue Hole, as though in anticipation of some small pleasure or adventure known only to itself.

From the depths came a sudden and violent roiling of the water. It seemed the very engines of hell itself were driving a giant underwater turbine. Out of the violent, turbid waters, a vague form suddenly materialized and the frog vanished, as though it had been a figment of my imagination. Then quietly and slowly, the form sank into the water, leaving no evidence of its presence except for a diminishing whirlpool, a slowly abating vortex, a barely perceptible eddy as witness to its existence.

I knew that I had witnessed a remarkable thing, but my mind balked at accepting the vision as real. Had my longing to see and perhaps conquer such a creature so impressed itself upon my faculties that reason was suppressed and overwhelmed, while my wildest imaginings became a chimera of reality?

With trembling fingers, I searched my tackle box for an artificial lure, a replica of a frog fitted out with two wicked treble hooks cleverly attached to the body of the decoy. I tied it to my leader and, in breathless anticipation, launched the bait.

Were I a swearing man, I would affirm by the angels of heaven itself that what follows is truth. Still, I am not given to swearing, for does not the Bible forewarn against the taking of such oaths? Therefore, I can only attest to the following events with all the veracity of one whose very word is known to be as good as his bond.

The previously detailed scenario was repeated as precisely as though photographed, and more swiftly than the eye could see or the mind comprehend. Suddenly, I found myself attached by a thread of nylon to a fighting machine from the netherworld, whose ferocity was beyond my comprehension and whose repertoire of tricks and ruses exceeded my experience. In brief, I was badly overmatched, and I quickly recognized that my poor skills were completely inadequate for the contest.

There is a period of time in everyone's passage from callow youth to security in the strength of manhood when one doubts one's untested self. It is a question of unproven courage. In the moment of truth, will the guiding principles of one's life support one in the epic struggle between integrity and expediency? Does one choose the path of honor and completeness as a man, or does he opt for the broken condition of moral impairment as he seeks unfair advantage as a means to achieve his ends?

I derive no satisfaction from what follows, for only a fatally flawed and inadequate persona could find pleasure in these events. I cannot even throw myself upon the mercy of my court of readers by pleading youth and seeking the forgiveness my fellows. I was man-grown, yet in the blunt and sometimes brutal language of the Book of Books, I had been tested and found wanting!

In a desperate effort to rid itself of the painful bite of the barb in its mouth, the fish jumped clear of the water, fully revealing itself to me for the first time. The muskellunge swung its giant head, first right, then left, in a bid to shake the hook from its mouth. Its slender body writhed in midair, and the sunlight glistened off the water-darkened surface of its skin. The sheer force of its rush to freedom and the height of its great leap carried it out of the sheltering depths of the Blue Hole and into the shallows of the main stream.

Now, the sport of fishing is based on a concept of fairness, which gives the quarry a fighting chance. It is that which gives meaning to the word *sport*. The failure to honor one's adversary is to reduce the *sport* to a shameful killing. But I was beyond thought or knowledge at this point. My reaction was to cover the muskie with my body in the shallow water, wrap it in my arms and, by brute force, wrestle it to a spot on the creek bank. To my shame, this reaction denied my adversary the honor that one valiant foe deserves as his right from another. I can give no concrete estimate of the size of the Leviathan imprisoned in my arms, but its weight seemed that of a half-grown shoat. As I grasped the giant at the midpoint of its body, its tail left a trail of wetness in the dry sand.

But make no mistake, Justice must be reckoned with and Right will win! Man has always recognized that his very unworthiness may become a force against him in his struggle to impose his strength and will on the natural order. It is said that "the mills of God grind slowly, but they grind exceeding fine."

In a rapid reversal of this sentiment, the mills began to grind exceeding fast. The great fish continued to struggle beneath me, the treble hook buried deep in its flesh, and answering the demands of Justice, the second treble hook buried itself in the fleshy mound at the base of my right thumb.

I found myself shackled to my prize in a classic reversal of the roles of captor and captive, tormentor and tormented. As I rose to my knees to deal with this new and unexpected problem, the fish continued to thrash wildly, sinking the barb more deeply in my hand and setting the point firmly under the bone.

At last, as though to prove the old adage that justice is tempered by mercy, the hook in the mouth of the fish tore free, releasing us from our bondage to one another. Though the pain in my right hand was excruciating, I grasped the fish's gills with my left and dragged it to the lip of the Blue Hole.

Releasing it to its element, I offered a silent paean of thanks for a painful lesson on the order of relationships as they are meant to be. To paraphrase the timeless observation of Pogo, "I have met the enemy, and he is me!" As I returned to Spencer to have the hook surgically removed and the damage to my thumb repaired, I consigned my fishing gear to a trash bin behind City Hall.

Though I will continue to enjoy the hills and streams of my

homeland, I will seek to live in peace and harmony with God's other creatures. Never again will I seek to find value in my own eyes, or in the eyes of my fellow man, by the domination and death of any living thing.

I vowed that day to pay homage to my ancient opponent by revealing to no one the location of the Blue Hole. I intend to remain true to that vow.

The Summersville Courthouse Incident

For obvious reasons, I cannot personally verify what is popularly known as The Summersville Courthouse Incident—it took place some twenty-five to thirty years before I was even born. Nevertheless, more than a hundred years after the event, if diligent inquiry is made of the old-timers occupying the park benches of Summersville's Courthouse Square, some may be found who will give you their version of the affair.

For some reason, many residents deny any knowledge of the happenings. Despite some minor differences in detail, however, those who do consent to speak will find major points of agreement. This indicates to me that, at its core, there is a central body of truth in the story.

At the time of this event in the late 1890s, the incident was widely discussed and was even reported by one major daily and two weekly newspapers. All remain in circulation today, and I rely on their reporting of events, knowing that no responsible public journal would ever dare risk its reputation and readership by printing a false account. If I can read it in one of these papers, that is proof enough for me.

About 1895, the citizens of Nicholas County, West Virginia, voted to replace the rickety old frame County Office building, with its public whipping post and pillory dating from 1824, with a grand new court house and jail. The new building was two stories high, plus full basement, and it was constructed of hand-dressed native sandstone. A substantial slate roof and an impressive cupola housing the town bell crowned the structure.

The cost was enormous, given the state of the public treasury at the time, but was amply justified by the desire of the populace to bring Summersville and Nicholas County into the twentieth century in a manner befitting a modern county seat of government. It was, and is today, a handsome building and a source of pride to the citizens of the area.

Summersville, in the late 1890s, was a pretty little town. Its Main Street was lined with a variety of businesses, and its well-kept homes reflected favorably on the more than two hundred residents of the place.

In the vicinity of the common border between western Nicholas County and eastern Clay County, lies a richly timbered and nearly inaccessible warren of steep hills and dark hollows known locally as The Booger Hole. It was thinly populated by a group of outlaws and renegades, bootleggers and bushwhackers, known as the Water Moccasin Gang. All were active sympathizers with the Confederate cause, which had ended so disastrously for them thirty years earlier. Many were still in bitter denial of the outcome of the War Between the States. It was a point of honor with them to refuse to call it "The Civil War," for that term implied that the subservient states were in rebellion against a politically superior power. They saw the states as autonomous equals and rejected the centralized authority of the federal government.

The Water Moccasins lived by poaching, thievery, and moonshining. Their *purpose* in life, however, was to terrorize and demoralize those of their neighbors who had chosen to align themselves with the Union forces during the recent conflict. If they could not have victory, they would have revenge.

In no sense could the Water Moccasin Gang be considered representative of the residents of the two counties, most of whom were fine, public-spirited people, eager to leave the war behind them as they moved into a new century.

One supporter of the Water Moccasins, and an active participant in their terrorist activity, was Bartholomew Hindren. He was called "Black Bart" for uncertain reasons. Whether for the unwashed condition of his filthy hide, the color of his heart, or his ugly moods, his name was entirely appropriate, and he tried in every way to justify it.

Bart was a throwback to a much earlier time. He lived alone in a shallow cave at the base of a cliff. The opening had been walled up with rocks chinked with mud. A curtain of animal skins covered the doorway and shut out the inclement weather and nosy neighbors. Uncovered, the entry served as a smoke hole for his cooking fires and provided scant ventilation for his dark quarters.

Bart's nearest neighbor was Walden Castor, a widower whose wife had died in childbirth. He lived a few miles from Bart with his fourteen-year-old daughter, Libby, just east of the Clay County line, in the vicinity of Dille. Libby was a pretty young thing, shy and eager to please like her mother, and just beginning to show signs of the beautiful young woman she would become.

Walden had opened a vein of coal on his property from which he dug his house fuel. One day, as Bart followed a wounded deer, he passed near the opening to Walden's mine. Hearing a faint cry for help, he investigated and found that the roof of the mine had caved in, trapping the badly injured miner under a huge boulder. The doomed man's last thought was of his daughter, Libby. Before dying, he exacted a solemn promise from Bart that he would see that the orphaned Libby was taken care of. Leaving the unfortunate Walden in his mine, in lieu of a more appropriate burial place, Bart hurried to the nearby house to inform Libby of her father's death.

For several years, Bart had felt the keen need of a woman in his bed. He had made a few attempts to persuade local females to cohabit with him, but none were sufficiently possessed of the pioneer spirit to stay the course. Bart's primitive living situation, coupled with his filthy personal habits and dark spirit, always forced him to go back to his solitary life. Now, he saw a possible permanent solution to his ongoing problem.

Here was a young woman who was old enough to serve his needs, yet young enough to be submissive to his will. Bart would honor Walden's dying request to see that Libby was taken care of. What more appropriate way to keep his promise than to "take care" of her himself?

Though Libby wept and begged to be delivered to the care of

a family of her acquaintance, Bart told her that she now belonged to him. Her dying father had given her into his care. She would, therefore, accompany him to his home, where she would serve him as his wife. If she refused, she would be severely beaten. He then administered a sample of the kind of treatment she could expect if she persisted in her obstinate refusal. Bloody, disconsolate, and weeping, Libby gathered a few items of clothing and carried them to her new home with Bart.

Through the next five years, Libby lived with her captor in his mountain cave. Once, she ran away, but having no idea about where to go, she was soon recaptured and roundly beaten by Bart. Her lack of knowledge of these mountains equipped her poorly for survival, and she was weakened by a series of pregnancies.

Bart wanted no "young'uns" whom he would have to provide for, and a child might limit her service to him. As soon as her condition became obvious, he would beat and kick her until she aborted the fetus. Within a few weeks or months, she would find herself pregnant again, repeating the whole brutal cycle. She was so dispirited that she found herself unable to resist his insistent demands. Lacking the means to resist, it was better to meekly comply than to be beaten into unwilling submission.

One summer day in her nineteenth year, following a particularly savage battering, Libby sought the comforting warmth of the sunshine outside the cave. Bart was away with his Moccasin comrades and would probably not return before nightfall. Suddenly, she became alerted to the presence of another person, an older man, on the hillside below the cave. As she tried to slip away unseen into the shelter of the cave, he saw her and spoke to her.

"Why, girl, what are you doing way out here by yourself?" It was the first human being that she had seen, other than Bart, in the five years of her captivity.

The stranger introduced himself as Laban Donahue, traveling from his home near Strange Creek to Summersville. Appalled by the extent of her injuries and concerned for her safety, he spoke kindly and offered to take her to a doctor in the county seat town.

At first Libby refused, out of fear that Bart would follow and kill them both. Despite that, Laban persuaded her that the only hope of ending Bart's reign of terror lay in escape. Pausing only long enough to throw a blanket around her thin shoulders and to secure a pair of moccasins for her feet, the fugitive pair set off over the shoulder of Powell's Mountain.

By nightfall they were within sight and sound of the lumber mill at Birch River. Libby resisted Laban's suggestion that they seek refuge in the tiny hamlet, fearing that they may encounter an acquaintance of Bart's, so they made a rude camp at the edge of a clearing. They spread their blankets in a laurel thicket and shared Laban's traveling rations of venison and cold biscuit.

The warm rays of the morning sun awakened Libby to her first full day of freedom in five long, tormented years. Breaking camp was no large chore, and within minutes they were moving down a beautiful mountain valley following old deer and Indian trails. It was such a peaceful scene that she was almost persuaded that her recent ordeal had been only a bad dream.

However, the pain in her tortured limbs and the bruises on her body bore undeniable testimony to the reality of her experience. They traveled slowly, keeping to the wooded slopes of the mountain rather than risk being seen and recognized by those they might meet on the road below. By evening they were at the widening of the valley, the Forks of Muddlety Creek. Summersville, and safety, was less than ten miles away. By noon tomorrow her long nightmare would be history. Again, they made camp in the dense forest and sought the comfort and rest of their blankets.

The screeching of the steam whistle at the mill on the right fork of Muddlety Creek awakened the fugitive pair. They ate the remains of the venison in Laban's bag, washing the dry meat down with generous gulps of water from a spring-fed stream. Preparation for the final leg of their journey was accomplished by shaking out and folding their blankets and pulling on shoes and moccasins. Three hours later, they crested a small hill and saw, spread out below them, the lovely village of Summersville, with the Nicholas County Courthouse at its center. For the first time in years, Libby found release from her conflicted emotions in the tears she shed.

Painfully conscious of her tattered garments and of her pathetic physical appearance, Libby was tormented by a desire to run away, rather than face the pitying stares of the townsfolk. Still, with no real alternative, she forced herself to follow Laban through the great oak doors of the new courthouse. The office of Sheriff A. W. Bodner was just down the hall.

Before she permitted herself to be remanded to the care of Dr. J. H. Fulton, she insisted on filing charges against Bartholomew Hindren for kidnapping, assault, and battery. The charges were entered, pending a determination as to whether the alleged crime had occurred in Nicholas County or Clay. A later charge of rape was added, though the Prosecuting Attorney, W. A. McCloskey, felt that it could not be substantiated and would be difficult to prove. Her five years of cohabiting with Bart seemed to satisfy the requirements of a common-law marriage. Her consent to the arrangement would be assumed.

Since the jail was temporarily unoccupied, Libby was permitted to use the space designated for the housing of female prisoners, pending more satisfactory and permanent arrangements. Within a few days, she began to regain her strength and vitality. As her plight became known in the town, many citizens made donations of clothing and basic personal items. The possession of a comb and mirror, though she expressed horror at what she saw reflected therein, brought a sparkle to her eyes and made buoyant her spirit. Clean undergarments and a presentable dress to cover her near-naked condition produced a sensuously euphoric mood, heightened the color in her cheeks, and added a sprightliness to her step.

As she regained her strength, she began to busy herself about the courthouse, cleaning, running errands, and making herself useful in many small ways. She was locked in her cell at night, for her own protection, but otherwise had full run of the courthouse and, for that matter, of the town.

As her paranoia and fear diminished, her personality came alive and blossomed. She captured the attention and dogged devotion of the jailer, Bill Bascomb, a middle-aged bachelor, who served also as janitor and general handyman.

According to the practice of the time, the jail and a large courtroom were located on the second floor of the Courthouse, with the first floor reserved for county offices. The basement housed public restrooms, a maintenance shop, and a small two-room apartment in which Bill lived.

Libby quickly became a fixture of the place, and the county officials began to wonder how they had ever gotten along without her. Within a few days, she was cleaning the jail cells and the jailer's rooms, and cooking light meals for herself, the jailer, and the occasional inmate.

As jailer, Bill was allowed a small daily stipend for the feeding of prisoners. The meals were catered as needed by the proprietor of a local boarding house. Now, having Libby to cook meals for himself and his prisoners, Bill experienced a small wave of unprecedented prosperity as he pocketed the meal allowance in addition to his salary.

Perhaps it was inevitable that, given Bill's devotion and considerate treatment of her, romance would bloom, and that she would begin to share herself with him in other ways. Though she continued, officially, to occupy the cell at night, after the county offices had closed and the building was quiet, she furtively descended the stairs and entered the quarters of her jailer/lover.

Their affair soon became the worst kept secret in the history of Nicholas County. Though the jail and the jailer lent an undeniable sense of security, Libby began to worry that, given her high profile in the courthouse, Bart would soon learn of her presence there and would come to seek retribution. Already she had heard rumors of a darkly sinister man making guarded inquiries about her around the town.

One of Bill's collateral duties as jailer was that of making coffins for any prisoner who might die while in his custody, and for any indigent person who expired within the county. The coffin was just a rough pine box, of the "wooden overcoat" pattern. The coffins were unlined, "one size fits all," to accommodate cadavers of any dimensions.

A few coffins were made in advance and stored in the basement workshop to answer the demands of almost any catastrophe, such as logging accidents, mine disasters, floods, fires, or outbreaks of disease. When a prisoner died, or an indigent person expired, the body was brought to the courthouse basement and placed in a waiting coffin. Then Bill, in his own good time, went to the bell rope on the second floor of the building, where he tolled the bell thirteen times.

His signal alerted the appointed volunteer pallbearers who, at the end of the workday, converged on the courthouse to attend to the burial in Potter's Field. This was a sop to the local convention than no one should be buried unattended. Thus, the social conscience was salved and the necessity of storing unrefrigerated and unembalmed bodies was circumvented.

Given their common concern that Bart might suddenly appear to seek revenge against them both, they were not surprised when Sheriff Bodner appeared with a request from the Clay County Sheriff that Libby be confined and held for extradition and trial in Clay. It seemed that Bart had filed charges there against her for allegedly stealing a small cache of gold coins he had hidden in the cave. He was also taking action, as Libby's common-law husband, to have her father's house and property deeded to him. At that time, women were permitted to hold property in their own name only if they were single. A married woman's property normally was given over to the husband.

Although full of apologies for having to do so, Bill reluctantly locked Libby in her cell. They began immediately to devise a plan that might deliver them from danger and provide a means of escape. The Clay County courts were known to be sympathetic to the Moccasin cause, and Libby knew that if she were delivered there for trial, she was a doomed woman. They must, therefore, move quickly.

After much intense discussion, it was determined that Libby must inexplicably and completely be made to disappear. Bill, too, would evaporate, though his vanishing act would be harder to explain. He was, after all, a county official. Even so, by the time his absence was noted, they hoped to be long gone and forever lost to the world.

The plan to which they resorted seems unnecessarily complicated, but we must allow for Bill's flair for the dramatic and for Libby's desire that their disappearance be attended by an aura of mystery. Libby must hold herself in constant readiness for a long and precipitous journey.

Bill would prepare by fashioning a special coffin of only slightly more generous dimensions than normal, in which the next deceased to reach his basement workshop would be placed. Then Bill would unlock the door to Libby's cell. When she heard the bell toll thirteen times, she must make her way unseen to the makeshift morgue, lift the lid to the coffin, and crawl inside, lying face to face with the cadaver therein. Bill would soon come to nail the coffin shut.

The extra dimensions of the coffin would not only give them sufficient room to occupy the tight space, but would provide a little more air for breathing. At day's end, the pallbearers would assemble, transport the coffin to Potter's Field, and bury it in a pre-dug grave.

As soon as the pallbearers had completed their work at the gravesite and darkness had descended, Bill would quickly appear with two fast horses and a shovel. He would uncover the coffin, pry off the lid, and rescue his lovely Libby. Together they would re-cover the coffin, mount their horses, and ride off into the night. With luck, they could be forty miles away by morning and boarding a train to parts unknown. Their tickets were already purchased and secure in his vest pocket. Bill was pleased. The plan was sound. All was over except the waiting. He whistled an off-key tune as he thought of his future with Libby.

Late the following day, a body was brought in from Peter's Creek. An unidentified man had been killed in a gunfight during a log-camp gambling dispute. The victim was a slightly built man of less than medium height.

After he was laid in the coffin, Bill unlocked Libby's cell, then returned briefly to his basement shop for a final check on preparations. A short time later, the bell was heard to toll thirteen times—the prearranged signal to the pallbearers and to Libby. She delayed only long enough to ensure that the stairs were clear, then quickly made her way to the basement workroom and climbed into the coffin with her unknown companion, carefully avoiding looking at his face.

It was a tight fit, but she would be fine for a short time. Soon Bill would return from the bell tower. He would secure the lid to the coffin with ten short nails and deliver it to the custody of the pallbearers, who would make quick work of the burial. She was unaware, however, that an unseen pair of piercing blue eyes, burning with intensity in a darkly bearded face, watched her every move from behind the stacked coffins in the workroom.

To all appearances, the plan unfolded flawlessly. Libby settled into her uneasy quarters with her silent companion. Within a few minutes she heard the rapping of a hammer as the nails were driven, securing the lid on the coffin. At five o'clock, the pallbearers appeared with a horse and light wagon. The coffin was loaded without comment, though one of the pallbearers was later remembered to have said, "Gee, this guy must weigh a ton. Why don't the skinny ones ever die?" The sun was just setting over the Muddlety Bottoms when the burial party finished their work and turned back toward the town, eager to get home to their waiting families and their evening meal.

Meanwhile, in the palpable darkness of the coffin, buried under the rocky soil of Potter's Field, Libby patiently awaited Bill's arrival. It was a little weird being in the tight confines of the coffin with a dead stranger, but she could tolerate it for a short time. The air was becoming just a bit foul, and she did wish Bill would hurry.

She had no way to estimate the passage of time, but she was beginning to regret having consumed that last large cup of coffee just before she heard the tolling of the bell. Surely . . . surely, he would be here soon. Breathlessly she awaited the soft sibilant scraping of the shovel on the mounded earth. But no sound reached her in the silence of her tomb.

She began to experience panic, imagining that the air trapped in the coffin would be consumed before she was rescued. If only she had thought to bring a light, a candle, a match.

Aha . . . a match! She remembered having put a single match in the pocket of her dress. She felt in her pocket and grasped the match as though it were her only salvation. With a trembling hand, she brought the match head against the inside of the coffin lid and raked it firmly across the rough surface of the pine boards. Darn! The matchstick snapped near its sulfurous head.

"Be careful now," she coached herself. "Grasp the match securely and draw it firmly across the wooden lid. Be prepared for burned fingers. Don't drop it! This is your last chance. Do it NOW!"

The implement sputtered a blue flame and flared briefly yellow before delivering a painful burn to her grasping fingers. The flame went out and darkness returned. It had been a short respite from the blackness, but it was long enough for her to recognize the pale, sightless eyes of her lover, Bill Bascomb. A pair of train tickets protruded from the pocket of his vest. Her last conscious remembrance was of opening her mouth in a silent scream.

The absence of the star-crossed lovers was duly noted the next morning. Inquiries revealed that no one had seen either of them after the body of the gambler was delivered to the basement late on the previous day. Sheriff Bodner assembled the anxious courthouse workers to try to reconstruct events and solve the mystery of the lovers' disappearance.

"But the bell tolled. That must have been Bill ringing the bell," the sheriff observed. "Did anyone see him go to the second floor?"

"I saw someone on the stairs just *before* the bell was tolled," responded the county clerk, "but I'm pretty sure it wasn't Bill. This man was taller and was extremely dirty. He left a very bad smell in the hallway, and I just know that wasn't Bill."

Though most suspected the pair had simply eloped, a close search of the basement was conducted. The body of the Peter's Creek gunfighter/gambler was found hidden under a pile of boards for coffin making. Sometime later he was identified as an itinerant worker who went by the name of Leander Kincaid, but the folks on Peter's Creek doubted that was his real name. Since no relatives had appeared to claim his body, the pallbearers were reassembled and he was soon properly buried in Potter's Field.

Curious as to just who might be occupying the grave intended originally for Mr. Kincaid, the burial site was opened and the coffin lid was removed. There, together for all eternity, lay Libby Castor, her lips forever frozen in a silent scream. Beside her was Bill Bascomb, her erstwhile lover, a pair of train tickets protruding conspicuously from the pocket of his vest.

Sheriff Bodner, succumbing to a rare moment of sentimentality, quietly turned to his crew and said, "Let's cover them back up again boys. They wanted to be together so bad, it seems a shame to bust them up now. And boys, let's just keep this to ourselves. We don't know what happened here, but there ain't no use of making a federal case out of it. We'll just tell the Clay County Sheriff that the prisoner escaped. That's a lot less trouble for everyone."

A year or so later, curiosity drove Laban Donahue to return to the cave where he had found Libby. Observing no sign of life in the rude accommodations, he entered to find Bartholomew Hindren stretched out on his bed. Though *rigor mortis* had stiffened his limbs, he did not appear to have been dead long. A heavy bear skin rug covered the body. The stench in the airless space was unbearable.

Laban hastily summoned the Clay County authorities. Finding no evidence of foul play, they speculated that Black Bart had simply fallen asleep and that his trapped body odors had accumulated beneath the bearskin rug, causing his death by suffocation. Though it was unusual, a hastily assembled coroner's inquest officially confirmed the suspected cause of death.

Not only had Laban solved the mystery of the demise of Black Bart Hindren, he inadvertently answered a much weightier question when he revealed that when he found him, Bart's whiskers were definitely tucked *beneath* the covers of his bed.

Many Nicholas Countians remain in a state of denial about this story to this day. They say that it never happened. Some even deny that there ever was such a person as Libby Castor and will state their opinion that Bill Bascomb was just a petty thief who simply absconded with the jail's feed-bill revenue. It is their privilege to believe what they will, to bury their heads in the sands of their own disbelief. Anyway, if you have an open mind, walk just west of town some moonlit night. Take the road to Potter's Field, and stand quietly on the brow of the hill overlooking Muddlety Road.

Listen carefully, and above the sighing of the wind in the trees, you may hear the faint echoes of a heartrending scream, the ultimate expression of utter despair. It is Libby, eternally reliving the moment of her chilling discovery and the shattering of her dream of deliverance. Some will insist that it is *only* the wind or the distant scream of a panther in the dark woods, but I submit to the overwhelming evidence of the accumulated facts of the case. I believe, not because I will, but because I must. Try as I may, I can do no other.

Nicholas County Courthouse, Summersville, West Virginia

PART 2
Semper Fi
1942–1945

"Do Ye Know Where Looneyville's Ay-ut?"

Among the earliest settlers of the headwaters of the Pocatalico River were the Looneys. They were of rugged pioneer stock—hardworking, industrious, and honest. In Roane County, the name Looney is one to be reckoned with, and there, none of the levity attaches to it that must be dealt with elsewhere. Growing up among the Looney families, it simply never occurred to us to associate the name with *loony bin* or *lunatic asylum*.

The area settled by the Looneys came to be known as "Looneyville." My mother's home was at Looneyville, and my parents lived there for several years after their marriage. Since I was born at Gandeeville, a place settled by the Gandee family, and having encountered some of the hilarity with which many outlanders treated the former's name, I was always truly grateful to have been the only one of seven children of my family not born in Looneyville.

The story is told of a scion of the Looney family who was drafted into the army during the early years of World War II. His name and birthplace were the subject of much good-natured fun, the more so since he was of a completely naïve and trusting nature.

On one occasion his drill sergeant, exasperated and perhaps amused by Looney's evident innocence, mused, "Looney! Looney! Looney! You really *are* a little bit loony, aren't you? Where in West Virginia did you say you were from, Looney?"

"Well, sir," the hapless Looney drawled, "Do ye know where Looneyville's ay-ut?"

The Pot Walloper

It is the unremarkable that is sometimes remembered best and remains with us longest. And often the best training for our future lives comes to us in innocent and uncalculated ways. Some of my best and most practical training and work experience came early in life at the hands of my sister Faye.

Three-and-a-half years my senior, Faye had a heavy load to carry, particularly through her high school years and most especially after our mother's death. At that time, she and I were the only children remaining at home. Both of us had morning and evening chores to do, but during Mom's illness, an increasing share of housekeeping tasks became Faye's responsibility.

I was charged with chopping wood for heating and cooking, and caring for the cow, pigs, and chickens—all best done before dinner. But Faye arrived home an hour later than I, often in near darkness, and was faced with the immediate task of starting the evening meal.

After dinner, I was as free as a bird and had little or no homework to do in preparation for school the next day. But she still had a table full of dirty dishes to be washed and floors to be swept and scrubbed before she could even consider beginning her evening's homework. It was a heavy load for her, which she characteristically accepted without grumbling or complaining. But the injustice of the work allocation must have suggested itself to her for, in her own quiet and unassuming way, she sought and found a perfect and painless solution—me!

My only after-dinner chore was to carry in a supply of water for the night and the following day. When that was finished, Faye would be busily washing dishes. "I read a good story today. Want me to tell it to you?" Of course I did, for she was a marvelous storyteller. "Then why don't you just dry these dishes while you're standing there?"

Before I knew it, the dishes were done. Sometimes the story was spun out through other chores as well; not that I cared, for it was idle time for me and her stories were always exciting and entertaining. But I did take note that they were invariably continued stories, with a climax, crisis, or some sort of hook to draw me back to another session, carefully timed to coincide with the end of our work.

"I have to do my homework now," she would announce, "but we will finish the story tomorrow night"—thus assuring my willing and even eager cooperation the following evening. Usually, I could hardly wait.

After I entered the Marine Corps, I found that the one thing I missed most about my life on the farm was the solitude. Unaccustomed to constantly being in the company of more humanity than I could easily abide, I yearned for some time and place where I could be alone to think and to dream. My solution was to volunteer for all manner of jobs that promised to take me away from the omnipresent mob of marines. I volunteered to be an armed security guard on merchant ships anchored in the harbor. I made myself available to guard the United Services Organization (USO) building in town after a series of break-ins. It was quality time!

All USMC privates were subject to up to thirty days per year of KP, or kitchen duty, in which one peeled the proverbial potatoes, assisted the cooks, swabbed greasy decks, cleaned equipment, and "walloped" pots and pans. Most young men believed that such chores were women's work, to be avoided at all costs. But Faye's training and my need for time alone persuaded me that instead of being terminally boring and morally offensive, such work could be made to serve my purposes.

The pot walloper position seemed ideally suited to my temperament and met all of my requirements. All other jobs would require my presence in the galley both before and during meal service—the busiest, most hectic, and noisiest time of day. Pot walloping, while presenting the appearance of a truly daunting task due to the mountains of dirty cooking vessels to be washed, actually went quite quickly and certainly demanded little expenditure of brainpower;

the mind could turn to other pursuits as the hands worked. After performing my primary duty and swabbing down the scullery area, my time was my own until after the next meal. At most, I worked about five hours each day.

The scullery occupied its own section of the galley, to better contain the heat and the bad smells. And since I was alone in the area at the time, I was practically unsupervised and could select or prepare my choice of foods. Best of all, it was a job no one else wanted, and I had the run of the camp at a time when everyone else was occupied in other areas. I tried to present the cooks with well-walloped pots and did so without complaint. The result was that I was accepted for such duty whenever I volunteered.

When my unit was in the field, we subsisted on field rations (C-rations) and had no need of a galley or scullery. At such times I was occupied with my regularly assigned duties in demolitions. But when the battalion went into garrison, we were subjected to endless rounds of mind-numbing training exercises. To escape that boring drill, I often volunteered for mess duty and invariably requested assignment as a pot walloper.

Kitchen staff, pot walloper far left

The downside of walloping pots was chiefly in the title. It did lack that certain air of dignity and panache that one desires, but then I never exactly waxed lyrical over *yardbird* or even *private*, and I had no plan to make a life's work of it. In the scullery, I was never addressed by any title other than Pot Walloper, but I was left to my own devices and that suited me just fine.

Thanks to Faye's training, I had found something that I could do well, and I had stumbled onto a way to retain my sanity, even though my dignity might occasionally suffer. Now if I can just keep Peggy from reading this, I'm home free. But if she ever offers to tell me an exciting story, or if I hear a strident voice loudly demanding the presence of the pot walloper, I'm outta here!

Fire in the Hole!

A farmer slips a stick or two of dynamite into the hole he has dug under an old stump in his pasture field. He tamps the earth carefully over and around the charge and, lighting the fuse, shouts, "Fire in the hole!" as he runs for cover. A few seconds later, the stump erupts in a cloud of smoke and dust, and splinters rain down on the pasture.

A "powder monkey" drills a series of boreholes in the side of a mountain at the site of a new super highway or the location of a proposed high dam. Carefully, he charges each hole with a precisely calculated amount of explosive. Each charge is armed with its own detonator and is linked to every other charge in the series by an intricate network of thin wires. A small handheld machine capable of sending a tiny electrical current through the wires is connected to the maze. The warning shout, "Fire in the hole!" causes lookouts stationed a half-mile away to relay the ominous cry, "Fire in the hole!" The dynamo is then activated, and instantly the earth shakes and rumbles as an entire mountainside erupts in a deluge of broken rock and pulverized dirt.

This scene is repeated hundreds of times a day with minor variations as, deep in the earth, miners blast tunnels through seams of coal and drillers shock their oil-bearing sands into new productivity. The common denominator in each scene is the boisterous cry, "Fire in the hole!" as the power of explosives is unleashed to accomplish its purpose.

Growing up in the oil fields of West Virginia, I was certainly no stranger to the clamorous warning that sent all who heard it scrambling for cover. But in this, as in so many other things, it remained for the Marine Corps to put "new wine in old vessels" by lending a whole new meaning to the concept. And I can hardly thank them enough for having so furthered my education.

Boot camp at Parris Island, South Carolina, was a tightly scheduled series of evolutions from reveille to taps. With thousands of recruits all attempting to use the same facilities at the same time, tight scheduling was a necessity. Each platoon of 64 trainees was given an inflexible window of opportunity to use drill fields, rifle ranges, mess halls, and "heads," or bathrooms. Reveille sounded at 0430 not by bugle, but by the drill instructor beating on a bucket with a swagger stick. We were given fifteen minutes to accomplish the three S's: *shit, shower, and shave.*

Allow me to set the scene: a large multipurpose room served all uses related to personal comfort and sanitation. Across the back of the room, behind a shoulder-high partition, a dozen showerheads jutted from a wall, each designed to accommodate four or more persons. Each showerhead could only be turned *On* or *Off.* There was no need to try to regulate the temperature, the only choice being COLD.

On the starboard (right) side of the room ran a metal trough through which a current of seawater was pumped. A series of faucets dispensing fresh water jutted from the bulkhead above the trough, permitting shaving, toothbrushing, rinsing, and spitting into the sea water, which drained into Port Royal Sound via a series of sewer lines.

Another larger and deeper trough ran the length of the port (left) bulkhead, through which a similar current of seawater was pumped. This trough was fitted with a wide board through which a number of large holes had been cut, each appropriately sized for its obvious purpose. No doubt about it, the Marine Corps spared no effort or expense to make its facilities not only adequate, but also ergonomically correct.

On the fourth side, a large double door was centered, flanked by urinal troughs. We learned early on to take nothing to the head with us except a toilet kit and towel, for no provision was made for placement of clothing or other articles.

So we draped our towels about our necks or loins and, otherwise naked, dashed for the facilities. Dignity and modesty were left behind, along with self-consciousness. Our DI frequently admonished us, "Now hear this! When I holler, 'Head Call,' I don't wanna see nothin' but backsides and elbows—and them just a quiverin'! I wanna see 64 bare butts disappear through them double doors at the same time, or I wanna see a whole lotta blood on them door frames!"

Inside the doors, a mad scramble occurred as the most urgent business was conducted at the two urinals and then forty bodies competed for space under the showers or at the shaving trough. Along the port bulkhead, at least twenty bodies settled themselves over the *other* trough, where they grunted and strained as each attempted to accomplish his mission within the designated timeframe.

And at least twice in the allotted fifteen minutes, someone at the head of the line of seated "meditators" would reel off a basketball-size wad of toilet paper, set it afire, and drop it into the gently flowing stream of flushing water. One by one, twenty rumps would rise briefly off the seat as the flaming torch passed slowly beneath them. As they arose momentarily, looking for all the world like a spectator wave at an athletic contest, each would cry out the time-honored warning, "Fire in the hole!"

When I became a demolitions man for the coal mines, working daily with the explosives that gave legitimacy to the expression, I half expected, with each shouted warning, to see those marines in the area assume a momentary half-crouch before resuming their places.

After Parris Island, the cry "Fire in the hole!" somehow lost some of its urgency.

Doing The Laundry, Marine Corps Style

You never miss the water till the well runs dry.
—Rowland Howard

Though it appears to be an insignificant chore, doing the laundry looms large on the list of things to be done by troops in the field. When I was deployed, we seemed to be in a perennial drought, so water was provided only in sufficient quantities for drinking and sponge bathing—often a personal ration of two quarts daily. Doing the laundry easily dropped to the very bottom of the list. But if sanitation was to be maintained, it had to be done eventually, and it was never far from the top of our minds.

Marine units deployed in the field for more than a day or two were normally equipped with the Field Transport Pack, which provided for one change of clothing, including underwear and socks. At the end of the day, a bivouac area would be seen to "blossom," with tomorrow's underwear and other items laid out to dry and be sanitized by the sun. Careful rotation, with special attention to the socks and underwear, would see a marine through several such days.

You may imagine that many crude remarks were invented and raunchy stories told about personal sanitation among troops so deployed. One of the favorites concerned a platoon of marines who had been in the field for many days. One morning at roll call, as the troops were brought to attention, the lieutenant announced, "Good news, men. Today we get a change of underwear. Brown, you will change with Gillespie. Carlson, you will change with Johnson," etc.

"The Racks" at Parris Island prepared us for self-sufficiency when deployed. They were waist-high platforms in the sandlot behind the pine board (PB) huts. Each recruit was issued a ten-quart galvanized bucket, a fiber scrub brush, and a cake of very caustic lye soap. Soiled clothing items were laid on the platform, soaked with water, rubbed with lye soap, and vigorously scrubbed with the brush. After rinsing, they were attached to a clothesline with tie strings for drying.

The Marine Corps had not yet found or invented a satisfactory iron or ironing board, so none was provided. Ironing was accomplished by folding the rumpled laundry items as neatly as possible. They were then inserted between the canvas cot and the thin mattress pad, where they were "pressed" by body weight while we were sleeping. Needless to say, the results were somewhat humbling, which may have been the intended purpose.

Only large bases had permanent laundry facilities. Larger ships at sea were equipped with laundries, though often they were inadequate to serve the needs of embarked marines. In those instances, the troops became quite inventive in providing for their laundry needs. Lines hanging overboard to which laundry was attached when underway draped the sides of the smaller ships. There, it was thoroughly beaten and pounded by the bow wave until taken in for drying. When dried, the fabric was saturated with salt from the evaporated seawater. From this comes the term *old salt*, meaning someone who has been at sea for so long that his clothing is encrusted with sea salt. The term *old salt* was a coveted term of approbation—so much so that newer items of clothing were often soaked in sea water and bleached in the sun to make them appear to be well-worn. Newly issued clothing was the mark of a newcomer, or recruit—not that of an old salt.

In the islands, we were never far from the sea. Fresh water was always in short supply, so we often did our laundry by going for a swim in the sea, fully clothed, at the end of which the freshly "laundered" items were laid out to dry in the sun.

After the Tarawa campaign (see "The Battle of Tarawa"), we subsisted for a month or more on the precious canned water we had brought with us from Samoa. During this time, we were limited to the standard field ration of two quarts of water per man, per day. It is amazing what a well-motivated person can do with two quarts of water.

A pint of water in a helmet cover is adequate for shaving and, using the same water, a thorough washing of the crotch and underarms. This was considered necessary for prevention of a nasty infection in those areas, aptly called *the crud*. A tiny bit of fresh water was squeezed through the salt laden socks, after which they would be used to "rinse" the crotch and underarms. Only a small amount of fresh water was needed to brush the teeth. A Lister bag was set up under a tripod, usually in front of the dispensary. The Lister bag was a canvas bag of about 35 to 50 gallons, resembling a cow's udder with four teats, or dispensing valves, from which one with great patience could coax a drink of water. The porous canvas allowed for cooling by evaporation. It was an imperfect arrangement but a welcome solution, USMC-style, to the water problem.

Eventually water evaporation units were set up to distill seawater into fresh. Soon the operators of the evaporation units had their own thing going. Small, hastily constructed windmills were set up on the beach. Using five-gallon buckets, tubs, and cracker tins, they pilfered enough water from the evaporators to go into business for themselves. A dasher foot on the end of a rod running from an eccentric windmill shaft used the power of the wind to agitate the laundry endlessly. They took in washings from their fellow marines, charging a couple of dollars per load, making more money than the Marine Corps paid them.

During my frequent month-long tours of mess duty as pot walloper in the galley, I learned a new method of doing the laundry. Food was cooked and kept warm by steam, which circulated in the giant vats, urns, and steam tables. In the scullery, where the pots and pans were washed, a petcock was installed in the steam line. A short length of hose was forced over the end of the petcock and dropped into a tub of water. The soiled clothing was put in the tub with laundry soap, the steam turned on, and soon the water was hot and bubbling merrily away. It was, by far, the most painless and satisfactory way I ever found to do my laundry. Unfortunately, I was not on permanent mess duty, and after returning to my regular duties with my company, I sorely missed my improvised laundry in the scullery.

Today I look back on Marine Corps days with nostalgia and amusement. But I do not miss sponge baths, water hours, or water rationing. One of my greatest luxuries is a shower with an endless supply of hot water. Indeed, "you never miss the water till the well runs dry."

The Battle of Tarawa

In April 1943, as a member of the Marine Corps 19th Replacement Battalion, I was shipped to Pago Pago, Tutuila, American Samoa, where I was assigned to the 2nd Defense Battalion, 2nd Marine Division, as a 75mm gun crewman. Within a few months, we were in the midst of a hurried reorganization as we were redesignated the 2nd Anti-Aircraft Artillery Battalion (AAA).

Our 75mm guns, relics of WWI, were given to a native Samoan self-defense force. We were given 90mm antiaircraft guns and began an intensive training program in their use. It became clear that Samoa was unthreatened, and that we were being prepared for some larger purpose.

Our light artillery, .30-caliber and .50-caliber machine guns and 20mm and 40mm weapons, were attached to the division's infantry component and sent off to Auckland, New Zealand, for amphibious training. It was a time of frenzied activity as we prepared for our new and as yet undisclosed mission.

A multitude of speculative stories, or scuttlebutt, were circulated as a number of island groups were nominated for possible invasion scenarios. We considered ourselves to be that *well* trained. Alternatively, we would be disbanded and assigned as replacements for battle casualties in other AAA units. We considered ourselves to be that *poorly* trained. But the *favorite* piece of scuttlebutt had us returning to the United States to become the nucleus of a newly formed division-strength invasion force.

In early September, that last enduring dream was laid to rest when a convoy of LSTs (Landing Ship, Tank), escorted by a few destroyers (DD) and destroyer escorts (DDE), entered the harbor. The LSTs were beached on the Pago Pago waterfront.

Soon we were busily moving aboard the LST 20 with guns,

ammunition, and provisions. We knew little of the art of combat loading (positioning materials and provisions so that first-needed items would be first off at our destination). Most of us had never even seen an LST, a weird looking vessel designed for grounding on a beachhead, whose massive bow doors opened up to a huge ramp, permitting vehicles to roll on and off the ship.

USS *LST-20*

Guns, ammunition, and perishable provisions were packed in the cavernous interior (the Tank deck). Trucks and various items in trailers were loaded on the open main deck (the Truck deck). A large area forward of the superstructure was designated for storage of gasoline drums and fuel oil, secured by chains and covered by layers of baled sandbags.

Spaces below decks were very cramped. Officers and ship's crew were billeted in spaces designated for that purpose, with marine NCOs filling in the empty bunks. We marine privates were issued a folding canvas cot and told to find a place wherever space afforded—in vehicles or on the Tank deck. Following the example of others, I lashed my cot to the port railing on the open Truck deck and covered it with my poncho against the elements. Many simply spread a blanket on the layers of sandbags bundled atop the fuel drums stored topside.

Except during inclement weather, we who were billeted topside were much cooler and more comfortable than those below deck. Their spaces lacked air conditioning or even adequate ventilation. During one extended storm, I entered the bow door compartment and slung a hammock between the giant wheels of the bow door/ramp mechanism. It was so comfortable that I slept there for much of our voyage.

We skirted Western Samoa and proceeded north to the Ellice and Wallis islands, where we joined a larger convoy consisting of personnel transports (APA), destroyers, at least one battleship (BB), and an escort carrier (CVE). The progress was leisurely, for the entire convoy was limited by the top speed of our LSTs, about six or seven knots.

The LST proved to be a surprisingly durable and versatile ship, and most served throughout WWII. Round bottomed, with the minimum draft at the bow to facilitate beaching and the displacement mostly at the stern, it had been designed for a single voyage. If necessary, it could be abandoned on the beaches of an embattled island and the loss would be minimal.

But it was also a miserably uncomfortable ship. Its design made for maximum roll and pitch. Freeboard at the low point of a roll was almost nonexistent. With the diesel engines in the stern, the bow met every wave with a resounding smack and a shower of spray. Engine exhaust ports were just below the waterline. The roar of the engines shifted constantly and disconcertingly from port to starboard, as first one exhaust port and then the other submerged. The pervasive stink of diesel fumes was everywhere. The air itself was heavy with the rank smell of the stuff. The evaporated water was tainted. Even the food from the ship's galley reeked of it.

We wallowed along at our top speed, so cramped for space that exercise was impossible. At times we must have looked like a refugee ship from some ragtag armada, laden as we were with camouflaged vehicles and miscellaneous cargo, every otherwise empty space being filled with bodies.

The ship's laundry was inadequate for the use of the marines aboard and so was restricted to the ship's crew. As previously noted, marines did their laundry by tying it to a line and dropping it overboard, where it was beaten by the bow wash until clean. Sun-dried, our clothing was heavy with evaporated salt, for we were denied the use of precious fresh water for rinsing. Showers were limited to every second day, and guards were posted in the heads to assure compliance. Again, this is how I came to understand the origin of the term *old salt* when applied to a navy or marine veteran.

At Funafuti, we dropped anchor for the first time as we rendezvoused with our infantry and light artillery components. Here we rested for a day as our officers conferred aboard the battleship. Landing boats were put into the water as a shark patrol, manned by armed marines, and we were permitted to swim in the ocean swells. It was the only exercise period we were to enjoy during the entire two months at sea.

We were told that our objective was Tarawa, in the Gilbert Islands. It had been heavily fortified and was defended by Imperial Marines of the Japanese Navy. For three days after our arrival, we lay offshore and enjoyed a front row view of the bombardment by the navy's heaviest guns and bombers. By day, a thick pall of smoke hung over the atoll. By night, it seemed that even the sand of the beaches was ablaze.

On the day before the planned invasion, I was assigned to a marine working party. To my surprise, we were directed to enter the bow door compartment—*my improvised bedroom*. Lifting the deck plates, we entered the bilges, and there, cradled in wooden forms, were two glass bottles, each containing about five gallons of pure nitroglycerin, a very unstable form of extremely high explosive. We carefully carried the capricious cargo to a waiting boat and accompanied it twelve miles west of the battle site to an unoccupied sand spit, where we buried it deep in the sand.

Aerial view of Tarawa with Betio Island in the foreground

Bow door compartment: my improvised bedroom

I do not know what eventually happened to the explosive stuff, but it is probably still there, buried under thirty inches of sand on a mid-Pacific atoll. But I will admit that I would have slept much less soundly had I known that there was enough nitroglycerin to blow the whole fleet to kingdom come riding only three or four feet beneath my butt.

The next morning, November 20, 1943, we watched from the safety of the ship's deck as the first waves of marines began their approach to the beaches. It was a disaster. The tide was too low for the boats to clear the coral reefs half a mile offshore. The stranded marines were forced to wade ashore in the 4- to 5-foot-deep water, completely at the mercy of a withering hail of machine gun and rifle fire from the bunkers ashore.

Hundreds died in the chest-deep water, where they washed to and fro in the waves. Those who lived to gain the beachhead were pinned down behind the scant shelter of a low seawall. Gradually, the landing parties began to find breaks in the reef and passage to shallower water inside. The narrow beach was soon filled with supplies intended to sustain the effort ashore. But in the confusion, no one knew what the materials were or where they were located.

Hundreds died in the chest-deep water

In an attempt to ground itself and unload its cargo, our LST broached on the reef. Fuel was urgently needed ashore, so our cargo was quickly pushed over the side. Along with many others, I was ordered into the water, where we swam as we pushed the nearly submerged drums of fuel the half-mile to the beach, past the bodies of our fallen comrades.

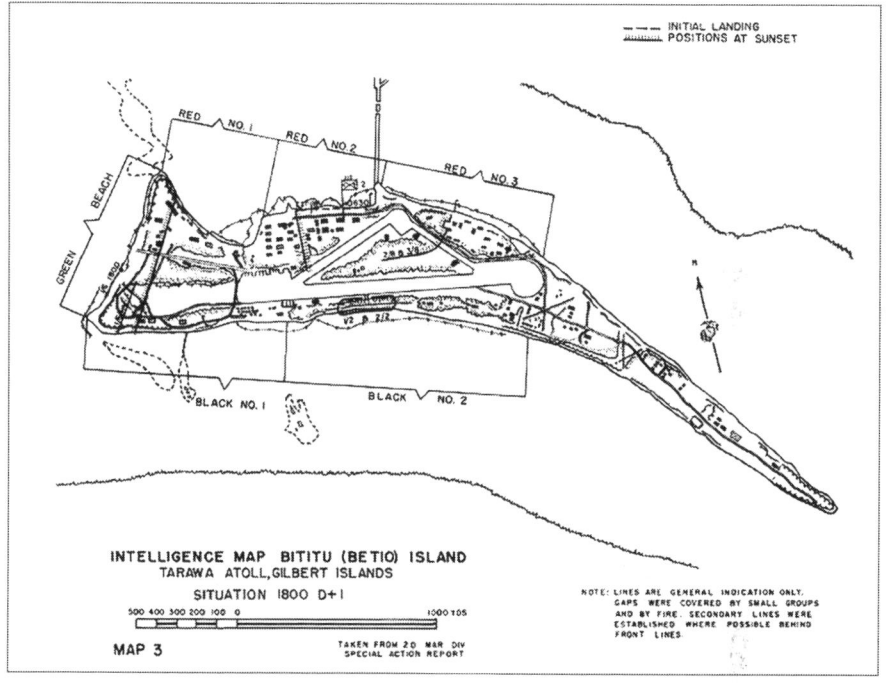

Red Beach 1

Assisting them was out of the question. They were already dead. A few boats not otherwise engaged were picking up corpses and delivering them to makeshift morgue vessels. Other boats with marines aboard were cruising the lagoon, firing at what I initially thought to be coconuts floating in the water. They were the heads of Japanese soldiers, trying desperately to escape the firestorm ashore by swimming to nearby islands.

Late in the afternoon, sunburned, waterlogged, hungry, and thirsty, I sought to locate my unit on the beach. I was unarmed, having left my weapon on the ship as I worked in the water. I watched from the safety of the low seawall as a group of marines assaulted a bunker. While the others laid down a covering fire, one carrying a satchel charge ran up the side and quickly dropped the pack inside a gunport. Smoke billowed from each opening as the charge exploded inside.

Laying down a covering fire

To my left, another marine with a flamethrower raced up to the rim of a shell crater and directed his weapon into the excavation. A Japanese soldier, a living ball of burning napalm, ran out of the crater to be immediately cut down by a volley of rifle fire.

Nearby, another crawled out from beneath a pile of debris with his hands in the air in a gesture of surrender. He was hastily rushed off under guard to a more secure area on the beach. I quickly armed myself with an M1 rifle salvaged from a fallen marine.

Marine with a flamethrower

As night fell, I found a supply dump containing food. I broke open boxes of canned chicken and grapefruit juice. Someone observed me and opened fire. There, I learned that the term "friendly fire" is a misnomer. When you are being shot at, all fire is distinctly unfriendly. Hastily leaving the supply dump, I ran to the sheltering outriggers of a 90mm gun. It was one of ours, and I was back among friends.

With the breaking of day, the fighting had moved beyond our area, and we got our first good view of the results of the battle. Dead bodies littered the area. Swarms of flies, too bloated to become airborne, covered the living and the dead. The cloying stench of death and decay was overwhelming.* Shell holes and bomb craters overlapped one another, and several corpses occupied each.

It was a surreal and thoroughly revolting scene. Somehow, we maneuvered our guns through the cratered landscape and by nightfall were in position and ready to answer the enemy air raids, which were to become a nightly experience.

---

* Dive bomber pilots reported that, flying at 1,000 feet altitude, they were sickened by the odor.

Initial body counts, subject to later revision*, estimated that six thousand Japanese and four thousand US personnel had died on that one square mile of sand. It was a heavy price to pay for such a tiny piece of real estate, but it did demonstrate the validity of the concept of amphibious warfare.

The valuable lessons learned at Tarawa were applied to later invasions, resulting in lower casualty counts. From that time onward, the tides of battle flowed in our favor. It was a decisive victory and a major turning point in the war in the Pacific Theater.

The largest of thirty-seven cemeteries on Tarawa

---

* Initial body counts, a phenomenon of warfare, are nearly always grossly inflated. Later estimates were lowered to about forty-five hundred to five thousand Japanese dead and twelve hundred to fifteen hundred US marines and navy.

From Innocence to Reality

My early to mid-teen years were spent in the peaceful, green hills of central West Virginia. There I completed the eighth grade on schedule and graduated to high school. In no way could I have been considered pampered or sheltered, for I was expected to do routine farm chores, and it was an unspoken understanding that if I wanted to continue in high school, I had to earn the money for books and clothing. So each summer I worked for neighboring farmers, hoeing corn, cutting brush, putting up hay, etc., earning $1 per 10-hour day.

I did not consider myself abused or underprivileged for having to do so. On the contrary, I was generally treated with kindness and consideration by employers, neighbors, and acquaintances, and I learned that giving an honest day's work for my wages was the way to earn the respect of both elders and peers.

It was during these years that I suffered the loss of my mother, my sister Evelyn and two of her children, and my home in a fire. The death of my mother and my sister were hugely traumatic events for me, and I dealt with them by burying my sorrow deep inside and for years refusing to allow them to rise to consciousness. I mourned my other tragedies and losses in my own way and considered them a part of life's unforeseeable events.

On the other hand, I did not expect to be exploited and so did not learn to guard myself against exploitation and abuse. My family and our community ethic of stoicism told me that if life delivered a low blow, I had to learn to deal with it and move on. Perhaps in this respect I was sheltered, but I do not consider that to be the case. I was, however, poorly prepared to deal with the real ugliness of life as I came to know it after enlisting in the Marine Corps at age seventeen, and especially after being exposed to the unsparing brutality of war.

As an active participant in the invasion of Tarawa in November 1943, I had never seen human death except by natural causes and was emotionally unprepared to see men shot, drowned, blown apart by explosives, and burned to death by flamethrower. This was violence on a scale that was wholly foreign to me, whether the victims were enemy or friendly.

Most of my first day in combat was spent working in the surf of that tropical atoll, moving materials onto the sands of Red Beach I. I moved ashore late in the day and spent most of the night in the shelter of the friendly outriggers of a 90mm anti-aircraft gun, trying to be as small and inconspicuous as possible.

The next morning, we moved out and began to maneuver our guns into position on the northern tip of the island of Betio. Almost immediately I was confronted by an open, gaping bomb crater or shell hole. It was eight to ten feet deep and twice as wide. There, sprawled in the grotesque attitudes of death, lay a dozen bodies of the enemy. A cloud of flies swarmed over each. The sickening stench of death was overwhelming.

On top of this hideous and outrageous heap of human offal was the body of a Japanese officer. He wore a sidearm and binoculars, and on his arm was a wristwatch. I knew that I might never have another such opportunity to capture valuable souvenirs, but I just could not bring myself to clamber down into that grisly hole and remove them from his body.

Within a matter of minutes, my platoon sergeant found me and assigned me to a detail burying Japanese dead. My scruples against handling dead bodies vanished quickly as we moved corpses into hastily improvised trenches and covered them with sand. Those in shell holes, including that of the officer with the souvenirs, were simply covered over where they lay.

A part of my hesitancy in souvenir hunting came from being warned of the enemy practice of booby-trapping the bodies of their dead. Consequently, we learned to attach ropes to the bodies and turn them over before attempting to move them to their final resting places in the trench. Souvenir hunting was both strictly forbidden and avidly pursued by officer and enlisted personnel alike. To proceed with caution was a safeguard many could have heeded with profit.

Once we had our guns moved into position and set up, most of our people began to spread out and explore the area. This was to ensure that no undiscovered "hidey-holes" remained to shelter enemy soldiers who might suddenly appear and start shooting. (One day later, a Japanese soldier was found hiding under a pile of debris and was captured without incident.)

A secondary purpose of the exploratory tour was to find undiscovered souvenirs. By that time, flags, pistols, etc., were already gone, but there was an abundance of rifles, both .25 and .31 caliber. One marine, whose identity was unknown to me, picked up a .25 rifle from the sand and, upon finding the action jammed with sand and grit, placed the stock on the ground and, holding the muzzle in his hands, delivered a sharp kick to the bolt. A look of surprise and disbelief flashed across his face as the weapon discharged, shooting him in the stomach. It was an unbelievably stupid thing to do, and even the greenest marine should have known better. He was evacuated to a hospital ship, and we never learned whether he lived or died.

Our searchlight battery and range detector sections were to our immediate north. Sandwiched in between our guns and a Seabee battalion to our south was an old Japanese pillbox/warehouse. All units were ordered to bury the dead and generally police up their own areas. This was quickly done, but contention soon arose over whether the pillbox was our responsibility or that of the Seabees. Since it was filled with the dead bodies of Japanese, neither group volunteered to assume jurisdiction.

The number of flies crawling everywhere was unbelievable. After days of feeding on an unlimited supply of human flesh, their distended yellow bellies were so large that they could no longer fly. They just buzzed and crawled—everywhere.

Eating became a creative art form. One hand was busily waved over the food, while the other manipulated the eating utensils. Macabre jokes on the subject were common currency. "Don't scare 'em away—they're good protein." It was often said that newcomers to the island were easily identified, for they brushed the flies off their food before eating. Seasoned troops just ate the flies with their food, while real veterans carefully picked up and ate the flies others discarded.

Within days, a scourge of dengue fever overwhelmed both our unit and the Seabees. The medics traced the source of the disease to the rotting bodies in that orphan pillbox. They had been killed by satchel charges and flamethrowers. The skin of the burned corpses had fried to a crisp crust, but under the charred surface, the flesh was in a state of liquefied suppuration. No one wanted the distasteful chore of disposal.

Finally, the area commander announced his decision about who "owned" the disputed territory. The Seabees won. The marines lost. We had some bodies to bury. A bulldozer, borrowed from the jubilant Seabees (at that point they would have given us anything), was set to scooping out a deep trench about eight feet wide and some sixty or so feet long.

Of course, as a private and a peon, I was automatically a part of the burial detail. We donned gas masks and moved in to do our disgusting work. It was immediately evident that the gas masks, designed merely to filter out poisonous gasses, were no match for this job. The masks were unbearably hot, and as we sweat, the goggles fogged up. Soon the masks were discarded as useless and handkerchiefs were substituted. They, too, were given up as of no benefit.

With our hands encased in rubber gloves, tying ropes around the limbs of the dead, they were unceremoniously dragged to the trench and covered by the borrowed bulldozer. All told, there were over thirty bodies to be buried. When finished, our clothing was discarded and burned.

No funeral rites or ceremonies were conducted. It was, without question, the most loathsome task I had to do during the whole of the war. My senses, which do have a good memory, can still smell the nauseating odor of bodies too long unburied. For weeks afterward, my sleep was disturbed by the thought that there were more bodies in other pillboxes on other islands, and if that were true, I already knew who would be chosen for the burial detail.

Other campaigns were to come. Guam, in 1944, was followed by Okinawa in 1945. But when I think of the horrors of war, the image that immediately comes to mind is that of Tarawa.

It's My Party

They come almost nightly to disturb my dreams, a file of anonymous marines in dusty battle dress marching into a westering sun. They have neither names nor faces, these weary young men of yesterday, these phantom companions of my long-ago youth. They move resolutely across the distant horizon of an old man's memory. To give them identity is to release a flood of associations too intimate, too precious, and too painful for conscious remembrance.

In other dreamtime scenarios, a ragged line of men abreast moves through the surf toward a distant island. They press relentlessly forward. They have no choice. To do otherwise is to be thrown back into the sea and to die. The island offers dubious haven, for there the enemy awaits to deny them sanctuary. Many stumble and fall, struck down as though by some invisible hand. Some rise and press forward. Others wash endlessly to and fro in the restless sea.

Where are they now, these brash and brave young men of another time? Do they, like me, lie awake in the late-night hours, tormented by transient scenes from an old horror movie that endlessly replays itself in the mind?

These marines have names—some well-remembered, while others are lost in the indistinct recesses of aging memory. But the faces are sharply etched on the indelible plate of recall. A lump rises in my throat and a mist comes to my eyes as I remember those who, once strangers, became comrades and finally friends, as we learned to rely on one another for our very survival.

I have made little attempt to maintain contact with those companions of my youth. It is a chapter that, once written, is better not revisited, for to do so is to awaken the unthinkable threat—to deal once again with the rising consciousness of mortality. To my knowledge, no reunions have been announced to bring us together.

Perhaps, like me, they find the exercise of remembrance to be painful. As I recall their faces, I weep for who we were and are no longer. I weep for the unrealized potential, for the dreams that will never be dreamed, for the stories that will never be told. How many survive, and who, and why? Who have lived to become as old as I, and who remain forever nineteen? Perhaps it is better not to know.

In my reverie I am reminded of a rock and roll song from the 1960s resurrected now as an advertising jingle for Burger King:

> It's my party, I can cry if I want to,
> Cry if I want to,
> Cry if I want to,
> You would cry too, if it happened to you.

My sleep is fitful in these later years and is often disturbed by ghostly reminders of another time. That is how it is with old men. We receive our nocturnal visitors, dream our poignant dreams, and shed our bitter tears.

> It's my party, I can cry if I want to.
> You would cry too, if it happened to you.

A Moment of Sheer Terror

Betio Island of Tarawa Atoll, in the Gilbert group of the British Mandated Islands (now Kiribati), lies less than one degree north of the equator. It fronts on the Pacific Ocean on one side and encircles a beautiful blue lagoon.

A necklace of low islands, of which Betio is the southernmost, defines the fifteen-mile-wide tropical lagoon and, in WWII, formed an ideal harbor for our occupying warships. The composition of the atoll was coral growth overlaid by a scant covering of sand. Occupying less than one square mile of territory, the boomerang-shaped island was about two miles long and less than a half-mile across the base, tapering to a narrow sandspit at the top. At no point was the tiny outgrowth of sand and coral more than six feet above sea level, except atop the concrete-block houses, which often reared to the dizzying height of ten or twelve feet.

Betio, once densely clothed by a forest of coconut palms, was now totally denuded by the bombing and shelling resulting from the Battle of Tarawa and the resulting invasion. The position of the USMC 2nd AAA Battalion on the extreme northern end of the tiny island had us squeezed onto a narrow peninsula that was less than a hundred yards across. At high tide, the water often rose perilously close to our tents, and the prospect of a typhoon with a tidal surge was a matter of no small concern. Fortunately, we experienced no such weather extremes during our five-month tenure there.

Aerial view of Betio peninsula, Tarawa atoll. Red Beach is to the left.

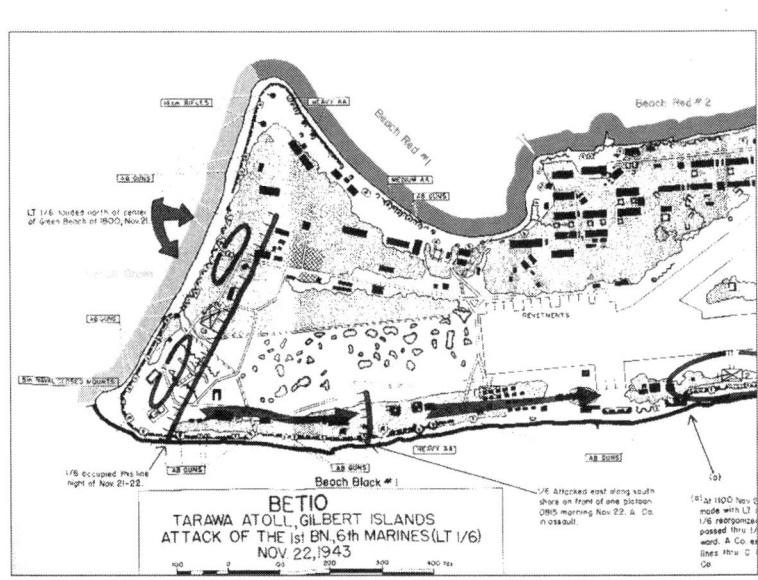

Map showing Red Beach, where I conducted my nighttime patrol.

On the seaward side, to protect a battery of eight-inch coast-artillery guns from the eroding action of the ocean waves, the Japanese had built a short section of three-foot-high sea wall with a four-foot-wide apron of concrete to counter the water erosion.

Only days into our period of occupation, when fears of a counter-invasion had begun to abate somewhat, our protecting naval force steamed off to fight the war in other areas. Our lagoon was left nearly empty of vessels, and we felt very lonely and exposed without them.

We settled into a routine that consisted of consolidating and improving our positions by day and answering enemy air raids by night. Under the circumstances, we were seeking and finding our level of maximum comfort, waiting for the time when other troops would free us to resume our place on the fighting front.

But lurking just beneath conscious thought in every mind was the troubling awareness that, while we had been successful in our invasion, the Japanese could yet turn the tables and do to us what had been done to them. A daily air patrol was dispatched to scan the ocean for any enemy ships that would constitute a challenge to our emplacement.

One morning a report came down from division headquarters that a Japanese fleet had been detected steaming in our direction. We began to prepare for our defense. The next night, we were made aware that radar had picked up echoes indicating the presence of several metal objects, possibly surface craft, in the nearby ocean to the east. We were ordered to immediately throw a defensive cordon around our area and to be alert to an invasion attempt from the sea.

One likely landing site was the Japanese-built seawall, for it offered both a gentle seabed gradient and a low concrete wall for shelter. A defensive line of riflemen was dug in around our battery. My responsibility, and that of at least one other marine private (we being the most expendable members of our force), was to each patrol a hundred-yard section of seawall, keeping especially alert for both swimmers and landing craft.

By what misconceived quirk of fate I had been directed to represent my companions on the outer perimeter of the battery, I could only imagine. If it could be said that the most frightened person in the company would be most alert to danger, and therefore quick to raise an alarm, then I was a good choice. But I suspected that my nomination had been made on the simple reckoning that a sacrificial lamb must be offered to the gods of war; therefore, why waste a prime ram when a scrub weanling would suffice. At least I could be easily replaced, and my demise would not be critical to the larger group.

As I began the surveillance of my area, a weak moon shone through the patchy low cloud cover. I moved cautiously, intently scanning the lightly breaking surf for swimmers/demolition teams and for landing craft, while looking frequently over my shoulder in response to the cold fingers of fear that raced up and down my spine. I hugged the wall as I walked in a half crouch, acutely conscious that I would be spotted by someone approaching from the water; I tried not to move when the moon slipped from behind the fitful cover of the denser clouds. My M1 rifle, with fixed bayonet, was carried in the high port position, ready for instant action.

But the gently breaking surf and the lightly tossing sea carried no hint of an impending problem on or beneath its calm surface. In spite of my misapprehensions, I could see no evidence of threat. Within neither sound nor sight was there any reason to suspect that a potential problem existed.

Feeling reassured and comforted that soon I would meet my watchmate, who was patrolling the neighboring hundred yards of the beach, I was keenly aware that a terribly disquieting reality frequently hides itself beneath the most placid appearance; i.e., things are not always as they seem.

I stopped and remained motionless as the moon illuminated the nearly white coral sand washed up onto the concrete apron of the seawall. As I halted, I thought I heard a faint whisper of sound behind me. I chanced a quick look over my shoulder. Nothing was there. I took two more steps as I resumed my cautious patrol. A faint soft scraping sound greeted me, the sound of something brushing lightly against the wall. I froze in place.

Given even a suggestion of trouble, a fearful mind will instantly flesh out the most fanciful details of a worst-case scenario. I knew and could see in my mind's eye the armed Japanese soldier who had presented himself two paces behind me. The creeping flesh between my shoulder blades told me that in another instant his knife would find entrance into my body. No confirming glance was needed to register his presence. *He was there.* I could *feel* him there.

In an instant I whirled to face him, rifle and bayonet at the ready. Incredibly, there was nothing there! Then as my knees grew weak with relief, my body bathed in cold sweat, I saw it. A small horseshoe crab, no more than four inches long, was crawling close to the wall, scraping his hard shell against the rough surface. I took an unscheduled break against the seawall, chuckling shakily in recognition of the incredible power of mind over matter.

We continued our alert watchfulness throughout the night, until the order came to "stand down." Then it was revealed that our primitive radar had picked up several empty fuel drums floating on the ocean currents. The reported approaching enemy fleet never materialized, but I confess that if fear is a devil that can kill, then I had been almost scared to death by demons that existed only in my mind.

Horseshoe crab

Love Battery

The lineage and history of Love Battery, 2nd Defense Battalion (2ndDefBn) is unknown to me prior to about 1941. At that time, I believe it was formed at Camp Elliott, California. Shortly after the Japanese attack on Pearl Harbor, 2ndDefBn was sent to American Samoa to defend that island from enemy acquisition.

In the confused days following the Pearl Harbor attack, Japanese ambitions appeared to include the acquisition of the Samoan Islands, Fiji, and the Ellice and Wallis groups. Fortunately, Samoa was never actively threatened and 2ndDefBn was able to set up its batteries strategically, providing for both coastal and anti-aircraft defense, while also helping to train a self-defense force of Samoan marines.

My recollections of Love Battery are less than adequate for this remembrance, for the battery was broken up within three months of my arrival and the personnel assigned to other units. But those memories that do remain are sharp and clear. The physical setting was unique, not to be duplicated during my Marine Corps tenure, being more typical of the far Southwest Pacific, perhaps, than of the coral atolls we would come to know farther north.

I came to the battery as a replacement in mid-April, 1943, to supplement the complement in preparation for changing to larger, more modern, and more powerful weapons. The battalion's antique 75mm rifles were less automated, and as I recall, were not fully capable of firing by radar direction. Fuse settings, elevation, and traversing were accomplished by manually following directions fed from a central fire control point. Accuracy suffered because too many steps were involved between aiming and firing, and opportunity for human error was too great. Better and more automated guns were needed, and the larger 90mm seemed to answer that need.

Four guns and a radar-driven fire control unit composed a battery.

The battalion consisted of four batteries (Dog, Fox, Love, and Mike), plus Headquarters and Service (H&S) Battery. H&S Battery consisted of an administrative, supply, and motor transport section. Hotel (heavy 155mm artillery) and Item (light 20mm, 40mm, and machine gun) batteries were attached from Division HQ. After the acquisition of 90mm guns, Hotel and Item batteries went back to Division.

Except for the commanding officer's jeep, our only motorized vehicle was a small tracked Caterpillar, which could be used to tow and move the position of the guns, if necessary. All other motor transport functions were supplied by battalion H&S Battery.

Towing a small trailer, the "cat" was used to make scheduled garbage disposal runs to a nearby lava overlook, where it was dumped in the ocean and pulverized by the wave action against the volcanic rock. The high point of the trip and the main attraction, which qualified it as entertainment, was seeing the sharks and other fish that appeared almost magically to feed on those tasty tidbits from our galley.

Speaking of the galley, I must pay tribute to the cooks, who did their best with the limited supplies on hand, which ran heavily to powdered coffee and milk, eggs, and canned tomatoes. I was amazed to discover that on the occasion that fresh eggs were received, we were permitted to specify individually how we liked them done. By and large, we ate surprisingly well.

A popular diversion was swimming in the seaplane lanes adjacent to the airport. Two deep lanes had been dredged in the shallow tidal cove, each perhaps a hundred feet wide and several feet deep. Use of the facility by the amphibian Catalina and Mars flying boats was infrequent, so we felt secure in using the channels for recreational purposes. In addition, the dredged-up material was often a productive source of pretty shells, including an occasional "cat's eye."

Neither land- nor water-based facilities were heavily used, and any incoming planes always made a warning "fly-by" pass before actually attempting a landing. Dive bombers and fighter planes were occasionally employed in towing a sleeve for the batteries of guns to use in live-firing practice. But we were confident that we could clear the area before danger from the air presented itself.

The pace of life was slow and easy in Love Battery. The guns were cleaned, oiled, and bore-sighted daily, for in that climate, neglect meant rapid corrosion and decay. Camp chores, working parties at Pago Pago's piers, regular four-hour turns at guard duty, and upkeep of personal equipment occupied the most of our time. The duties themselves were not onerous, with one notable exception.

Everyone, especially the unrated PVTs and PFCs, dreaded the pier-side working parties, for they seemed unending. When a ship arrived carrying cargo for the Marine Corps, we were sure to be called on to perform stevedore duties and unload the ship. Not only did the work involve very heavy lifting on the pier and in the stiflingly hot holds of the ship, but it ended only when all the cargo was unloaded. If that took 24 hours, then we stayed and worked around the clock, returning to the battery exhausted to face the immediate resumption of the daily routine of work on the guns, guard duties, and camp chores.

The only respite from our labor lay in exercising the revenge factor. Since we held the officers directly responsible for our assignment to the insufferable working parties—in which they shared none of the labor—our payback was directed toward them. The laboring marines were divided into two sections, one working in the holds filling the cargo nets and the other on the pier unloading the nets and reloading the contents onto waiting trucks. A member of the ship's crew operated the steam-powered winches and booms on deck, directed by hand signals from one of the gang on the pier.

We all *knew*, via the active rumor mill, that each officer was allowed a regular consignment of liquor through the Officers' Mess. Therefore, boxes and crates that seemed destined for the Officers' Mess were handled roughly, dropped on a corner, caused to accidentally fall off the truck, or otherwise be damaged in what was probably a futile attempt to get revenge by smashing their liquor bottles. I know of no instances in which we succeeded in our purpose, for all materials were well packed and crated to withstand rough handling. But we obtained great satisfaction in striking back, believing that we were hitting them where it hurt.

A low point for everyone was guard duty, especially at night, because by necessity, it took us out into the darkness, where the enemies were mosquitoes, rain, and mind-numbing boredom. The loneliest place on the planet was the guard shack at the entrance to the Love Battery, in which the voracious mosquitoes also sought refuge from the downpour. Their buzzing was the only accompaniment to the unidentified night sounds of the creatures of the swamp.

On one occasion, the mosquitoes drove me from the guard house, out of the dubious protection of the shelter, into the rain-drenched darkness, where in desperation I stripped three six-foot-long leaves from a nearby banana tree. Leaving my rifle and the mosquitoes in the shelter of the guard shack, I lay down under the tree and placed one of the 16-inch-wide leaves along each of my sides and the third overlapping them on top to complete my roof. To my surprise, my improvised shelter not only turned away most of the rain, but also some of the mosquitoes. Now a new worry intruded—being discovered by the corporal or sergeant of the guard and charged with sleeping at my post, a court-martial offense. Happily, my dereliction of duty has gone undiscovered up until now. And I believe that, after sixty years, a statute of limitation must surely apply.

Infrequent trips were made to a nearby banana plantation, where huge stalks of green bananas were harvested for ripening in the "dark box" situated behind each hut. I believe the location of the banana plantation was the site of an old failed Mormon settlement. The Latter Day Saints were, in the mid- to late 1800s, engaged in the search for a permanent home, and they established colonies around the world, including Samoa. I believe the place was to have been called "Mormon Valley" or "Happy Valley."

At scheduled intervals, a courier truck was dispatched from H&S to make "round robin" runs through each battery and into the port city of Pago Pago. This truck served as our "liberty" transportation on our one day off per week.

But however far our pursuit of happiness took us from camp, we were always eager to return in time for the once weekly beer call, usually on Friday afternoon. We were permitted to purchase two bottles of beer weekly, mostly "Golden Grain" or some other obscure brand that we pretended to disdain but drank anyway. Seldom did a nationally distributed brand of beer find its way out to the islands. But in spite of the assault on our unsophisticated tastebuds, this was easily the most popular diversion on the island, probably because at home most would still, on average, have been underage and prohibited from legally indulging in the beverage. Coca-Cola was also made available in the same quantities for those who did not drink beer or when beer was unavailable.

The individual batteries were situated several miles from one another along the seaward perimeter of the island. Love Battery was located near the inboard end of the airport/seaplane base in the middle of a huge swamp. Access was gained by means of what seemed like a miles-long causeway connecting airport to main highway, if I may be permitted use of the words *main* and *highway* to describe the narrow unpaved road that served the seaport side of the island.

I must acknowledge here that my sojourn in Love Battery, and later in Fox, served me well as a buffer to my rather abrupt entry into adult society. The men of the unit were older, and while there was a "pecking order" in place, there was no hazing or harassment of their younger counterparts. There was also an honor system in place that did not permit thievery from one another. We appropriated freely from other units and from the government, but we regarded that not as stealing, but as simply reclaiming that which was already ours. I will always have warm feelings for the men of Love and Fox batteries. They were excellent mentors and role models.

If my experience with Love Battery could be summed up in a single word, it would have to be borrowed from the title of W. Somerset Maugham's 1921 story "Rain," which was set, appropriately, in Pago Pago, Samoa. I had read "Rain" in high school. As a lifelong resident of moderate rainfall areas, I fancied that I had seen world-class downpours. I was unprepared, however, for the almost unceasing torrents that fell from the Samoan skies. Rainfall there exceeds 117 inches per year, according to the World Fact Book, most of it occurring between November and April, the rainy season.

The unrelenting rain was accompanied by oppressive heat and humidity, contributing to athlete's foot and other fungal infections. The "others" appeared under the arms and in the groin, areas that were never dry. Huge pustules of infection formed in spite of the best efforts of the medics, who swabbed on gallons of various infection-killing potions and tinctures. Virtually everyone suffered from this malady, which we called Jungle Rot or Chinese Crud. The medical corpsman, with his swabs and bottle of liquid fire, was an accustomed sight. We often joked that the "docs" treated our coughs and our crotches from the same bottle and with the same swab.

One member of Love Battery, soon after my arrival, provided a comic opera of amusement that impressed itself indelibly on my memory. A standpipe provided fresh water near the center of the compound. Having just returned to his quarters after a shave and shower, he sat nude on the edge of his bunk to attend to an ugly eruption of "crud" by thoroughly drying his crotch, before applying shaving lotion to his face. The shaving lotion slipped from his fingers and dropped in his lap, thoroughly drenching the raw, blistered area between his legs. With a great bellow of anguish, flinging toilet articles in every direction, he made a tormented dash for the standpipe in the center of camp. Turning on the water, he thrust his beleaguered parts under the cooling flow as his unsympathetic onlookers laughed uproariously.

The nearly constant rainfall and the saturating humidity produced hordes of hungry *anopheles* mosquitoes, causing endemic *lymphatic filariasis* or *elephantiasis* in the native population and frequently infecting the visiting marines. The condition, popularly called *muu-muu*, was characterized by gross swelling of the feet, legs, and genitalia of both males and females. Medications are now available to curb the disease, but in 1943, the only known relief lay in early detection and removal of the patient from the tropics to a more temperate climate. It was much feared, though many marines would have accepted a mild case of *muu-muu* in exchange for a ticket home.

Fortunately, at that time there were no snakes in Samoa, and no monkeys, but there were fruit bats. An abundance of these tropical mammals, often called *fox bats*, colonized the jungled forest in the vicinity of Love Battery. Except in size and ability to echolocate, these nocturnal animals are quite similar to our much smaller common bat, and as harmless.

Sometimes reaching five feet in wingspan, the fruit bat navigates by sight and by scent. It is responsible for the pollination of most tropical fruits around the world and relies on that source also for food. Native Samoans, as well as other indigenous people, often capture the fruit bats and eat them, considering them a rare delicacy.

Fruit or fox bat located on Samoa

Without the fruit bat, it is safe to say that there would be virtually no tropical fruits. They were usually seen flying about at the close of the day or hanging by their feet in great clusters in trees, their wings draped about themselves during daylight hours. When disturbed, they would fly away startled with a great and noisy beating of wings. They are not dangerous, but most marines imported their own inborn prejudice against all bats and indiscriminately applied them to the harmless fruit bat. They were the subject of much scuttlebutt about their viciousness, completely outside the realm of truth, but they were weird-looking animals.

Troops in search of entertainment found nothing ready-made. A hurried trip to the port city of Pago Pago was permitted once a week, but there was not much there to attract one's interest—just the usual collection of straw-thatched *fales*, or Samoan homes, with a sprinkling of rusty tin-roofed shacks. The Samoans seemed to have no need to call attention to their own importance by building elaborate houses. Everyone from the high or "talking" chief on down appeared to practice pure democracy in housing. The *fale* was typically several coconut logs set upright in an elongated oval pattern on a slightly elevated platform of packed earth, covered by a roof of grass and/or pandanus thatch. The sides were left open to permit the free passage of the cooling nighttime breezes. For sleeping, mats were rolled out on the earthen floor under draped mosquito nets. The single room served all living purposes and arrangements. Meals were served family style on a cloth spread on the floor.

Samoan fale exterior

Samoan fale interior

I became acquainted with a young Samoan Self-Defense Force marine who invited me to his home for a midday meal. The family sat on the floor around a cloth on which was centered a large bowl of stewed tomatoes, a much favored dish. In it, a single large serving spoon was placed. The accompanying dishes were fried plantain (a variety of banana), raw native fruits, and baked breadfruit. The company was pleasant; the meal was adequate, if a bit bland. The only off-putting thing about the entire arrangement to me was that there were no individual serving pieces, giving new meaning to the term *finger foods*. The stewed tomatoes were eaten by dipping the shared spoon into the communal bowl to the accompaniment of loud slurping and appreciative grunts and groans of pleasure. My approach was to put my own tastes and prejudices aside, determined to do in Samoa as the Samoans do.

None of the above is intended to disparage the Samoan lifestyle. It was primitive, simple, and worked quite well for these open and friendly people. I found the Samoans to be invariably warm, accepting, uncritical, and sociable. They were collectively, except for the disfiguring ravages of elephantiasis, the most robust and handsome indigenous people I have encountered.

After our meal, my friend's family invited me to attend a *siva-siva*, a ceremonial dance or gathering, with them that evening. I accepted in hope that I might get to witness an authentic *hula-hula* dance as performed by real Polynesian dancers, but alas, my hopes were not to be realized. I would later learn that the Samoans do not dance the hula, regarding it as a vulgar imported affectation. In time, I would view the Hawaiian hula and would find it to be a dance of a whole different genre.

The gathering was called to order by the village chief, and it appeared to me to be a rather convivial form of town meeting. The language was Samoan, with which I was not conversant. Regrettably, like most marines, I had learned only the more vulgar expressions of the language. It seems that exposure to a second language always results in first learning the forbidden words and expressions. The meeting proceeded in an informal but not unstructured manner. The presiding chief had the situation well in hand at all times.

Through it all, the chief, or head man, sat with his retinue of princesses, surrounded by a group of village virgins. Without creating doubts or casting aspersions on the individual state of their virginity, I came to understand that these were simply the young unmarried girls of the village. They did no actual dancing, but individuals did pantomime a few scenarios, accompanied by vocalizations in the form of a guttural chant, which I found unspectacular, therefore uninteresting. The Samoans do have beautiful harmonious voices when singing a cappella, but that was not to be a part of our evening entertainment.

I know nothing about the status or lineage of the princesses. Whether or not they were in a political line of descent as a birthright, they did seem to enjoy a special status above the others.

The Samoan positions of political power were elective, with perhaps some overtones of decadent inherited privilege. But I should say nothing on this subject because I know nothing.

A prominent feature of the *siva-siva* was the frequent passing of a large bowl of a ceremonial drink called *kava*, which I understood to be mildly intoxicating. The base for the drink was traditionally made by chewing the kava root to a pulp and spitting it into a container, where it was allowed a period of fermentation, to which was then added an unknown quantity and variety of liquids. I had no difficulty in passing the kava bowl without sampling the contents. The initiates, to the contrary, seemed to enjoy it immensely. Though I cannot be sure, I suspect the object of the gathering was less ceremonial and informational than social.

After about three months in Love Battery, the quality of our lives took a quantum leap for the better when we were disbanded and most of us were incorporated into Fox Battery. And that, as they say, is a whole 'nother story.

—Sidney D. Lowe & Charles B. Scott,
December 23, 2005

Fox Battery

In terms of environment and location in American Samoa, Fox Battery was a planet removed from Love Battery. Instead of the swampy jungle that confined us to the causeway on which Love Battery was situated, we were relocated to a beautiful island beach. The mountain reared itself directly behind us. Here, the main road to Pago Pago ran directly through the camp. A passing truck or jeep, though infrequent, was no longer an event for discussion and speculation about who and where.

A much appreciated bonus was that our new location beyond Pago Pago and across the harbor was farther removed from battalion headquarters (H&S Battery) than any other of the units. Some of us believed that we were thus spared the pressure and harassment that closer proximity to our supervising authority might have brought. We liked that.

Except for the constricted rocky beach on which Fox Battery was located, the mountain plunged precipitously into the sea, and a slender ribbon of road clung tenaciously to its densely jungled flanks. Our narrow strip of real estate was shared with a small village of less than a dozen *fales*, or homes of an extended Samoan family. It was a setting worthy of a Dorothy Lamour movie or a slick travel poster. Huge breadfruit and mango trees shaded the base of the mountain and the fales beneath them. Papaya and guava grew lush in the sunny places. The villagers subsisted on their daily catch of fish from the ocean and their harvest of tropical fruits; several fat hogs fed on the surplus. Coconut palms grew on the fringe of sand and rock with their slender trunks leaning, yearning, toward the water. The gentle surf washed the peaceful shore, its sibilant sound lulling us to sleep at night as the cooling breezes wafted through our huts.

Actually, I dislike calling them huts, for that word implies that they were shacks or shanties. They were inexpensively but sturdily constructed, quite comfortable, and perfectly adequate for our needs and for that tropical climate. Sheathed in plywood on the exterior to about four feet above the deck, then open almost to the roof line and enclosed with screen wire mesh, they were designed to capture the free passage of any breeze. A shutter panel of plywood, hinged on top, provided for their closure as needed during times of heavy or blowing rain. A sheet-metal roof completed the simple structure, intended to house twelve men. I liked living in them. They were home to us, however rustic and temporary.

A serious defect of the open-sided huts was that the mesh screen enclosure provided little resistance to the entrance of the minute coconut bug. This almost microscopic tropical pest was somehow able to introduce itself through the mesh of the screens. It was attracted particularly to light and to sweaty skin. The bugs flew mostly at night and having once lighted on your skin, were unable or unwilling to resume flight. They did not bite; they just crept and crawled on the skin. They were tiny, hard-shelled, and virtually indestructible. On a hot and humid night, they were practically guaranteed to drive their chosen victim crazy.

A short distance down the unpaved, potholed road was a larger village, named *Nu'uuli* (Noo-oolie), of which our small outpost seemed to be a suburb. From our vantage point on the beach, the snug little harbor lay at our feet at the head of which was situated the port city, Pago Pago. Suddenly our closed-in world had opened to new vistas, and our spirits lifted accordingly.

A few hundred feet up the steep ascent of the mountain behind us, a cascading natural pool had been tapped, and from it, water was piped into the camp. It was serviced by a short inclined tramway on which some marine officer had practiced his engineering skills. I would give him an easy "A," if I were grading the project. Thus, an ample supply of cool, pure mountain water was provided for bathing and other domestic purposes and was shared without restriction by marines and villagers alike.

Showers were located within the camp, consisting of a single open-sided room with a four-foot-wide length of burlap or target cloth material screening the interior from public view. The high point of the day was a refreshing shower after a period of training or maintenance on the guns. It was made more exhilarating and memorable if we were joined in the shower by a couple of the lovely uninhibited girls of Nu'uuli. To them nudity was no big deal, but they did have the good sense not to remove their sarong-like lava-lava wraps when showering with a group of randy young marines. I can recall no instances of misbehavior by members of either group. I would also award the girls an "A" on their expertise in showering without ever exposing themselves beneath their garments.

Traditional lavalava dress

Ordinarily, the older women especially preferred to go topless, their lavalava wrapped and fastened at the waist. If marines were in the area, the quick fix was to hitch the garment up above their breasts and *voila!*, they were fully covered.

The story is told of a missionary to one of the Pacific island societies who, embarrassed and scandalized by the women's topless mode of dress, issued a T-shirt to each of the provoking women and ordered them to be worn. Imagine his surprise and outrage when the next morning the women appeared in their new T-shirts, having solved the problem of the unaccustomed restrictiveness by cutting a pair of holes in the front of the uncomfortable garment through which their breasts protruded.

Toilets, which the Marine Corps called heads, were across the beach on the waterfront and were set on pilings six or eight feet above the lightly breaking surf, much in the style of an open-sided country privy. It was a most simple and functional affair—a covered platform extending over the water, on which was set a long board with eight or ten holes cut in the top. It was accessed from the beach by a twenty- to thirty-foot-long ramp. It too was screened by a short width of the ubiquitous target cloth.

My favorite and most consistent memory of Fox Battery in Samoa is of a small group of marines sitting in the head at day's end, trousers at half-mast, companionably discussing their take on the events of the day while smoking cigarettes and intermittently raising small geysers on the surface of the water below. Bring your own paper, please. The toilets were flushed naturally and very effectively by the twice daily cycle of the tides—the world's first and oldest sewage treatment plant.

Because the sea floor and shoreline consisted of broken-up pieces of lava rock, ours was not a good swimming beach. The shallow gradient required wading out several yards across sharp rocks to reach water deep enough to swim, a problem of major magnitude for the tenderfooted marines. But it was no obstacle at all for the Samoans, they of tough feet, for they had never worn shoes. Due to the position of the heads, we would not have used it for swimming in any case. But no such scruples inhibited the villagers, many of whom went to the bay regularly for bathing. The ladies' preferred swimwear was a pair of rayon or cotton panties below and nothing above. Except for the attendance of a company of enthusiastic marines ashore, the women would no doubt have opted for "skinny dipping." Social conventions can only dictate a change in fashion up to a certain point. Following their saltwater swim, the villagers often rinsed off in the communal shower.

Our presence imposed upon the Samoans must have been at least a minor irritant and obstruction to their settled way of life, but as far as my personal observations took me, the blending of the two cultures produced no unusual or unexpected conflict. When they were annoyed or offended, the mild invitation to eat our own excrement for breakfast ("I kai, Maline"), was answered by our bland directive for them to embark on a solo sexual adventure, both delivered automatically and without heat or rancor. Beyond this I saw very little evidence of serious friction between the two groups.

Meanwhile, the days proceeded apace for each group. Life appeared to be quite easy and unhurried for the Samoans. The women busied themselves with home, family chores, and—assisted by the young boys for climbing trees—gathering breadfruit, coconuts, mangoes, and other fruits that composed the staples of their meals. The men occupied themselves with fishing, using cast nets and spears. Occasionally a pair of young men would pursue a free-roaming hog through the cluster of huts and fales. One would grasp the animal's ears and bulldog it to the ground, holding it while the other tied the feet together. Then thrusting a stout pole between its feet and powering it to their shoulders, they would carry the squealing animal away at an easy trot, presumably to an area for either confinement or slaughter. When possible, a game was made of work, which was accompanied by a great deal of shouted admonishment, cajolery, and good-natured laughter.

Once I witnessed an event of a more tragic nature when a mother sent her twelve-year-old son up into a huge breadfruit tree to collect a fruit for dinner. The child fell from a height of over thirty feet to the ground. They carried him away unconscious, and although I was unable to learn the extent of his injuries, I did understand that they were quite serious.

The marines' time was fully occupied with training on the new and unfamiliar 90 mm guns. Classes and practice sessions were held to familiarize us with their operation, nomenclature, and maintenance. Each crewman was cross-trained in the duties of at least one position other than his own primary one. The gun captain was the gunner, loading and operating the firing mechanism, aided by the assistant gunner/breach loader, who was also the gun captain-in-training. The

Azimuth trainer and the Elevation trainer sat at their control wheels, ready to manually aim the gun if the central fire-control section should be disabled or knocked out. The fuse setter operated the fuse pot, arming the projectile and setting the point at which it was programmed to explode. Most of our firing was done with proximity fuses, which were preprogrammed to explode in contact with, or in close proximity to, a targeted plane. The intention was for the four guns to simultaneously fire a salvo, throwing up a pattern of bursts that would explode at the same time, bracketing the targeted aircraft. It was hoped that the bomber would be disabled by shrapnel or concussion, or that the aim of the bombardier would be so disrupted as to cause the bombs to fall wide of their objective. Sometimes it even worked out as planned.

90mm gun crew

Three or four ammunition passers and a "hot brass" man to throw the expended casings out of the gun pit completed the nine- or ten-man crew. With so many related activities being carried out, a high degree of close cooperation was required to produce an effective, smoothly operating gun crew.

When the guns were being towed or moved, the outriggers and platform were folded in the trail position. On reaching the site of permanent emplacement, the outriggers and platform were lowered into place, giving the gun stability in firing. The sandbagged revetment walls would then be raised to a height of seven or eight feet, involving the hand filling and placement of hundreds, if not thousands, of sandbags. The company Caterpillar bulldozer was then employed to push up a levee of sand or dirt against the outside of the sandbagged walls. Boxes of ammunition were stacked against the inner walls, creating a ready-at-hand supply of ammunition within an essentially bombproof enclosure. A direct hit would have been required to knock us out of action, and we felt very secure within our homemade cocoon.

A one- or two-man watch was maintained on the guns at all times. The purpose of the guard was to protect the gun and to raise an alarm if a threatening situation developed. In the event of an air-raid alarm, he was also expected to uncover the gun, open ammunition boxes, and otherwise make the weapon ready for action while the rest of the crew assembled.

Much later, after the Samoan interlude, and following the Tarawa campaign, I was chosen for cross-training in demolitions. In addition to clearing the area of dud projectiles and bombs, it became my job to blast away any obstructions and to use the small bulldozer to dig a recessed site for each of the four guns of the battery. When the revetment walls had been raised, I then used the bulldozer to form the surplus dirt into a protective levee around them. Since the gun pit provided the safest haven during an air attack, at such times I went there and served the gun as an extra ammunition passer.

The morning after an air raid was a busy time for the crew. The expended brass casings had to be gathered and sent back to the manufacturer for recycling and the supply of live ammunition renewed. The firing mechanism and breech block was field-stripped, cleaned, and lubricated. The gun tube was thoroughly swabbed with caustic soda to remove any corrosive traces of burned gun powder, oiled, bore sighted, and covered, in preparation for the next air attack. Fortunately, the Japanese advance did not extend as far as the Samoan Islands, but for the first two years of the war these islands stood as the front line of defense of US-controlled territory.

It was obvious to even the most unaware of us that our peaceful interval in Samoa was about to come to a close. The announcement that a movement or evolution was about to happen usually was made by our NCOs at morning formation. The brass were never forthcoming with information about future activities. It may be that except for those few at the very highest levels, even they were uninformed. It was just as well. Had we known earlier, we would probably have defied censorship rules by telling our families of our destination. Many had already worked out a prearranged code to let their folks know where they were.

But suddenly, just when we were becoming reconciled to sitting out the war in a boring backwater of inactivity, however idyllic, there came the announcement that the time had come to pack our seabags. Characteristically, we were given none of the details as to when and where we were going. Eventually, we got ourselves organized into work parties and got on with the job of loading mountains of equipment on our LST 20. Only after days and weeks at sea, almost on the eve of our baptism of fire, would we be told that our destination and objective was the island of Tarawa in the Gilbert Islands.

The LST on which we were embarked was certainly more comfortable than a troop ship might have been, but it was still very restrictive. It was less crowded in terms of there being fewer troops aboard, but it was also much smaller. Consequently, many looked forward eagerly to getting off the ship and on solid ground. Of course, at that point we had no idea of the ordeal that awaited us ashore. We had been encouraged to believe that the naval and aerial preinvasion bombardment was so intense that nothing could remain alive and functioning on the island. We expected that resistance would be light. But time would prove this preassessment very wrong. And time would find many of us quite willing to have gone back to the restrictive discomfort of the ship. That voyage and its aftermath have been covered extensively in my earlier vignette "From Innocence to Reality."

For the next few days and weeks, we were engaged in burying dozens of dead Japanese soldiers, improving our gun positions, and clearing the obstructive debris of war. The wrecked and torn hulks of LCVPs, amphibious tractors, tanks, and other war-ravaged equipment, both Japanese and American, were deemed unworthy of the cost of salvage and left to rust away where they lay. They were pushed aside only if they were in the way.

Recent photos of the beaches of Tarawa still show the recognizable remains of equipment ever sixty years later. And lately, a grisly discovery was made while excavating the site of a building project: a mangled American tank with the skeletons of the marine crew still inside. They were removed and given a belated burial.

For the next five months we resisted air raids, maintained the guns and equipment, and waited for relief. It came in late March or early April 1944, when we were relieved and replaced by an Army AAA unit. Leaving tents, guns, and other paraphernalia in place, we picked up our seabags, and with rifles at "sling arms," marched off to board a Victory ship, SS *Meteor*. Our destination was the Territory of Hawaii, specifically the island of Kauai, where we remained until nearly the end of 1944.

During this interval of relative peace and tranquility, we received new equipment and concentrated on training for the next phase of the war. I was assigned to a newly formed demolitions squad and received training in the use of such explosives as dynamite, TNT, shaped charges and Primacord. We touched only briefly on the niceties of disarming bombs, projectiles, and booby traps, the preferred method of disposal being to clear the area, cap them with a block of TNT, and detonate them.

Although assigned for accounting and administrative purposes to H&S Battery, I would continue to operate as though assigned to Gun 4, Fox Battery. The best part of such detached duty was that as long as I did my job, I had little or no immediate supervision. The worst aspect of such duty was also that as long as I did my job, I had little or no supervision. As an area was cleared of dangerous explosive ordinance and the guns set up and emplaced, aside from answering air attacks with the gun crew, I had virtually nothing to do. It was a situation I quickly found boring and, ultimately, quite depressing.

Kauai was an island where, for the civilian population, sugar was king. Vast sugar cane fields dominated the landscape and provided for the employment of the predominately mixed-oriental workers and their families. The burgeoning military population soon came to outnumber and overwhelm the static civilian residents and the island's infrastructure. Our camp was situated between the towns of Lihue and Kapaa, at Lydgate Park, in an old sugar cane field now recycled as a golf course. Nearby was the mouth of the Wailua River, a favorite place for swimming. On our one liberty day per week, that and drinking beer in the local taverns became routine activities. We soon adopted the refrain of bored teenagers worldwide, seeking the path of least resistance—"There is nothing else to do." That, of course, was untrue, but in this case was nearly so.

Here the older men, those who had been longest in the war zone, were rotated back to the States and given well-deserved leaves home. My coauthor for this piece, Charles B. Scott (Scotty), was among those rotated at that time. They were destined to soon be assigned to other units and shuttled back to the Pacific region. We, the new nucleus of the old battalion, received replacement personnel, guns, and equipment, and we were made to understand that after a short period of retraining we, too, would be reassigned to the forward area.

Scotty, meanwhile, after his home leave, was assigned to Camp LeJeune, North Carolina, and promoted to sergeant. There he attended Infantry School, Searchlight School, and 90mm Anti-Aircraft Artillery School. After reassignment to MCRD, Parris Island, South Carolina, for a brief period, he returned to Camp LeJeune and joined a replacement draft. He was enroute to Okinawa with Dog Battery, 5th AAA Battalion, when the war ended.

Fox Battery, 2nd AAA Battalion, in the interim, was itself headed back to war. On Christmas Eve, 1944, we were trucked to Nawiliwili

Harbor at Lihue to board an old and rather decrepit freighter of Dutch registry, HMS *Aquaprince*. (See "Ships I Have Known" and "Beer Call.") After an uneventful voyage of several days' duration, and brief calls at Eniweitok and Kwajalein in the Marshall Islands, we cruised on to the beautiful, newly secured island of Guam. There we left the *Aquaprince* and set up our guns, temporarily, in a lovely coconut grove just north of the port city of Agana.

We were located on a bluff overlooking a still incomplete seaside airport being built to accommodate the largest bomber in use at the time, the B-29. By then, Guam was out of the anticipated range of Japanese bombers. Our days and nights were used to send occasional patrols into the jungles and mountains of Guam, searching for small hidden groups of Japanese soldiers who had escaped during the fighting and who maintained themselves by stealing supplies from the American occupying forces. In reality, we were there as a part of the gigantic buildup of forces awaiting the Iwo Jima and Okinawa campaigns. After a month or so of relative inactivity, we re-embarked in LSTs for the short cruise to Saipan, where we laid up in the harbor to await the formation of a convoy in whose company we would sail on to an unknown destination. There I was to have an unusual, cherished, and very pleasant experience.

One day as I stood in the chow line for the midday meal, I heard my name being paged with the directive to return to my bunk immediately. Leaving my place reluctantly, for I was near the head of a long line, I returned as ordered to find my older brother sitting on my bunk. He was ashore on Saipan with an Army Field Hospital unit. I knew that he was overseas but had no idea that we occupied the same part of the world. He had inquired of an acquaintance in the Fleet Post Office as to the location of my unit and, learning that we were aboard ships in the Saipan harbor, had hitched a ride on a boat and come looking for me.

We sat up comparing notes on items of mutual interest until morning, when he had to rejoin his unit, with the expectation that he would obtain permission to return later in the day. Fate was to dictate a different outcome, however, for later that day I was dismayed to hear the petty officer of the watch announce, "Now hear this! Set the special sea detail. Make preparation for getting under way." Within a matter of minutes we were on our way to rejoin the war.

Within the next few days we were given our destination, Okinawa, along with a briefing on the terrain (mountainous), enemy forces (many and annoyed), anticipated level of resistance (stiff and tenacious), poisonous reptiles (snakes and scorpions), and characteristics and culture of the native population (little known).

We proceeded to an offshore group of islands, Kerama Rhetto, less than fifty miles from the objective. There we anchored in a tight little harbor that was packed with allied shipping. So closely spaced were the ships that there was virtually no room to maneuver. Destroyers on the perimeter kept us under a dense smoke screen for the next three days, as hordes of enemy planes buzzed above us like a swarm of hungry mosquitoes.

As chance would have it, on the third day at midmorning, a sudden wind came up and blew away our protective cloud of smoke. Immediately the planes overhead swooped to the attack and every ship in the harbor commenced firing at them. I have never, before or since, seen a more intense anti-aircraft barrage. All of the enemy planes were shot down or driven away, until only a single attacker remained, a single-engine torpedo bomber. He flew very slowly across the massed formation, as he appeared to be seeking out the very best target. He must have been disabled, for he did not maneuver, but flew straight and level, at stall speed and masthead height.

Anti-aircraft gunners are taught to lead, or aim ahead of, their target to compensate for the normal speed of the plane. So low and slow was he that the gunners aimed too far ahead, just in front of the intended point of impact. The bomber crossed the harbor and returned, again low and slow. The larger guns on the ships could not fire for fear of hitting their own ship or another. But the 30mm, 50mm, 20mm, and 40mm caliber onslaught was as intense as before.

Again he succeeded in reaching the opposite shoreline, though smoke now poured from the engine. Again he turned, and began his third perilous crossing. At about midway across, he was hit in the tail and went out of control, crashing and burning on the deck of an LST near us. Later we learned that the LST had sustained little damage in the crash. It was amazing to me that he could have survived for so long.

By the following morning, April 1, 1945, we were in position just south of Bolo point and opposite Yontan (Yomitan) Airfield, our assigned objective. We watched from the deck as the first waves of infantry stormed ashore. They were unopposed at the beaches, and we moved ashore just behind them. The LST beached and we landed with dry feet, a totally unaccustomed and unexpected experience. Our point of landing was at the narrower part of the island, opposite Ishikawa City, and the infantry quickly seized the advantage by driving completely across to the opposite shore.

Pictured here are the men of Fox Battery, 2nd Defense Battalion, 2nd Marine Division, who went ashore on Betio Island, Tarawa Atoll, as soon as organized resistance ceased November 25, 1943, and fired against Japanese planes in twelve night raids on the island during December 1943, and January 1944.

Fox Battery set up its guns on the cliffs of Bolo Point, with an open view of the South China Sea to the north and the west. A light rain was falling, and that night and the nights of April 1 and 2, we slept in the mud. I think I have rarely been so tired, cold, wet, and miserable—I even fancied that the soldiers in Europe were fortunate to have temperatures so low that the ground was conveniently frozen; no mud for those lucky bozos! I knew better at the time and have lived to regret and rescind my thoughts. That night, as Japanese 5" guns in the mountains northeast of us took us under fire, I said, "To heck with this, I'm sleeping warm and dry tonight." My buddy and I found an empty utility trailer and appropriated it for a temporary bedroom. I have rarely had a better or a sounder sleep, oblivious to the 5" shells falling around us.

Within the space of another day, the naval and ground artillery fire had silenced the 5" battery in the Okinawan hills. With that, except for frequent air raids and bombings, the immediate threat to us in Fox Battery had ended, and while the battle raged on, we were in relative safety and comfort.

The Okinawans in the area, presumably for reasons of military security and their own personal safety, had been confined in temporary compounds, leaving homes and villages unpopulated. Many had escaped confinement by taking refuge in the hills. Numerous goats and a few horses roamed the locale, temporarily set free by the fortunes of war. Cultivated fields lay barren, untended, and forsaken.

The Japanese had, uncharacteristically, chosen not to defend the landing beaches, but to fortify selected strong points inland. The marines were enabled to push rapidly across this rather narrow isthmus of land without meeting significant opposition. Where was the enemy? No one believed that they had given up so easily.

The marine infantry was designated to subdue the wilder, less densely populated northern end of the island, while the army would advance on the more agricultural and thickly settled south. The marines immediately began their push toward the city of Nago and the Motobu peninsula. Although the defending forces fought fiercely at times, the marines were eventually able to overcome the opposition and secure their area of responsibility. After about three weeks of battle, winning rapid advances, the northern part of the island was declared secure.

But the army encountered a much different situation in the south. The greater concentration of defending troops and fortified strongholds was in the more easily defensible south, principally Naha, Shuri Castle, and Sugar Loaf Hill. There, the army found itself stalemated by the fanatically determined forces of the Emperor of Japan. The deadly impasse continued while the marines struggled to bring their northern zone of conflict under control. When that had been accomplished, the marine forces were immediately directed to supplement the army effort against the passionately dedicated Japanese defenders, who preferred death to surrender or defeat.

Before the battle ended on June 21, 1945, American casualties at sea and ashore had mounted to a staggering 12,000 killed and nearly 38,000 wounded. The American navy ship casualties were 36 sunk and 368 damaged. Seven hundred sixty-three aircraft were destroyed.

Japanese losses were much greater, with 128,000 killed and 7,400 captured; 17 ships were sunk and more than 4,000 aircraft were destroyed. Perhaps it is significant that both top commanders were killed during this final battle of WWII. US Army Lt. General Simon Bolivar Buckner was killed by artillery fire, while Lt. General Ushijima, the overall commander of the Japanese forces, committed suicide shortly before the end of the battle rather than accept defeat.

Upwards of one third of the total civilian population of Okinawa perished in the fighting. Out of an estimated 300,000 civilians at the beginning of the battle, at the end only 196,000 remained. When the smoke had cleared, counting the Okinawan conscripts in the Japanese army, Okinawans suffered casualties nearly equal to military losses on both sides. In the final analysis, it is usually the civilians who pay the highest price.

One day after northern Okinawa had been secured, a friend and I planned a hike into the hills to search for the Japanese battery that had shelled us soon after our landing. We each made up a small pack of rations, cigarettes, and chocolates, checked out for the day, and shouldering our weapons, headed into the hinterland. Toward midday we reached the objective area but could find no trace of the guns we were searching for. No matter—we just wanted to get out of camp for a while anyway.

Turning, we started back by a different route. The hillsides were covered by a rather dense and scrubby growth. Soon we rounded the shoulder of a hill and were surprised to find a camp. Thinking that this might be the camp of a group of Japanese holdouts, we approached cautiously, to find an old Okinawan man and his teenage daughter. They were as surprised as we. They appeared to be terrified, not knowing what to expect of us but, anxious not to give offense, made welcoming gestures. The camp was very crude—a rough shelter made of a scrap of canvas, a few pieces of sheet metal, and cardboard around a crude frame made of tree limbs. The girl was cooking something in a container of tin holding two or three gallons.

Conversation was impossible, so without appearing threatening, we expressed an interest in the food they were preparing. The concoction had boiled away until only a small amount of gray-green pasty substance remained. The girl was shaping small patties of the stuff and baking or drying them over the fire. The man was working with a small basket of what looked like immature green soybean pods gathered from the fields. The girl made us to understand that she was making their meal and offered us a sample. We each took a small bite of the glutinous, rubbery substance and found it to be, at least to our tastes, almost inedible. They did not appear to be starving, but observing nothing else to eat around the place, we assumed that they had nothing else. We emptied our packs of edibles and gave them a key-chain GI can opener, leaving them well supplied with a meal or two. As we walked back to our own camp, we wondered what made them happier, to have the few meals we had given them or to be rid of our threatening presence.

For all sides, Okinawa was the bloodiest battle of the war in the Pacific. It had been the largest amphibious invasion of the Pacific campaign and, though unknown to us at the time, was to be the final battle of the war. The next phase, we thought, would surely entail the invasion of the home islands of Japan, for judging by the tenacity of their forces to date, nothing short of that would bring them to surrender. Well in advance of the cessation of hostilities on Okinawa, the preparation of resources, facilities, and forces for that eventuality had already begun. We believed that it would be a bloodbath.

It was with heartfelt relief that we received the news of the dropping of the atomic bombs and the eventual surrender of the Japanese authorities. (See "A Farewell to Arms.")

With that, though I was given an opportunity to remain for further deployment with the battalion, I chose to return home, thus ending my association with Fox Battery. I later was told later that they had deployed with III Amphibious Corps to Tiensein, China, to disarmament, repatriation, and occupation duty. I returned to San Diego for a few days, and then was sent on to Camp Perry, Bainbridge, Maryland, for discharge on October 30, 1945. Scotty was discharged on November 27, 1945.

Although it was a positive and defining experience for me, shared with a great group of young men, I would not wish to repeat the experience. But if I were to do so, I can think of no better group with which to share it than the marines of Fox Battery, 2nd AAA Battalion.

—Sidney D. Lowe & Charles B. Scott,
December 24, 2005

Dangerous Dan McGrew

Two half-brothers (same father, different mothers), James Webster and Freddie Hart, both fifteen years old, were members of my USMC boot camp platoon. Although they shared an absentee father, their mothers were neighbors and friends. I cannot imagine how this could possibly be; perhaps you can work it out.

The family relationships were a bit murky, but the two boys had grown up as brothers and best friends. Both were strong, handsome, likeable, and free-spirited. They appeared three years older, not younger, than their platoon mates. Webster was a physical phenom—a brawler whose *joie de vivre* was something to behold! His half-brother, Hart, was marginally more retiring and introspective. Both were guitar players, singers, and raconteurs, at their best when surrounded by a circle of admirers as they told filthy stories and sang bawdy songs.

They knew 105 verses of "Dangerous Dan McGrew"—though not the version found in the anthologies—and they sang them all with great gusto. Hart's mother, angered that her son had lied about his age and enlisted without her consent, complained and secured his release near the end of the boot camp period. Webster's mother, apparently having had enough of her rowdy son, chose not to challenge his enlistment. Though the authorities knew his true age, Webster was sent overseas at age fifteen. He was assigned to a different unit than mine, and I lost contact with him after boot camp.

Approximately one-and-a-half years later, having completed the Tarawa campaign, we were in retraining camp on Kauai, Hawaii. One evening I walked through a neighboring battalion area. I heard the chords of a guitar and a familiar voice coming from a circle of marines in a tent, singing the interminable verses of "Dangerous Dan McGrew." The unforgettable words were the same. The voice and the joy with which it sang were the same. I pushed my way into the tent and there he sat, the centerpiece of his favorite scene. Surrounded by his cheering fans, with a cold brew at his elbow, he belted out chorus after chorus of his favorite song. It was vintage Webster in concert. He couldn't have been happier, and for that matter, neither could I. What a pleasure it was to see him again!

Hart, according to his sibling, had reentered the Marine Corps, present location unspecified. I never saw either of the brothers again. But a few years ago, browsing through a cheap record shop, I picked up a country album and there on the cover, large as life, was Freddie Hart who, according to the liner notes, had enjoyed a long and modestly successful career as a recording artist after a youthful hitch as a marine. I studied the photograph, seeing in it the same handsome ruggedness I remembered in my old friend. I kept the album and thought of giving him a call, but I didn't; perhaps the memory would prove better than the reality.

In the meantime, my daughter went to her computer and googled him. Oops! Wrong Freddie Hart. But while it lasted, it was fun believing that I had reconnected with one of my old buddies. Now I wonder more than ever . . . whatever became of Webster and Hart?

Shelter Buddies

My memory fails me as to the exact date of the following events, but it must have been in late 1943 or early 1944, following the Gilbert Islands campaign. The place was one of many forgettable, and therefore forgotten, uninhabited atolls in the general area of the central Pacific known as Micronesia, where our battalion of US Marines conducted practice field exercises in preparation for further participation in the expanding Asiatic/Pacific theater of WWII.

When in the field, we lived in a type of two-man pup tent called "shelter halves." Each man carried half a tent which, when joined to another, formed a simple but quite functional rudimentary shelter. In our battalion, the system permitted each marine to select his own "shelter buddy" from his squad or gun crew, a valued privilege since we were so seldom allowed to exercise individual freedom of choice. A singular responsibility accompanied the privilege, however, since custom demanded that shelter buddies watch each other's backs, defend one another in altercations, and cover for one another in various ways. In other words, one's shelter buddy was critical to one's very survival, and lifelong friendships often developed from this buddy system.

In permanent encampment, we were accustomed to having each Saturday morning devoted to various inspection activities. There was almost always a personnel inspection with the troops in the uniform of the day, during the course of which a simultaneous inspection of their living quarters was held, where cleanliness and general orderliness were emphasized. At least once a month, an equipment inspection and/or sanitation inspection was also scheduled. When we were engaged in field exercises, the inspection schedule was relaxed but never abandoned.

If the sanitation inspection, euphemistically called a *short-arm inspection*, was ordered, the troops formed a single file, facing right or left as appropriate, while a medical officer, accompanied by two medical corpsmen taking notes, "trooped the line" fore and aft, searching for hemorrhoids, hernias, and other physical anomalies. They also were vigilant for evidence of bodily vermin and venereal disease. Since we had been deprived of female companionship for many months, I never heard of a single case of VD being discovered and but one case of crab lice, though there may have been others. But "hope springs eternal" in the heart of a true military medic; hence, frequent inspections. It is of my inadvertent involvement with that one case of "crabs" that this story is concerned.

Calculated to hone our amphibious skills, we were engaged in a practice landing and invasion of an uninhabited sandspit a couple of miles long. It was not only unpopulated, but was barren of vegetation of any sort. We had just completed the off-loading of equipment and weapons when the CO made the decision that instead of returning to our ships, we should remain ashore for a few days to become accustomed to living apart from the supporting naval vessels in which we were embarked. On Saturday morning, word was passed to fall out and form up in a single file immediately in front of the sick bay tent for a sanitation inspection. Once there, we were instructed to disrobe completely, stack our clothing by the right foot, face left or right, step forward three paces, and stand by for inspection.

We knew the drill quite well from past experience. The medical officer would pass behind us, trailed by his note-taking assistants. The order was given to "bend forward and spread 'em." As each marine bent forward, he grasped each posterior cheek in his hands and "spread 'em," giving the inspecting officer a full and unobstructed view of each exposed orifice and its condition. The note-taking corpsmen duly recorded any hemorrhoids or other anomalies as the doctor loudly announced his findings. The right to privacy had not yet been invented, and all hands knew immediately the condition of each of his fellows. The process was completely impersonal and objective, but it was so dehumanizing that it was detested thoroughly by all.

Reaching the last man in the file of nude bodies, the doctor paused as the senior corpsman gave the order to face about. Each marine then turned simultaneously to face in the opposite direction so that the inspecting team could retrace its steps without the necessity of repositioning themselves relative to those being inspected, now from the front side instead of the rear. I have always suspected that when that doctor went shopping for a new car, he had the salesman turn the vehicle so that he could see both sides without the necessity of moving himself.

The frontal phase of the inspection consisted of an examination for crab lice, venereal disease, and hernia. Under the illumination of a powerful flashlight, the pubic hair was visually scanned for lice or their eggs. Finding none, an inquiring finger was poked into the groin area with the instruction to "turn your head and cough." If no evidence of hernia was felt, the attention was turned to uncovering nonexistent cases of gonorrhea or other social diseases. Stepping back one pace, the inspector ordered each man to take himself in hand, "peel it back and milk it down." In the event that no suspicious fluids were expressed from the suspect member, the attention was then shifted to the next man in line until the entire company had been scrutinized. The best thing that I can find to say of the short-arm inspection is that it accomplished in a few minutes what might have taken a couple of hours or more if done individually, thereby saving the medical staff much time. The price paid was in the coinage of human dignity, but dignity was in such short supply that there was never much to lose.

In mid-afternoon following the inspection described above, a close friend who had been my shelter buddy until assigned to a different gun crew approached me. He was a big kid whose distinguishing feature was a bumper crop of wiry red hair that covered much of his body. I will not identify him here; we will simply call him "Red." Red explained that he had been found to have crab lice in his pubic hair and had been ordered to disinfect, shave his private area, and report back to sick bay within 24 hours for a confirming reexamination.

The immediate problem was that there were areas of his body that he could not handily reach. He did not feel comfortable asking his current shelter mate to assist in such an intimate grooming and wondered if I might agree to help him out in his time of personal crisis. Although I had serious misgivings, a valued friend desperately required assistance, so I agreed to stand by and render the service expected, even demanded, of a shelter buddy.

I must explain that in those days, before "Don't ask, don't tell" became current policy in questions of sexual orientation, homophobia ran rampant in the Marine Corps. Any two men who became close friends and spent a significant amount of time together to the exclusion of others ran a real risk of being thought of as "funny" or queer.

The immediate problem confronting Red and me was that of finding a place where our task could be accomplished without being observed, for neither of us was willing to run the risk of being labeled "acey-deucey." We agreed to meet immediately after evening chow call, since that was the time when the troops were accustomed to going to the ocean for a refreshing swim to wash away the grime of the day.

After the evening meal, we casually walked down the beach to where we hoped to be able to do our work without falling under observation and suspicion. Red had his toilet kit tucked under his arm, and each of us carried a towel over his shoulder. Regular toilet soap turns to crud when used with salt water, so we each had a chunk of soap especially made for salt-water use. It was marginally better than none at all, closely resembling grandma's homemade lye soap in its caustic cleansing power. Those who used it hated the evil stuff passionately and used it as sparingly as possible.

Arriving at what we deemed a safe spot, I took my soap for a swim while Red began to shave those areas that were readily accessible to him. He was armed with a pair of four-inch blunt-nosed sewing kit scissors and a rusty old blunderbuss of a three-piece safety razor, with a blade rendered nearly useless by use and long exposure to the salt air of the tropical islands. It was an instrument that might have been invented by a medieval torture master.

While I lay on my towel being air dried by the equatorial breeze, Red finished his work to his satisfaction. Turning the now thoroughly dulled Gillette over to me, we decided that the best approach would be from a rump-up position, allowing the lingering rays of the setting sun to shine where it had never shone before. I proceeded with my tonsorial task to the accompaniment of pained and embarrassed outbursts from Red. It was a race against the light. We won, if you will pardon the expression, but only by a hair.

We arrived back in camp in near darkness, and Red passed an uneventful second inspection the following day. While he may or may not survive to remember the event, sixty years later it remains an indelible happening in my memory. If I am ever requested to reenact the scenario, I am delighted that my razor blades will be made of modern surgical steel. I will also be armed with a practiced knowledge of human anatomy not available to me until that time.

The Laziest Man Alive

As lazy as Ludlum's dog, that leaned his head against a wall to bark.

—John Ray

The Marine Corps of the World War II era was a highly segregated society. Officers occupied the top level, NCOs the middle tier, and lower-rated men ranked last in the pecking order. Officers did not fraternize with enlisted men. Orders were handed down through the NCOs, and we peons seldom glimpsed the officer caste.

Most of my officers' names have been long since forgotten, with the notable exception of 1st Lt. Glass, who, in the evening hours, often visited the enlisted bivouacs, chatting briefly with the men in his charge.

Lower-rated men were assigned quarters, six men per 16' x 16' pyramidal tent. Officers' quarters occupied a separate section of the camp. Three or four NCOs occupied a single unit. Lower ranked officers were assigned two to a tent. The colonel and executive officer each occupied an entire tent alone. Officers took their meals in a separate officers' mess.

In the rear areas, contracted professionals did the officers' laundry. Their crisply starched uniforms stood in stark contrast to the drab, rumpled appearance of the enlisted men and further increased the divide between us. The enlisted marines assigned nicknames to officers according to their real or imagined personal attributes. They were usually unkind and often unfair in their assessments. Our colonel, a blond, crew-cut, Germanic type, with a face so frozen in a disapproving frown that a smile might have shattered his visage, was known as "Mad Max."

It is in the nature of man to minimize his activities to the greatest degree possible. Uncorrected, many quickly revert to unrepentant slobs, uncaring of their personal habits and the condition of their habitat. And laziness feeds on boredom. The tents of the enlisted men were closely inspected and were, of necessity, kept clean and in good repair. Our tents were swept and swabbed daily. Not so the officers', whose quarters were not inspected. Their preferred method of cleaning was to kick the debris from the floor of the tent into the company street, where it would be picked up by the daily enlisted "police" patrol.

Lower-rated men were assigned quarters, six men per 16' x 16' pyramidal tent.

One second lieutenant was notorious for the disreputable condition of his person and his tent. He regularly stayed late in his bunk, and his uniform often appeared to have been slept in. His personal cleanliness was frequently called into question. He drank heavily, necessitating frequent nighttime trips to answer the call of nature.

Tiring of such nocturnal activity, and resenting the interruption of his sleep, he had his men dig a deep hole outside his tent and beside his bunk. A length of 3" pipe inserted in the hole at a shallow angle was positioned adjacent to the side of his cot and the hole was backfilled. A crude funnel, fashioned of sheet metal, was inserted in the "business end" of the tube.

This was not American ingenuity at its finest, but it worked. The lazy lieutenant had only to roll onto his side in the night when he felt the need to relieve himself. He apparently did not always aim well, because under the hot tropical sun, the odor of the improvised urinal began to permeate the area, to the objection of all with the exception of Lt. "Slob."

The arrangement came to the notice of Mad Max on one of his walk-about inspection tours of the camp. The jury-rigged urinal quickly disappeared, but for the remainder of my time with that battalion, Lt. "Slob" remained known unofficially as "Piss Call." I have no doubt that he was "The Laziest Man Alive."

A Good Night to Die

The summer of 1945 was a time of intense activity on the part of the Japanese air forces against US military on Okinawa and in the surrounding ocean. As successful opposition on the part of the US forces increasingly depleted the store of enemy planes and pilots, the Japanese turned more and more to kamikaze, or suicide, raids.

Their pilots were unskilled, sent out soon after completing flight training. Many were trained sufficiently to make only that single one-way flight. Their most effective use was to load their planes with explosives and deliberately crash them into US ships. In this role, they were devastatingly effective, for there is no sure way to prevent a pilot with suicidal intent from crashing into his target.

We on shore were given ringside seats to such attacks almost daily, some of which resulted in crippling or sinking the targeted ship. Of course, our enemy could not sustain such a practice of sacrificing planes and pilots for long, for they were already desperately short of both. As the suicide bombing of ships at sea diminished, the high altitude bombing of installations ashore on Okinawa escalated.

The US Air Force, with its huge (for that time) B-29 bombers, was mounting regular firebomb attacks on Tokyo and other large Japanese cities. They came from home bases in the Philippines and used Okinawa as a refueling and jumping-off point, enabling them to carry less fuel and a larger bomb load. At Yontan, they were refueled and parked in protective revetments, ready for an early morning takeoff. Often, the pilots arrived back at Okinawa after nightfall, to refuel and rest briefly before returning to their Philippine bases.

The B-29s were so unwieldy, especially if they had been damaged by Japanese anti-aircraft fire, that it was often difficult for them to land successfully. They had to traverse a narrow canyon on approach in order to gain maximum use of the relatively short runway. Our AAA mission was to protect Yontan airfield from enemy bombing raids, and so we were situated on high ground overlooking the airport, near the mouth of the canyon. Night after night we were awakened on our hillside by the sound of returning B-29s and the almost inevitable crash of one or more crippled planes against the canyon walls.

A view of Yontan Air Field looking northeast in 1945,
with the East China Sea in the background

And, of course, while the Japanese were being bombed, they were also bombing us, sometimes more than once per night, in an effort to knock out the airport that supported such a devastating rain of fire on their cities. Usually between midnight and 2:00 a.m., we were aroused from our sleep by the urgent wail of sirens and sent racing for our 90mm guns, to make the guns and ammunition ready for action.

Dazzling white fingers of searchlights

The range section locked onto the approaching planes, usually at an altitude of 12,000 to 18,000 feet. The searchlight's dazzling white fingers of probing light soon illuminated the bombers, and we opened with patterned bursts of fire intended to cause them to take evasive action, disrupting their run and hopefully causing their bombs to miss their target. We had long since learned to watch for the release of a "stick" of bombs, following them down the searchlight beams. Only those bombs that stayed in the beam of light as they approached the earth were to be feared. Those straying out of the beam would fall wide of our position.

It was 10:00 on a cloudless night in July 1945. A bright new moon bathed the earth in brilliant light . . . a perfect night for bombing. We had just turned into our beds, hoping to get a few hours of sleep before the night's certain activities started, when the wail of sirens jolted us to our feet. As we clambered into the gun emplacements, the searchlights illuminated a flight of two Japanese bombers, flying straight and level, at an altitude of about 10,000 feet. Approaching the airport, they took evasive action.

We watched the searchlight beams for the stick of bombs to be released, but none came. The planes flew on out of range. A few minutes passed, and we had word from the range section that they were returning at a very low altitude. We readied ourselves for a low-level bombing run and were surprised when we could not depress the guns sufficiently to lock onto the planes, which were flying at near ground level.

To our consternation, both planes landed on the airstrip and began to taxi between the rows of waiting B-29s, slowing briefly as they came to each revetment. We could not see the details of the action, but it became clear that they were dropping off demolition teams at each B-29. Soon the field was lit up by row upon row of burning planes, all having a full load of fuel and bombs, having been readied for an early morning takeoff.

With no opposition on the ground, the enemy bombers blew up virtually every plane on the field. They could easily have picked up their raiding parties and taken off again. But evidently, they had not been briefed on further action beyond the demolition of the planes, for at that point, the teams dispersed and took no action to escape.

Soon the rattle of small arms fire was heard coming from the direction of the airport, as our riflemen retrieved their weapons and began to search for the scattering enemy soldiers.

We received telephoned instructions from our headquarters to throw a defensive perimeter around our battery and be alert for Japanese troops that might attempt to blow up our guns. The minutes ticked slowly by. After half an hour of waiting, a babble of unintelligible voices was heard on the dirt road leading up to our installation. Two unidentified figures were seen approaching in the moonlight. We challenged them, but they continued to approach, apparently in deep conversation, their arms linked. Again, we ordered them to stop, with no result. Both were shot and killed immediately. Neither was armed, and they carried no explosives.

It appeared that they had been sent on a suicide mission, and having no instructions for escape, simply walked down the nearest road until they encountered troops who would complete their mission for them.

We had, of course, encountered Japanese suicide troops earlier and on other islands, but those earlier soldiers could not have escaped and committed suicide to evade capture. Clearly, however, these soldiers could have escaped simply by getting back aboard their plane and taking off, but they chose not to do so. Their actions remain a mystery to me, and, I am sure, to all of those present on that bright July night in 1945.

It must have been a good night to die.

Farewell to Arms

The end of WWII in the Pacific Theater came quite suddenly and unexpectedly. We knew nothing of the dropping of two atomic bombs on Japan, which convinced that nation's leadership that continuing the war would mean annihilation for their people, until quite a while after the fact.

We had heard vague rumors of peace feelers being proffered by Japan, but nothing of substance had been released. If our officers knew more than we, they kept it a closely guarded secret. We knew only that, having participated in three major campaigns—Tarawa, Guam, and Okinawa—we were scheduled for the last big push northward to Japan's home island of Honshu. We were prepared to find old men, women, and children among the last fanatic defenders of the Empire.

The time for embarkation was imminent. The build-up to shipping troops and supplies had begun, and we anticipated a general "mount-out" within a matter of days.

The first atomic bomb was dropped on Hiroshima on August 6, 1945, followed three days later by a second bomb on Nagasaki with catastrophic effect. The Japanese capitulated soon thereafter and, for us, the war was over.

On the last night of the war, I was guarding the 2nd AAA Battalion brig, a makeshift affair consisting of a couple of pyramidal tents in a barbed wire enclosure. The miscreant marines inside had been found guilty of minor infractions and were serving short terms of "brig time." No one had ever escaped or had attempted to do so.

To escape would mean forfeiting the unit support system. No matter how much one might hate the system, there was nowhere else to go, so few even tried.

My instructions were to release the prisoners in the event of an air attack so that they might seek the shelter of foxholes outside the barbed wire. The enclosure, in many ways, was superfluous, serving only to restrict freedom of movement and as a reminder of their status as prisoners. When the "all clear" sounded, the prisoners always came meekly back to be confined behind the barbed wire from which they could easily have escaped at almost any time.

My tour of duty as guard was from 4:00 to 8:00 p.m. As my shift was about to end, and the final rosy tints had faded in the western sky, ships offshore and in Buckner Bay began firing over the island. Assuming that an unannounced air raid was in progress, I released the prisoners to seek shelter.

As the darkness deepened, searchlights were playing random patterns over the night sky, but no planes were in evidence. Soon the big guns ashore were firing at will with no particular concentration of fire, which would have indicated the presence of targeted planes. I was worried because it was all so chaotic and I had no idea what was taking place. Were the Japanese attempting to mount a full-scale counterinvasion? The undirected firing continued for many minutes. My relief guard arrived more than an hour late.

"What's going on?" I inquired of the corporal of the guard. "The war is over!" he announced. "The Japanese have surrendered."

I didn't believe him. It was too much to take in, too good to be true. The "prisoners" began to gather round to hear the news and to be reconfined. Only after returning to my area were my tentmates able to convince me that perhaps it was over, after all.

Within a few days, a bulletin was posted on the company bulletin board with two pieces of news. The first and most important was a schedule for the rotation of eligible marines back to the United States on a point system. Overseas time was awarded as one point for each month. Those with "good time," decorations, and awards, such as Purple Hearts, were given extra points. "Bad time," disciplinary actions, etc., had points deducted. I no longer remember the cutoff point, but the bottom line was that I was eligible for rotation home and, hopefully, for discharge.

The second bit of news was that our mission had changed from invasion duty in Japan to occupation duty at some unspecified location in China. Volunteers were sought, hoping to persuade some of those going home to remain and accompany the unit to duty on mainland Asia. For me, it was a no-brainer. Though I would miss my buddies of nearly three years, the choice was easy. I had no desire to see China. I would go home.

A Casual Company was created to temporarily contain those marines who had chosen rotation over continuing with the unit. Within a few days, we had been assigned to a squadron of destroyers, with departure a few days hence. Each ship would accommodate a few marines for the voyage home.

Almost immediately a strong Pacific typhoon bore down on Okinawa. We had often practiced the drill for storm alerts, but in spite of three years of island-hopping all over the Pacific Ocean, had never encountered a storm of typhoon strength.

We were ordered to "dead man" our tents, digging trenches about two feet deep on each of the four sides. Logs were placed in each trench, the tent guy ropes were attached to the logs, and the trenches were refilled. We were confident that we could ride out the storm. My seabag was packed. My rifle and "732 gear" (helmet, cartridge belt, pack, etc.) had been turned over to the supply section in preparation for the voyage home. My only remaining equipment was my bedroll, seabag, and folding cot. I was ready. Bring it on!

The storm hit with a fury. Immediately our dead-manned tent ropes snapped and the tents went flapping away with the storm. Pelted by wind and rain, and having no place to go, I fortunately remembered a Japanese "fighting hole" I had found on a hillside nearby. With seabag on shoulder and bedroll under my arm, I dashed for the sanctuary that an unknown Japanese soldier had so generously and unwittingly provided.

He had been a good workman, that enemy soldier. The tiny opening to the small cave was just large enough to accommodate a man crawling in on his belly. Inside, the cave had been enlarged and deepened to allow a man to stand, using the opening as a fire port. Two disadvantages, I noticed as I crawled inside, pulling my seabag and bedroll after me, were its limited field of fire and the reservoir created by deepening the hole, which soon began to fill with water.

Overhead, my Japanese benefactor had thoughtfully built a platform of sturdy bamboo large enough to accommodate myself with bedroll and seabag. There, in relative comfort and security I rode out the storm, as I watched the water in the hole below rise to the level of the opening and spill over the edge. I was apprehensive about the stability of the ground above, but it proved to be a good and safe shelter. Thank you, my enemy, whoever and wherever you are.

I remained in the shelter of my cave for two nights and a day before venturing out to view the aftermath of the storm. The area was devastated. We had no permanent buildings, and the surroundings were flattened and scoured. Even the officers' mess tent was gone. How dare a mere typhoon spit in the eye of the brass in such a way?

The most immediate impact on me was that my transportation home, the destroyer squadron, had chosen to ride out the storm at anchor in Buckner Bay. Under the impact of the typhoon winds, the ships had slipped anchor and were washed onto the rocks along the shoreline. My ticket home had just become a TS slip.

USS *Nevada*, our ride home

Another month passed in relative inactivity, boredom, and fruitless speculation. We invented endless scuttlebutt about our date of departure and our mode of transport, to the point that we came to believe in our own creation. Finally, word came that I would be detailed to the marine detachment aboard USS *Nevada* (BB 36), that grand old veteran of two wars, many battles, and a survivor of Pearl Harbor.

Though there were several like myself who were supercargo on *Nevada*, I was the only one from my Casual Company to be detailed to that ship. I was driven to White Beach, where I joined a small group of other "war-refugee marines." Our ship was anchored some distance from shore, and while we waited for a barge to take us alongside, I observed several large piles of weapons, helmets, and other surplus materials being loaded aboard LCVPs and LCs. Inquiry revealed that they were to be taken beyond the reef and jettisoned in deep water. I quickly found a .30 caliber carbine in acceptable condition, broke it down, and shoved it into my seabag. That and a small live anti-personnel bomb became my only souvenirs of World War II. Only after my marriage in 1946 did it occur to me what an absolutely stupid thing it was to have that live bomb around. It was unceremoniously consigned to an outdoor privy where it still rests today. The carbine was kept with a loaded clip stored safely in a place separate from the weapon.

USS *Nevada* was heaven, if for no other reason that we casual passengers were assigned no duties. Our grungy uniforms, both utility and khaki, were consigned to the ship's laundry and returned to us clean, starched, and pressed. It did not hurt that the ship was so big that those aboard did not feel even moderately heavy seas. The food was wonderful and served in unlimited quantities. Showers were endless and unrationed. No regular crew's quarters were available to us, but we were taken far below decks, to the ship's magazines, where at night, we were assigned sleeping space on the ammunition conveyor belts. We were given the run of the ship during the day.

It was a very leisurely cruise home. Every navy ship must conduct regular drills and maneuvers at specified intervals in order to maintain its Readiness and Efficiency ratings. In the heat of war, it is often difficult to find opportunity to conduct all of those required drills. The destroyers in the homeward bound convoy towed targets for practice firing. We did drills with the onboard pontoon biplane. We practiced man-overboard routines, submarine alerts, and fire drills. After about three weeks, we arrived in Honolulu, where we were given one day ashore while the ship took on fuel and supplies.

I will not bore you with the details of what I did, or wanted to do, during that day ashore, but will say only that the day was in no sense long enough. The next morning, we were embarked on the last sea leg of the long journey home.

A week later we docked at Long Beach, California, where we were met by semi-trailer busses and transported to the marine base at San Diego. There we were given cursory physical examinations and told that we would be shipped to Camp Perry, Maryland, for discharge within the next few days. Requests for liberty would not be granted. Pay would be withheld until we arrived in Camp Perry, where we would be given our final separation papers and funds.

We spent a week in San Diego and another on a troop train enroute to Maryland, passing through Amarillo, Oklahoma City, St. Louis, Cincinnati, and Charleston, West Virginia, my ultimate and final destination. I was discharged at Camp Perry and given two days' travel time, arriving in Charleston on October 30, 1945.

Within the next two days I had met my future wife. I had survived a nasty war with no visible scars. Now I had lucked out again. She is still with me more than 56 years later. I am definitely on a roll. My lucky streak remains unbroken.

War's End

Sent: Sunday, May 06, 2007 10:55 PM
To: Sidney D. Lowe
Subject: The Old 2nd Defense Battalion

Sidney,
In going thru some old records, I came across this handwritten report. It brings back memories. And thanks for the memoirs you sent last year. I hope you are hanging in there.

—Alan MacLane

War's End

Written on Okinawa by Alan MacLane
Friday, August 10, 1945

At eight o'clock on Friday night, Dean Minnick and I were at a show, sitting on an oil drum and generally viewing with distaste several rather stupid "Community Sing" shorts, followed by *Old Acquaintance*, starring Bette Davis. We left the show and went to his mess hall for a good hot cup of joe. While standing outside, we noticed several searchlights probing their fingers through the dark sky. Suddenly, far to the south, red tracers from a 20mm gun began pouring into the sky, following one another on a curve into oblivion. My first thought was of a Condition Red, and I began to head back for the marine area. Then all over the camp, men began to shout and whoop. The air activity began to increase, and soon the sky was filled with rockets, star shells, and tracers of all colors of the rainbow. "The war is over!" The word spread like wildfire.

We rushed to the nearest radio in time to hear WXLH closing its news broadcast. I looked at my watch. It was 9:13. The announcer's voice was tense with excitement:

"We repeat the flash that we have just received. Radio Tokyo has just broadcast that the Japanese government has forwarded to the Allies, through the neutral governments of Sweden and Switzerland, a formal request for peace under the Potsdam agreement. As yet, we have received no confirmation of this report from Washington."

Those were the words, stating a fact: Japan was surrendering. I didn't get excited. I don't know why; perhaps it isn't my nature, but probably it was because the truth of the statement was too great to grasp in those few short minutes.

Meanwhile, people all over the island were going crazy. Beside the .20s, .50 and .30 caliber machine guns opened up. Everywhere was the sound of M1s and carbines being fired into the air by their happy owners.

From the show area came one tremendous shout as the news was given over the speaker. The picture stopped, everything stopped, and people gathered together in little knots to discuss the good news and watch the celebration.

Later that night, after more rational thought and more news reports, we realized that it was not really the end. There were loopholes. Perhaps this was just another false rumor, such as had preceded by several months the German capitulation. We waited eagerly for more news.

On Saturday it was confirmed that Friday night's news was true, but that still did not mean peace. The Japanese had included one provision, that they be allowed to keep the emperor as head of the government. Would this be accepted by the Allies? That was the question, and we argued it out among ourselves. Strictly speaking, this was not unconditional surrender.

During the next few days, the suspense, the awful waiting for the end, was the hard thing to take. The Allies received the surrender officially, but decided they didn't like the one condition. So it was thrown back in Japan's lap; it would be up to them to make the next decision. For on Sunday, the Big Four sent their reply stating that the emperor could remain, provided he would take all his orders from the Supreme Allied Commander. This would make him merely a puppet, a tool to help control the people.

The Allied answer reached the Japanese on Monday, and then there was more waiting—Monday, Tuesday, and then, Tuesday evening, Tokyo Radio announced that Japan's final answer was on its way. From Washington came the word that no announcement would be made until midnight our time.

At twelve, I had my ear glued to a shortwave receiver and from London heard that the reply was in Switzerland and still had to be coded, sent to the four capitols, decoded—and then the results made known.

Meanwhile, rumors and scuttlebutt were flying everywhere. Some said the Japanese had turned down our answer. Others declared that Jap planes had landed on the island and peace negotiations were in progress here on Okinawa with General MacArthur and Admiral Nimitz. Again, we waited for the straight dope from Washington.

It came Wednesday morning on the seven o'clock news broadcast. President Truman announced that the Japanese had surrendered unconditionally. True, the peace wasn't yet signed and consequently V-J Day had not been proclaimed, but the ceasefire order had been given, and as far as we were concerned, the war was really over. Wednesday, August 15, 1945, was made a Holiday Routine, and at precisely 12:15, two bottles of cold beer were issued free to every man in the battery.

PART 3

A Sailor's Life and Beyond
1945–2013

Stumbling Toward Paradise, Part 1

On October 30, 1945, I returned to Charleston, West Virginia, a newly discharged Marine Corps veteran, having neither plans nor prospects for the future. The next night, I accompanied my sister Faye to her night shift job as a nurse at Charleston General Hospital.

Within the next few minutes, I was to meet Peggy O'Dell, the young woman who would alter my perception of myself and slowly but irrevocably change the direction of my life. Within the next few days, we mutually decided that we would like to know each other better and began to keep regular company. She soon told me that she was "sort of" engaged to marry a young man in her home community but was not wholly committed to the relationship. She also invited me to her home in Nicholas County to meet her family. I hadn't figured it out yet, but I had already been selected and targeted.

Me as a newly discharged marine

Though at that time I had only one single experience of driving (a 5-ton USMC truck), I determined to buy a car so that I might drive Peggy on her next visit home. Her brother Vernon ("Pete") expected to be discharged from the army on Friday. Her father, Roy, would be in town in his REO Speedwagon logging truck to meet him and to return Peggy and him to their home.

Planning to relieve Roy of at least one passenger, on Friday afternoon I purchased a 1936 Chevrolet Straight 8 4-door sedan—the

Peggy, just before we met

only car in Charleston I could afford to buy. Incredibly, I declined the offer to test-drive the car before buying, probably because I had neither a license nor driving experience and did not wish to expose my ignorance to critical commentary.

As I exited the used car lot, I pulled out onto Capital Street, a one-way artery, headed in the *wrong* direction. Ignoring the blaring of horns and flashing of lights, I bucked the heavy rush-hour traffic. Finally, I began to understand that my fellow motorists and a host of wildly gesticulating pedestrians were all trying desperately to tell me something.

Demonstrating great presence of mind and enviable self-control, I quickly turned into a street intersecting from the left. I was now on Quarrier Street, another one-way street, and of course I was again going the wrong way. Almost

The Chevy Straight-8

immediately, I was forced to seek refuge on the sidewalk under the marquee of the Capital Theater.

One of Charleston's finest, in his immaculate blue uniform, approached. "Having a little trouble, are you, son?"

"Yes, sir," I responded, "I've just got out of the Marine Corps and am unfamiliar with the streets here and I sorta got going the wrong way."

"Well, now," he said, "let's see if we can't get the Marine Corps out of trouble."

Stepping into the street, he halted all traffic and helped me to get off the sidewalk and turned in the right direction. Shaken but undeterred by the incident, I proceeded back down Capital Street to Washington, then north to Morris, where I met Peggy at our prearranged spot.

Driving isn't so tough, I thought. *I have taken on the worst that Charleston has to offer, survived three crises in three minutes, and I'm still alive to tell about it.*

The plan was to follow Roy and Pete in their truck, since I had little knowledge of where we were and abso-

Peggy's brother, Pete O'Dell

lutely none of where we were going. Peggy and I proceeded up-river past DuPont, Cedar Grove, Montgomery, and Gauley Bridge. Leaving the nightmarish traffic of US 60 and the Great Kanawha Valley behind, we anticipated smooth sailing on State 39 for the remainder of our journey.

By 9:00 p.m. we were at Gilboa, approaching Summersville, when we received the first indication of trouble. The flashing red lights of a police car pierced the darkness ahead.

"Uh-oh," I remarked to Peggy, "that had better be an accident up ahead and not a roadblock."

Peggy's father, Roy O'Dell

We were not to be so fortunate. The police were stopping all traffic, checking for drunks and unlicensed drivers. Pete was driving the truck and, like myself, was unlicensed. The policeman asked him for his driver's permit. His father offered his own license instead.

"Officer, my son is just out of the army today," he said, "and hasn't had a chance to get a license. Can't we just let him get by on my credentials?"

"All right," the policeman readily agreed, "just take care of that license right away, though, won't you?"

"Yes, sir, and thank you, sir," Roy replied.

Meanwhile, knowing what was to come, I was trying desperately to think of a way out of my predicament. Not knowing that Pete was also unlicensed, I asked Peggy to go up on the passenger side of the truck and ask her father to come back with me so that he could vouch for me with his permit. She did so, and Roy and the policeman walked back to my car together, but on opposite sides of the truck. Roy took his seat beside me as the officer approached my window.

REO Speedwagon

"May I see your driver's license, please?" he asked politely.

Roy offered his own credential for the second time in as many minutes as he said, "Officer, this lad is just out of the Marine Corps today and hasn't had a chance to get a license. Can't I vouch for him with mine?"

The officer hesitated for only a second as he returned Roy's permit to him. "I guess that will be all right, Mr. O'Dell," he smiled, "but you folks be sure to take care of that licensing right away."

"Yes, sir. Thank you, sir!"

As you can see, following WWII, a grateful nation would hardly permit a returning veteran to get into trouble, no matter how hard he tried.

Stumbling Towards Paradise, Part 2

In "Stumbling Toward Paradise, Part I," I wrote of my first driving experience and my visit to Nicholas County, West Virginia, with Peggy to meet her family. It was a trip with lasting consequences, for I met a tightly knit family whom I liked very much and who seemed to accept me for what I was, in spite of my limitations and shortcomings. After all, one does not expect much of one who has so little to offer.

Peggy at the family farm, Nettie, West Virginia

As chance would have it, I would also stumble into a meeting with Peggy's fiancé and set in motion the first of a chain of events that would lead to the termination of their engagement; thus, I would significantly and inadvertently move forward on my journey toward Paradise.

Since two of Peggy's brothers and two sisters were at home that weekend, together for perhaps the first time in several years, there was a shortage of sleeping spaces. I was forced to sleep with her brother Pete by default. He still teases me about his being awakened during the night to find himself tightly wrapped in my amorous embrace. "I didn't sleep a wink," he said the next morning. "After being awakened the first time, I was afraid to go to back to sleep!" I *think* he was only teasing!

On Saturday afternoon, Peggy and I decided to take a drive around the community, since it was my first time in the area. As darkness approached, we pulled into an intersecting road, intending to turn and go home. It was a dirt road, which after recent heavy rains, was a bottomless quagmire. Ten feet off the paved highway, we were hopelessly stuck.

Peggy observed that she thought that an evening bus was due soon, which would take us to within a mile or so of her home. We could then walk on home and have her father or brother return with the log truck to pull us out of our mudhole. Though my ego was threatened, it seemed the best plan available.

After waiting for perhaps thirty minutes, we hailed the lights of the approaching bus. Entering, we took an unoccupied seat among the several passengers, one of whom, though I was unaware of it, was her fiancé. They exchanged greetings as we found our places, and I thought I detected a palpable uneasiness in her.

"Do you know that guy?" I asked, for it was obvious that she did.

"Oh," she responded with pretended nonchalance, "he's just a neighbor boy. His name is Edward."

At the Nettie General Store, we exited the bus, along with most of the passengers, including Edward. As we walked in darkness toward her home, I stopped momentarily to search fruitlessly for a match to light a cigarette. As I did so, I noticed that someone was following about 50 feet behind.

"Keep walking," I said to Peggy. "I'll catch up with you in a moment."

Turning, I walked toward our fellow traveler, whom I now recognized as Edward, the young man on the bus. He stopped, warily, as I approached.

"Hi, Edward," I greeted him. "Do you have a light?"

"Sure," he replied, as he lit my cigarette.

"Thanks," I said, as I hurried forward to rejoin Peggy, who was now thoroughly uncomfortable.

"What's wrong?" I asked.

"Oh, nothing you won't learn soon anyway," she said. "That's the guy I'm engaged to marry."

"I knew that," I lied, as though I had planned the entire encounter. "I just introduced myself to him. I didn't want him to think that I was intimidated by him following us."

Peggy and me on our wedding day

On Sunday afternoon someone drove up in front of the house, and Peggy quickly ran out to greet him. She returned in a few minutes, red-faced.

"Is something wrong?" I inquired.

"That was Edward," she replied. "I just broke our engagement."

Paradise suddenly seemed attainable.

194 ❦ AN INDOMITABLE SPIRIT

The Case of the Elusive Exhortation

In June 1950, I began a course of study at West Virginia Wesleyan College, a small but well-accredited four-year school related to the Methodist Church. Although I had been expelled during my senior year of high school (1942–43) and had not returned to complete the required class work for graduation, Dean Schoolcraft agreed to allow me to matriculate at Wesleyan pending a demonstration of my ability to do college-level work. Since in high school I had been a mediocre student at best, I wanted to demonstrate that ability to myself as well. I had found the ordained ministry an appealing field of endeavor but wanted to take a few college courses to test the waters before making a full commitment. I was a Marine Corps veteran with a wife and two small children, and I had recently been laid off from my job as a coal miner; the time seemed right to explore a change in occupational fields.

A few weeks into the summer class schedule, I was invited to a meeting with Dr. Sidney T. Davis, a professor in New Testament Studies. He was sponsoring a student ministry group and was recruiting a few students to provide a part-time ministry to several small churches whose full-time pastorates had been discontinued. I agreed to become a part of the group, for it promised an ideal opportunity to put my plan to the acid test.

Three students, Charles Hanna, Max Cramer, and I, were to share the ministry of a six-church

Me upon entering West Virginia Wesleyan College

country circuit about sixty miles away, near Elkins, West Virginia. Each of us was to be responsible for conducting Sunday services in one of two churches on alternate Sunday mornings. Charles was appointed to Montrose Church and Union Chapel. Max agreed to supply another pair of churches located near Parsons and Davis. I would fill the vacancies at Israel and Kerens. Charles would use his car for transportation, dropping Max and me off at our respective locations before proceeding to his own appointment. Any offerings would be devoted to defraying car expenses. We planned to test the hospitality of our parishioners for lunch and dinner and would remain in the community for general visitation in the afternoon and for evening services in the church not visited that morning. Fifth Sundays were left without regularly appointed services, making time for special events in our respective neighborhoods.

Time in transit to and from our appointments was spent brainstorming—discussing experiences and finding solutions to problems. And there were problems to be solved, for we lacked the wisdom and experience that would come only with practice. For example, while the preparation and delivery of a single sermon was not a totally insurmountable task, two such exercises per Sunday was a different matter. Cross-visitation by members between churches was sufficient to make the preparation of fresh material each week seem advisable and even necessary. And a succession of such exercises stretching seamlessly over fifty-two weeks per year and on into an indefinite future was daunting indeed. For many young preachers, such a scenario soon assumed nightmarish proportions. Some may have been reluctant to acknowledge and share this with others, for to do so may have appeared to call the legitimacy of one's vocation into question.

Six other students shared a parish of twelve churches in the vicinity of Fairmont and Bridgeport. Uniformly, it was a warm, rich, and enlightening experience for neophyte preachers. Each of us had an unequalled opportunity to see something of the expectation, pain, and pressure experienced daily in the regular pastorate, and I am grateful to have been a part of such a group. We learned a great deal and tried to minimize the formation of bad habits and practices that might have carried over into our respective ministries at a later time.

My friend and neighbor Ed Thomas lived nearby and was a member of the Bridgeport group. Early one Sunday morning, Ed's scheduled appointment was cancelled for some reason and he was at home. I was also at home, although my service at Kerens was still scheduled, for despite a heroic struggle, inspiration had failed to make an appearance to fill my dismally empty head. Reluctant to become the source of my own public embarrassment, I had sent Charlie and Max on without me. They were hardly gone when Ed spotted me moping drearily on my porch.

Ed Thomas

"I thought you were scheduled to be at Kerens," he challenged. "What happened?"

"Well, if you must know" I answered morosely, "I just couldn't get inspired, so I don't have a sermon. And I'm not going out there just to stand up like an idiot with my mouth hanging open and have nothing to say."

"Listen to me," Ed lectured, sternly playing the Dutch uncle role, "inspiration has been grossly overrated. You may not have a sermon, but you do have an appointment. Get your coat on. You and I are going to Kerens, and I'll bet you have a sermon by the time we get there."

We walked to the nearby highway and stuck our optimistic thumbs in the air. A passing farmer and his wife promptly picked us up, and we rode in the back of their pickup truck all the way to our destination. After a brief but pointed homily on the etiquette and sanctity of keeping appointments, Ed left me alone with my thoughts until we were dropped off beside the road at Kerens church.

Perhaps it was inspiration incognito. Perhaps it was all of that fresh air blowing through my cranial emptiness. Or perhaps it was just another confirmation of the adage that necessity is the mother of invention. But by the time we walked into that church, I had a sermon. And we were not late, but just in time. I will not say that it was my best effort, but I found something to say.

As my homiletics professor commented later in critiquing a sermon of mine to my seminary class, "Well, you weren't very good. But you *were loud!*" I had learned at Kerens Church that especially when you haven't much to say, it is good to say it with emphasis.

In 1992, Ed and his wife visited with Peggy and me in our home in Albuquerque. I remembered and remarked upon the incident of the elusive sermon, recalling it as one of life's more valuable lessons. Happily, after over fifty years, Ed had forgotten it or professed to have done so, perhaps out of kindness. It is probably just as well.

Israel Methodist Church congregation

I Baptize Thee . . . For Sure!

My experiences with the West Virginia Wesleyan College Student Group Ministry were, if not all positive, at least valuable and instructive. They gave me the golden option of evaluating the Methodist ministry from an inside perspective, though barely inside and without the necessity of a total commitment.

I reserved the option of returning to coal mining, although I did not wish to exercise it, for mining was hard, dirty work and extremely dangerous. If a rock fall or a gas explosion did not kill you, black lung disease probably would. It just took a bit longer.

One of the expectations of the country churches of that time and place was that their pastors would conduct annual revival meetings of several days' duration. Student pastors were no exception. My two churches, Israel and Kerens, scheduled their combined evangelistic campaign in late fall, before the onset of severe weather. A favorite time for such an effort was in midwinter, after inclement weather had mandated the closing down of work in field and forest and when families had more free time to devote to church activities.

One of the anticipated benefits of evangelization was the recruitment of new church members. But before new members could be enrolled, candidates had to be prepared for membership by submitting to the rite of baptism. Baptism by sprinkling is the overwhelming mode of choice among Methodists today, with most being baptized as infants or very young children, though options remain for baptism by the pouring of water or by immersion. The rite of baptism is a highly symbolic gesture of submission to a standard of belief and purpose imposed by the early Christian Church, according to the dictates of Jesus Christ.

I do not know why sprinkling has become the favorite method of baptism practiced by Methodists, nor do I know why the pouring mode has been largely abandoned. At the risk of revealing my ignorance and appearing frivolous, I will assume that neatness and convenience account for the popularity of the former. The case of the latter would appear to be due to the sentiment that if you are going to get wet anyway, why not go whole hog and clinch the deal by opting for immersion.

Contrary to popular usage elsewhere, however, in the mountains of West Virginia in 1950, baptism by immersion remained a very viable, even favorite, option. Such rituals were often conducted in late winter or very early spring to facilitate the reception of the new converts into membership before their resolve and zeal had faded. This scenario not only presented an opportunity, but also a problem. The problem lay in the fact that at that elevation in late winter, snow often covered the ground and the temperature of open streams could be expected to approach freezing.

Norm Allers, a fellow student minister, had just completed a series of highly successful revival meetings. As a farmer measures his crop only after the corn is safely in the crib, Norm wisely refrained from assigning a firm number to his count of recent converts until they had been safely brought into the fold via baptism and formal church membership. It seemed prudent, therefore, to schedule a baptismal service promptly to prevent the lambs from escaping the fold and going astray. But the streams were still only marginally above the freezing point, and Norm's weak but willing flesh quailed at the prospect. His own church orientation was from a city in New York State where Methodists were almost universally baptized by sprinkling, and he himself had never personally witnessed a baptism by immersion.

He canvassed his class of prospects closely and convinced most of them to accept the option of sprinkling. One older man, however, steadfastly refused to even consider anything other than total immersion. Norm's inquiries into the proper procedure for such a ritual produced a plethora of advice. He was assured that one local Baptist pastor routinely wore chest high waders, even though his baptismal services were held inside his church in a temperature-regulated tank. Certainly, it seemed safe to trust a Baptist minister in the proper conduct of a signature Baptist practice.

Norm carefully considered his options and decided to eschew the use of the waders, though one of his members had already secured the consent of the Baptist clergyman to borrow the item in question. In his mind, it would be cheating to ask someone else to enter that ice-cold water when he himself had chosen the easier path. Why, it would be little short of cowardly, and Norm Allers was not a coward! The baptism would proceed with the presiding official, himself, being no less wet, cold, and miserable than the presenting supplicant. A baptismal service was scheduled for a Sunday afternoon in the not-too-distant future.

The congregation assembled as planned on the bank of a local creek, where the seasonal floods had scoured out a pool of water of sufficient depth. Norm entered the water with an audible gasp as the icy liquid rose toward the level of his waist. He was accompanied by his candidate eager for immersion. A third member of the triumvirate, knowing of the novice minister's inexperience, had bravely volunteered himself to assist his pastor in lowering the penitent parishioner backward into the water and raising him upright again.

Tucking his book of ritual inside his jacket for temporary safekeeping, Norm placed his right hand on the candidate's back while grasping his wrist with the left. His assistant assumed a similar stance on the other side. Then to the consternation of the assemblage, as his victim was lowered backwards into the frigid bath, Norm quickly brought his supporting hand from behind the back.

Holding the man firmly beneath the water with his left hand on the man's chest, he retrieved his book of ritual with his right and began to read the entire service.

Sensing that something had gone seriously awry, the struggling applicant literally exploded from the creek bed. "What are you trying to do, drown me?" sputtered the indignant man.

"Nope," Norm responded calmly, "just trying to baptize you." Then following the whispered instructions of his more knowledgeable assistant, the procedure was repeated acceptably and according to form, with the supplicant standing in the water, dripping and cold.

No one suffered unduly in the case of the bewildered baptizer, except the well-baptized man who may have never regained his full trust and confidence in the good intentions of his pastor.

Travels with Tiger

My daughter Rebecca was less than four months old when we moved from West Virginia to Elkhart, Illinois, a little corn town situated on fabled Route 66, on the prairie a few miles north of Springfield. Soon after taking up residence there, a lady brought Becky a small striped kitten of the variety invariably named "Tiger."

There had been other pets whose circumstances dictated be found new homes, but Tiger remained. As an only pet, he soon became King of the Jungle, catered to by all as his status demanded. At home, he was in charge. But he proved to be a very poor traveler.

After my entry into the Navy Chaplaincy, following that service's requirement for frequent relocation, it became clear that Tiger was not well suited to the itinerant lifestyle. Not only did he fail to adapt well to each new home, requiring lengthy periods of adjustment, but when on the road, he became confused, restless, and irascible.

The ever elusive Tiger

Even a cat must answer to the requirements of nature, however, and having attended to his immediate physical needs, he invariably attempted to extend his liberty by seeking out a hiding place in which to soothe and repair his perverse temperament. On various occasions he escaped his human keepers in such diverse places as downtown Baltimore in rush-hour traffic, on a foggy mountain top in Bluefield,

West Virginia, and in the wide-open vastness of Montana cow country. We literally waited hours until Tiger, having communed with nature, his inner balance restored and perhaps driven by hunger, decided to reassume command of his company of bipeds.

On one occasion, while picnicking with friends on Cape Cod, a blinding flash of lightning and a roll of thunder announced the onset of a sudden summer storm. Tiger immediately "went south." As icy raindrops pelted us, we searched to no avail. As wailing children tearfully called out to him, he kept company with himself. Dusk came, and I announced that we would just have to go home. Perhaps we could return to the search tomorrow. By the faint reflected light of the few early stars, I saw the tearstained face of our son, Allen, as he looked heavenward for help.

"Please, God," he prayed, "don't let anything happen to Tiger. He's the only pet we have left."

"Come on, Mother," I said to Peggy. "Let's go find that darn cat."

Becky and friend taking Tiger outside

We found him, just ahead of total darkness, completely buried in a pile of leaves in a nearby grove of trees. Though he was temporarily lost to us many times afterward, there was never again a serious question of abandoning Tiger.

After all, he was the only pet we had left.

Out of the Mouths of Babes

When we moved to Norfolk, Virginia, Tiger the cat began to run with a very fast crowd. He strayed frequently and stayed away long. When he did return, often after an absence of several days, it was usually as a very sick and debilitated cat. His many "rumbles" and contested romances led to a series of quite serious and stubborn infections. Peggy and I concluded that both our pet and our budget would be healthier if Tiger submitted to the veterinarian's scalpel and was neutered. The big problem with this plan, however, was explaining it to the children and securing their agreement.

Rebecca, then five years of age, was particularly hard to convince. Finally, and most reluctantly, she yielded to my persuasion sufficiently to consider the plan, but only after demanding the right of informed consent. She proved to be a very tough negotiator in her self-appointed role as Tiger's ombudsman.

The questioning was sharp and to the point. What would the operation entail? Would it hurt? Would he cry? Might he die? We spoke of the purpose of the operation being to effect certain changes in Tiger and his behavior.

"Exactly what kind of changes? And what will he be like afterward?" she inquired.

"Well, honey," I explained, "you know that when Tiger goes out, sometimes he stays gone for a long time. And when he finally does come home, he is usually sick and needs to go to the doctor to get his cuts sewn up and his infections treated. After he has the operation, he will be a much nicer pet. He won't want to go out so much, and he'll just lie around the house and get fat and lazy."

It was too much information to be assimilated in such a short time. Becky thought about it for an extended period, working it all out in her mind. Finally, she came back with another question: "Just like you, huh, Daddy?"

Out of the mouths of babes . . .

The Prosecution of Mary Randolph

The sharp wind drove the cold rain in almost horizontal sheets. I sat in my office and watched the sodden skies unload on the Norfolk waterfront, thankful to be dry and in a warm place. No small boats moved between the ships at anchor in Hampton Roads and the naval base piers. Except for an infrequent truck or auto on the street, nothing moved but the wind and the rain. Even the seagulls had abandoned their ceaseless quarreling over food and sought shelter from the storm.

As I watched, far down the waterfront, a solitary figure came into view. I wondered what would drive someone into the streets on such a day. Shoulders hunched against the storm-driven misery, taking dubious sanctuary beneath an ancient umbrella that threatened imminent collapse under the insistent wind, the figure made no effort to avoid the numerous puddles of water flooding the street. As it drew nearer, I observed the flash of a woman's bare legs beneath the clinging wetness of her thin dress. *She must be on some terribly important business,* I thought, *and very cold and wet.* She wore a sailor's peacoat and men's government-issue oxfords, several sizes too large. Soon it became obvious that her destination was my location, the offices of the chaplain of Landing Ship Flotilla 2.

She entered with a great bluster of wind-driven rain. After I had shown her to the comforting warmth of a chair beside a steam radiator and had given her a hot mug of coffee, I inquired how I might be of help.

"My husband is Seaman Travis Randolph," she responded. "He is aboard the *Wahkiakum County*." And so began to unfold one of the most amazing and sordid stories I was to hear during my entire naval career.

I knew her husband by reputation. He was a seaman with seventeen years of service and was of such limited intellectual capacity that he consistently failed in his efforts at advancement in grade. But he was such a willing worker and so personally ingratiating that he had been allowed to reenlist several times, though it was against the navy's "up or out" promotion policy.

Mary and Travis had been married for about five years and had three children. His small family allotment and meager pay necessitated that they receive public welfare assistance, with occasional emergency financial supplementation from the Navy Relief Society. I knew all of the above as the Navy Relief Society liaison person for my squadron.

As Mary began her story, I learned that about a year prior to this time, Mary had proposed that she seek employment to help with the family finances. Though Travis protested, she took a night job as a waitress in a neighborhood bar. This permitted one parent to be at home with the children while the other worked.

Through her employment, Mary soon met and yielded to the blandishments of a shore-based sailor, Mack Davenport, who frequented the bar. He began to visit her in her home while Travis worked, and inevitably, she became pregnant by him. Soon afterward, he requested that she accompany him to Naval Base Headquarters, where he had some unspecified business to conduct. She told me that she innocently agreed, and soon they were ushered into the base commander's office.

Awaiting them there were the base commander, a chaplain, and a young woman who was also obviously pregnant. The commander was brief in his summation. The young lady who stood before him had appeared, charging Mack with paternity in the case of her unborn child. She sought the relief of marriage and child support through a family allotment.

"Do you acknowledge paternity?" asked the commander.

"Yes, sir," Mack replied.

"Then will you marry this young lady and support her child through an allotment?" the commander asked.

"Sir," Mack answered, "the young lady standing here with me is Mary Randolph. She is also pregnant with my child. Since I can't marry both of them, I would prefer to wed Miss Randolph."

"Very well," ordered the commander. "Make it so!" He then turned to the chaplain and said, "Chaplain, you will immediately escort Seaman Davenport and Miss Randolph to City Hall, where you will ensure that they obtain a marriage license. You will then conduct their wedding ceremony."

This was too much, even for a chaplain like me who fancied that he had seen and heard it all. None of this fit my experience of the way the navy did its thing.

I interrupted Mary. "Wait a minute!" I protested. "Didn't you inform them at that point that you were already married?"

"No," she responded. "I thought that once we were out of the commander's office, Mack could excuse himself by saying that I had just told him that I was already married. Then we could just go back to the way things were. But Mack didn't say anything, and soon we were at City Hall. Events just spun out of control, and the first thing I knew, we were standing at the altar in Base Chapel being married.

"After the ceremony, I didn't know what to do. But I warned Mack not to apply for a family allotment for me, for that would be fraud, since I was already receiving an allotment from Travis. He agreed, but I learned much later that he was called into the Personnel Office and ordered to submit an application for an allotment on the basis of his recent marriage. So, we just went on as before. The extra family allotment helped a lot and we were getting along just fine. Meanwhile I had moved out of Travis's apartment and in with Mack, taking my three children with me.

"The new baby was born in Portsmouth Naval Hospital, and a few weeks later Mack suggested that we take a short honeymoon trip to see my parents in Pennsylvania. We stayed there for a few days, and Mack proposed that we go on to New York to see his parents, who had not seen their new grandchild. We left my three older children with my parents and went to New York, promising to pick them up on our return.

"After several days in New York, Mack wanted to leave the new baby with his parents while we went away for a weekend. I agreed, since we really had never had any time alone together. But I was beginning to suspect that Mack was Absent Without Leave. When I confronted him, he confessed that it was true. I urged him to go back to Norfolk, turn himself in, and clear his record. He reluctantly agreed, and since we really didn't know how things would go in Norfolk, we decided to leave the children with our parents for a few more days.

"But when we returned to Norfolk, Mack was immediately arrested and confined to the Base Brig awaiting court-martial on charges of desertion. Meanwhile, it was discovered that I was receiving two family allotments, and both were immediately cancelled. I was certain that I would be charged with defrauding the government. The county authorities were investigating me for bigamy. My children were gone. I had no money. And now I discovered that I was pregnant again with Mack's child. I had no choice but to go back to Travis. He was angry with me, but agreed that I could move back in with him. But I just couldn't tell him I was pregnant again."

"Wow!" I said, "That is quite a story! How do you think I can help you?" I naively thought that she would ask for a referral to the Navy Relief Society for emergency financial assistance. I anticipated making the referral and having her neatly out of my hair. How badly I had misjudged her faith in the powers of the chaplain!

"Well, I thought that you could help me get my children back," she responded. "And perhaps you could tell the base commander that I didn't really *intend* to defraud the government. After all, no one *asked* if I was already married. And I did warn Mack not to apply for an allotment. I was unaware that he was AWOL. We certainly needed the Welfare Dept. money. And now Travis and I are back together again. If you would do those things for me, then everything will work out just fine."

"But Travis doesn't know about your new pregnancy," I observed.

"No," she admitted. "I thought you could tell him about that."

"There really is nothing that I can do about your impending legal problems," I offered. "I cannot intervene in that. As to your children, I suspect that they are better off where they are, at least for the moment. But there is one thing that I *can* do. I can inform Travis of your condition. I really think he should know."

I reached for the telephone and dialed the number for the *Wahkiakum County*, which was docked some distance away. I spoke to the officer of the deck, who promised to have SN Randolph report to me as soon as possible. I then instructed Mrs. Randolph to wait in another room until I called her.

Within a few minutes, a navy sedan delivered SN Randolph to my office. I explained the situation to him as gently as I could and asked if he wanted to see his wife. "No," he said, angrily, "and I hope I never see her again." With that, he walked out of the room and returned to his ship.

When I told her of his decision, Mary was furious. She could not understand why he could accept her but could not accept her baby, which, after all, was her own flesh and blood.

After allowing her to unburden herself of her anger, I gave her a ride to a sheltered bus stop off base and had no further contact with her. I inquired of Travis a day or so later and learned that she had happily returned to live with him in their apartment. Within a short time, I was transferred to duty with the Naval Hospital at Camp LeJeune, North Carolina. I considered the incident closed as far as my input was concerned.

Several months after reporting to Camp LeJeune, I visited Commander Jack Strickland, the hospital's Medical Service Corps officer, in his office. After chatting amiably for a few minutes he said, "Padre, if you have a few minutes I'd like to tell you one of the most tangled tales I have ever heard." It soon became clear that he was telling me the same story that I have just related to you.

I interrupted by asking, "Could that lady's name have been Randolph?"

"How did you know?" he asked, amazed. "I haven't told that story to anyone for fear that I would not be believed."

The end of the story is almost anticlimactic. Commander Strickland, who had obtained a law degree while stationed at Portsmouth Naval Hospital, had been assigned to investigate and assist in the prosecution of Mary Randolph on charges of defrauding the government. It came to pass that the navy, in its wisdom, saw fit to dismiss desertion charges against Mack Davenport to avoid the embarrassment of having to charge the base commander with issuing illegal orders to one of his subordinates. The county welfare authorities agreed to not press charges against Mary if the navy would proceed with fraud charges. She was acquitted of fraud, since it was Mack, not she, who had applied for the family allotment and had done so without her knowledge. The bigamy charges were dismissed on the basis that her marriage to Mack had been illegally ordered by the base commander, or perhaps out of sheer embarrassment on the part of the navy.

By the time her fifth child was born, in Portsmouth Naval Hospital, Mary and Travis were so happy and well-adjusted that they decided to remain together permanently. They regained custody of the four absent children, and Travis's family allotment was reinstated, along with supplemental welfare assistance from Norfolk County. Travis, at that point, was within two years of qualifying for retirement on the basis of twenty years of satisfactory service. His commanding officer was so anxious to protect his retirement potential that he was permitted to reenlist for a final two-year term. After all, none of this was the fault of Travis Randolph, nor did it happen with his knowledge.

I must assume that they all lived happily thereafter, except perhaps for poor Mack Davenport, who was deprived of the comfort of Mary's companionship and presence in his life.

Is there a moral to this story? You bet there is! Honesty and clean living will pay off every time.

The Proper Baptism of the Padre

In the summer of 1959, my squadron (Amphibious Squadron 10) was employed in an ongoing series of amphibious exercises in the vicinity of Vieques Island, Puerto Rico. The scenario called for the marines to be launched on the landing phase of the operation by LCVP and helicopter. Since there was no secure anchoring ground off Vieques, the ships would then disperse to their assigned secondary missions, including "show the flag" visits to various Caribbean ports, returning after several days to re-embark the marines and transport them back to another landing exercise at Onslow Beach, North Carolina. At that point, we returned to our homeport in Norfolk to reprovision and start the process all over again with a different group of marines. Turnaround time was about three weeks for these exercises.

My base of operations was the flagship USS *Boxer* (LPH 2), an old aircraft carrier recently converted to rotary wing (helicopter) operations, but I often went circuit riding on other ships of the squadron. The high point of these boring evolutions was that we could look forward to at least one port call at one of the many exotic island groups of the Caribbean.

On one occasion, we had successfully launched the marines to their onshore operations when a huge storm blew in off the eastern Atlantic. I was aboard USS *Kleinsmith* (APD 134), an old Destroyer Escort used for close inshore support of the marine landing parties, and was looking forward to accompanying them to their next port of call, Kingston, Jamaica.

The wind had piled the sea into enormous swells, and the little *Kleinsmith*, not much larger than a minesweeper, was under the water more than on it, struggling up the face of an oncoming swell and surfing down the reverse slope, to be buried under towering mountains of onrushing water. The sailors often joked that they should be drawing submarine pay.

A signal was received from the flagship ordering me to transfer immediately to USS *Plymouth Rock* (LSD 29), which had requested a chaplain to conduct Divine Services. I was then to return to the *Boxer*, which was scheduled for a port visit to San Juan. The method of transfer would have to be the "bosun's chair," or highline, since the *Kleinsmith* had no landing pad.

Due to the violent motion of the ship, and the forest of booms and masts, a helicopter could not hover close enough to pick me up by sling. Soon the two ships had maneuvered into position and were running side-by-side, separated by a scant 75 feet of racing water. We were windward of the receiving ship, so the decision was made to pass the highline by means of a "messenger," a lightline attached to a weighted knot called a "monkey-fist."

A burly bosun's mate spun the line around his head several times, paying out a bit more line with each revolution until the weight achieved critical velocity. He then released the line, which flew across the open space as though shot from a cannon. The lightline was attached to a heavier line and finally to an even heavier one that would carry the bosun's chair in which I would ride. The hawser was made fast to the receiving ship and returned by pulley to the *Kleinsmith*, where a group of twenty or so sailors manned the free end, giving and taking up slack, adjusting tension to the pitch and roll of the two ships.

Though I had made this trip several times before, it had never been under such adverse conditions, and I admit to a bit of apprehension. Sending my Val-Pak and field altar kit across first in a net sling, I awaited the rigging of the chair. Soon I was strapped in and ready for the big adventure. At a signal from the *Plymouth Rock*, the sending crew suddenly took the slack out of the line and I found myself racing across the chasm and dropping toward the water only a few feet below my precarious perch. Midway, the two ships rolled toward each other, allowing the chair to plummet like a roller coaster toward the briny deep. The watching sailors cheered as my feet submerged and sent a drenching spray of seawater over me. In a moment, the ships had reversed the direction of their roll and I was again hanging high, if not entirely dry.

"Well, the padre finally got properly baptized!" they laughed, with evident good humor as I was hauled aboard the *Plymouth Rock*. In their view, they had completed an eminently successful operation, made even more satisfactory by my impromptu drenching.

Highlining between ships at sea

Following a quick trip to the bridge to greet the captain, I was ushered to the well of the ship, where Divine Services would be held. The well, a space designed to launch and recover LCTs and LCVPs directly from the sea, was now a vast empty theatre. "Now hear this!" the ship's PA system blared and echoed through the empty space. "Secure from all unnecessary work. Divine Services will begin immediately in the well deck. Knock off all skylarking. Maintain quiet in the vicinity of Divine Services."

I set up my portable altar as I waited for my congregation. Finally, a lone sailor appeared, making his way down the vertical ladder.

There were no chairs and no organ or pews in our church. After a few minutes of conversation, the sailor said, "Well, I'm ready if you are, padre!" It appeared that my congregation had just arrived. I abandoned my prepared formal sermon in favor of a more personal discussion of some biblical topic.

I was reminded of the story of a farmer who was the only worshiper at a church service. The sermon was long. At its conclusion, the farmer reminded the preacher that when he went out to feed his sheep and a single lamb showed up for the morning feeding, he did not give it the entire load of hay. My "lamb" was fed, but he had not gotten the whole load.

Now I fully understood the minister who once said, "I have preached to congregations so small that when I said 'Dearly Beloved,' he blushed."

The sailor made his way back up the ladder, and in a few minutes, the word was passed: "Now secure from Divine Services. Resume ship's work."

The *Plymouth Rock* did have a helicopter pad, and soon I was airborne and on my way back to my home base on the *Boxer*. My only regret was that I never did get to visit Jamaica. I would make many more such transfers from ship to ship, but that was the only occasion an unexpected baptism was part of the trip.

A California Interlude

During my navy career, we spent six years in Southern California, four of them in Fallbrook. In my opinion, San Diego County has some of the finest climate in the United States, sunny and virtually frost-free, tempered by its proximity to the ocean and the cool Japan Current.

Fallbrook was a small lazy community of avocado and orange groves adjacent to the huge US Marine Base at Camp Pendleton. Its setting, economy, and interests were strictly agrarian. I cannot imagine a more favorable place for family life and outdoor activities; we felt fortunate to be part of such a congenial community of people. Since I was at sea for four of those six years, we were thankful for the friendship and support of many friendly neighbors.

Our next-door neighbors were Buzz and Doris Kessel, a wonderful couple with five children, with whom our three became fast friends. Buzz tended a large avocado grove, while Doris busied herself with a host of activities related mostly to her children's 4-H and FFA projects. They were an enjoyable family with a multitude of healthy interests, and since our children were almost constantly together, we felt blessed to have them as friends and neighbors.

Becky was then about ten years old and quickly became a real tomboy, with four rowdy "brothers" who were fiercely protective of her and who included her in many of their activities. She learned to harvest oranges and avocados, prune trees, shear sheep, irrigate the groves, and many other things related to that lifestyle.

It was inevitable that, as they grew older, she would develop a huge attachment to Mike Kessel, a year or two older than she, and that their attachment would blossom into preadolescent true love. She wanted only to be near him; his attention and approval was the stuff of which dreams were made.

Allen, Becky, and the Kessel boys in the avocado grove

Mike was a prototypical young westerner, a lean and lanky lad, a gentle giant who preferred action to words. He was all to her that a teenage hero should be.

One day Doris had to make a trip with Mike to Escondido, a larger nearby community, and they invited Becky to ride with them. She, of course, quickly accepted. Driving past the post office, Doris stopped to purchase a book of stamps. As she got out of the car, Becky settled in to enjoy a moment in Mike's company, pleased to command his full attention.

Becky relaxed, yawned sleepily, and as she did so, felt a large cell of gas forming in her intestinal tract. She was sure that she could relieve her discomfort silently and demurely, but as Robert Burns once wrote, "The best laid plans of mice and men often go awry." In passing, the gaseous aggravation did not go quietly. She was mortified and glanced surreptitiously at Mike to gauge his reaction.

Gentleman that he was, he reacted not at all, but continued to watch the passing parade of people on the sidewalk. Frantic to say something, anything, to divert attention from herself, she said, "Did you hear that motorcycle go by?"

"Nope," Mike responded laconically, "but I sure smelled it."

On the Way to Okinawa

As my two years of shore duty as chaplain, US Naval Hospital Camp LeJeune, North Carolina, approached an end in the summer of 1962, I prepared myself for an assignment at sea. I hoped that it would be with a ship rather than a deployed marine unit, since the latter would include an out-of-country tour of at least thirteen months, unaccompanied by family. A sea billet would at least get me home more frequently.

When orders came, I learned that I would be assigned to the US Marine Corps Base, Camp Pendleton, California. A closer reading of the "small print" revealed that I would be subject to "further assignment" at the discretion of the commanding general, to whom I was to report. As they say, "The devil is in the details."

After reporting as ordered, I received my "further assignment": to 3rd Battalion, 7th Marine Regiment, 1st Marine Division. The "devil in the details" lay in the fact that 3/7 was scheduled for transshipment to Okinawa, where we would become 1st Battalion, 9th Marine Regiment, 3rd Marine Division. After a short but intensive training and conditioning period, we were pronounced fit for service.

On March 15, 1963, after a painful goodbye to our families and the short trip to Naval Base San Diego, we boarded USS *William Mitchell* (TAP 114) for the voyage to Okinawa via Port Hueneme, California; Adak, Alaska; and Yokohama, Japan. Already aboard were numerous civilian types, mostly women and children, dependents of US military personnel who were on two-year assignments at various ports in the Far East.

These longer assignments were considered a hardship on dependents, so military personnel were permitted to break their long tour with a period of Rest and Recreation (R & R). They could choose to visit another port for their R & R, or they could board a ship of the

On the way to Alaska

Military Sea Transport Service (MSTS), whose mission was to transport military units and civilian dependents to their overseas stations. This MSTS tour, called a "round robin," normally visited Japan, Okinawa, Republic of the Philippines, and occasionally Formosa—or Korea, Hong Kong, Bangkok, Guam, Hawaii, San Diego or San Francisco, and Alaska, before completing their circuit two to two-and-a-half months later in Japan.

Several ships were employed in this service, half following the route described; the others doing the round robin in reverse direction. It was a wonderful opportunity for travel and very popular with service families, since they not only visited exotic Pacific ports, but also usually got an extended replenishment and repair stop in a US port. They could even leave the ship in any port and catch the next ship in the round robin. This gave them an unrivaled opportunity to visit families in the US before returning to their overseas stations.

We stopped at Port Hueneme, California, to board two battalions of Seabees, one of which was to debark at Adak, Alaska. The voyage across the Gulf of Alaska was unforgettably rough. The frigid Arctic winds piled the seas into mountainous waves, which came crashing aboard, burying the bow and smothering the rest of the ship in green water and spray.

My bunkroom, which I shared with seven marine officers, was just under the main deck and forward of the superstructure. As the ship pitched and rolled with the waves, a seam opened in the deck overhead, allowing ice-cold seawater to drip into my face. Alarmed, I quickly found the first lieutenant, who was in charge of repairs, to report the situation, for I envisioned the ship breaking apart and our taking an impromptu swim in icy water.

"Oh, that thing again," he responded casually. "Don't worry about it. It happens every crossing. We weld it and it breaks open again." I switched my head to the other end of my bunk and prepared to spend the rest of the voyage with wet feet. I soon learned to pile blankets and towels under the leak to soak up the water and remained fairly comfortable.

Coming under the lee of the Aleutian Islands, we found a brief respite from the towering seas, but the bitter wind raged on. Our arrival at Adak Island was marked by a transitory parting of the clouds, allowing a few rays of weak sunshine to break through.

Adak was overwhelming, both in its isolation and its desolation. Not a tree relieved the bleak and windswept landscape; only moss and a sparse grass covered the frozen rocks and soil. The naval station personnel and their families turned out en masse to welcome us.

We were dressed in foul weather gear, which seemed appropriate to us considering the raw weather. They were coatless and in a celebratory mood on this, their loveliest day of the year. It was, they assured us, the first time they had seen the sun in several months.

Adak Island base

Proudly pointing to a collection of perhaps a dozen totem poles thrusting their grimacing visages skyward, and demonstrating the unflinching sense of humor that makes survival possible in such places, they proudly dubbed their wretched collection "The Adak National Forest." Quickly off-loading the dependents and the Seabees destined for that redoubtable place, we were back at sea by dinnertime, happy that we could spend so little time there.

After another few days at sea, we entered Tokyo Bay, where the captain and crew had a few very busy hours picking their way through the tangle of barges and local traffic plying their inner-harbor trade. Two harbor tugs warped us neatly "portside to" the pier at Yokosuka Naval Station. There we spent two days on shore leave while the ship took on provisions and fuel. We also dropped off most of our embarked dependents and took on just as many more for the next phase of the round robin. The weather became steadily and rapidly more tropical as we continued our voyage southward to Okinawa.

It was happenstance that brought me back to Okinawa on April 1, 1963, exactly eighteen years after my first visit there in 1945, but under radically different circumstances. I hoped that its designation as April Fool's Day would not be prophetic. The plain and unassuming appearance of the Okinawan capitol and port city of Naha contrasted starkly to the bright lights and glitter of Tokyo. Although the inhabitants wore the same basic costumes, the drabness of the Okinawan dress, as opposed to the bright colors of the Japanese, told us that we were among down-to-earth working people. We noted that in both Japan and Okinawa, the homes were unpainted, a concession to the free roaming spirits of the dead, who could penetrate walls but not a coat of paint.

Reflecting their economic prosperity, the thick straw-thatched roofs were rapidly giving way to more modern fireproof materials. Each tile roof was decorated with either a ceramic or cast metal shisa dog to scare away unwanted spirits and protect the household. The streets teemed with activity in this busy port.

As we were bussed northward to our permanent base, I noted that the distinctive lyre-shaped burial tombs, which had been such a prominent feature during WWII, evidenced good repair. During the battle, both sides had used them as fighting cover, which resulted in the destruction of the tombs and the scattering of burial pots and bones.

Ethnically, the Okinawans were more closely related to the Chinese than to the Japanese. Some eight hundred years earlier, the Chinese had invaded and conquered the

Testament to the local sense of humor

aboriginal occupants of the Ryukyu Islands, of which Okinawa was the largest land mass. Over the next few hundred years, control of the islands alternated between Formosa, China, and Japan, but the dominant culture and ethnic identification remained Chinese.

The islanders actively disliked and resented the Japanese, with their superior attitude, brutal measures of control, and particularly for their having impressed large numbers of Okinawans into Japanese service—the men as laborers and the females as "comfort women."

They would come to resent the American presence equally, as their farms and fields were preempted to accommodate the sprawling American bases.

The quiet self-effacing manner of the islanders seemed likely to be overwhelmed by the brash assertiveness of their American tenants and visitors. The two cultures did not mix well, and one could easily understand the native uneasiness with the "ugly Americans." Initially, they liked the easy Yankee dollars and the economic uplift given their economy, but in the end, cultural conflict came to mark their tenuous accommodation of one another.

In defense of the Okinawans, I think that no subservient culture could readily withstand an invasion by thousands of young, hormone-driven Americans who had been newly released from the cultural restraints of their homeland. Most Okinawans regarded them as uncivilized, and overwhelmingly, they were. Although many Americans were married, they easily left behind the humanizing influence of wives and sweethearts, treating their hosts as sexual amenities. They flippantly defended their behavior by quoting, "There are no married men beyond the 180th parallel (International Date Line)." Many formed liaisons with women from the local bars that sprang up around the camps and began living with them in a "ranching" or "shacking" arrangement, giving further affront to the Okinawan morality.

Fortunately for us, it would prove to be a very busy time. Almost immediately, we went into a guerrilla warfare–training regimen on the remote northern end of the island, leaving little time for us to spend in Camp Hansen, our base camp. As soon as the guerrilla training ended, we boarded USS *Bexar* (APA 237) for transport to Camp Fuji, Japan. We spent the next two months at about the 5000-foot level on Mt. Fuji in tactical training with the Japanese Self-Defense Force. It rained virtually every day, and for the duration of our stay there we were neither warm nor dry. Near the end of June, USS *Bexar* arrived to rescue us and return us to Okinawa's more equitable climate.

The *Bexar* was a very unhappy ship. That ships have distinct personalities is a fact known to all seagoing personnel, who may speak of a vessel as "happy," "unhappy," "grim," "depressing," or "spooked." A "bad" ship takes its characteristics partly, but not entirely, from the state of morale of officers and crew. Some ships remain unhappy ships despite changes in employment, leadership, and crew. I accept that but cannot explain it.

I hope that, in the case of the *Bexar*, the personality of the captain was the operative factor and that better days were ahead under new leadership. He was an irascible and unhappy man, determined to rule by the biting power of an acid personality. The captain hated marines and much preferred that they remain below deck at all times. Our poor colonel was always under the gun. Distinct white lines marked off the crowded decks of the ship, leaving room only for passage around equipment. One who ventured topside and stepped over a sacred white line was sure to feel the sting of the captain's tongue. He roamed the wings of the navigation bridge with microphone in hand. Spotting an out-of-place marine, he would scream for the colonel to "Get your @#$%& ^%#@^ marines offa my white lines, or we'll go to 'fist city.'"

On the southward voyage, we passed through a narrow strait that was crowded with the small sailing vessels of the local fishermen. The rules of the road require that sailing vessels be given the right of way, under the "burdened vessel" rule.

The captain, on this rare occasion, was absent from the bridge, and the hapless officer of the deck simply did not know how to navigate this confused situation without endangering the small boats. He properly called for the assistance of the captain who, in his usual foul mood, began to shout abusively, "I am surrounded by a bunch of #@$%^& idiots. Clear the bridge!"

After banishing all but the helmsman, he continued to vent his anger, throwing his $50 hat on the deck and stomping on it. Only a madman stomps on a $50 hat. But he soon had things in hand and retained control of the ship until we had transited the straits. I will give him credit for being a superb seaman and the best ship handler I have ever seen. We wished *Bexar* and her crew "happy sailing" as we returned to the gentler, kinder climate of Okinawa.

There, for the next three months, we would be designated the "ready" or "mount-out" battalion of Fleet Marine Force, Pacific. One battalion, called the Afloat-Ready Battalion, was constantly aboard ship, cruising the waters of Southeast Asia, alert for any contingency action in that troubled part of the world. The ready battalion was held in reserve, ashore. Meanwhile, we continued our intensified training program on Okinawa until our turn came to become the "afloat" battalion. A large part of that training was in our readiness to respond to emergency "mount-out" orders.

In late July, an urgent "frost call" came from Division Headquarters. We were to respond to an attack on the headquarters of the South Vietnamese government in Saigon by the Viet Cong. Within hours we were boarding military transport aircraft. We took off on a flight of several hours. The troops were calm but tense, for they believed, as I did, that we were destined for combat. Windows were all blacked out. After about thirty minutes, the flight crew chief came to me and said that the pilot had requested my presence on the flight deck. I responded and was a bit puzzled when the captain said, "I thought you might be more comfortable up here where you can see out."

Taking this as an invitation to get nosy, I immediately noted that the setting sun was on our port side. If we were heading for Vietnam, it should have been to starboard. I also spotted a line of islands that should not have been there, if my estimate was correct. As I glanced over the navigator's shoulder at the chart, he asked, "Padre, do you know where we are going?" I replied, "No, but I know where we are *not* going. We are not going to Vietnam."

At that point he informed me that this was a test of our readiness, that we were flying north toward Japan and that our next stop would be our starting point—Kadena Air Base, Okinawa. But in the interest of making the exercise realistic, the troops aboard were not to be told until after we landed and they had charged down the loading ramp into "combat."

We landed after about six hours in the air, and the marines on board performed flawlessly, taking up positions on the tarmac until the situation was known and orders given. When they learned that they had been tricked, they were understandably angry and disillusioned that their own leaders could be so duplicitous. I agreed with them, believing that once in the air, the "training" benefit had been achieved and the men should have been told this was an exercise. After all, if the troops cannot trust their own leaders to be honest and forthcoming in so crucial a situation, something vital to good morale is irretrievably lost.

At last, the point of our long training period was realized. We were designated the afloat battalion, or Special Landing Force, US Seventh Fleet. Boarding USS *Talladega* (APA 208), we sailed to the Lingayan Gulf, Philippine Islands, where we practiced a "turn away" landing, proving the soundness of our amphibious landing skills.

Several weeks were spent in Subic Bay, "Pearl of the Orient," before returning to Okinawa, where we took on reinforcements and were designated a Regimental Landing Team. We returned to Subic Bay on alternate shipping. USS *Okanogan* (APA 220) would be our home for the next five months, with side trips to Formosa and Hong Kong.

Olongapo, the port city outside the naval base at Subic Bay, was no "Pearl of the Orient." It had one main street, a one-and-a-half-mile-long "red light" district. Within days, the VD rate began to soar among our marines. Alarmed, the colonel ordered that a supply of condoms be placed at the quarterdeck and that each marine going ashore be required to take one. Some of the marines complained to me that this was an affront to their religious beliefs and that they would not accept the proffered condoms. I felt that the situation bordered on open rebellion and approached the colonel with an alternate plan. I proposed that condoms be made available at the quarterdeck and that each marine be *invited* to take one or more. I believe that the colonel was already searching for a way to retreat from his hardnosed stance, for he readily accepted my alternate plan. The VD rate quickly returned to a more manageable level and remained there for the duration.

As our scheduled tour expired, our return to Okinawa was interrupted by the assassination of President John F. Kennedy. We turned back to South Vietnam to cruise offshore for several additional weeks in readiness for intervention if a power vacuum should develop ashore. There was none, and we returned to Okinawa in late March, where we prepared for the end of our deployment and return to Camp Pendleton.

I flew to San Francisco by chartered airline. The remainder of the battalion returned aboard USS *Mann*, another troop transport, arriving a month later. In May 1964, I reported to Camp Pendleton's naval hospital for duty as chaplain. I departed from my assignment with 1/9 with some regret, for they were a good group of men.

One marine casualty marred our long cruise. The Marine Advisory Group in Saigon had requested the assignment of one marine officer to serve temporarily as observer/advisor to the South Vietnamese forces. A first lieutenant from Headquarters Company volunteered. We saw no more of him until our return to Okinawa at the conclusion of our duty afloat. He was waiting for us on the pier at White Beach. He recounted having accompanied a patrol into the jungles of the Mekong Delta. The patrol encountered no enemy forces until, at a brief rest stop, he decided to step into the bushes to answer an urgent call of nature. As he dropped his trousers, he presented a perfect target to a hidden Viet Cong soldier, who shot him through both buttocks. We wondered if the Viet Cong soldier had a sense of humor, or perhaps he just resented being "mooned" by an American marine.

Although I missed my family terribly during the long months of the cruise, I came to agree with the policy that left families in the United States. Given the brief time we were ashore on Okinawa and due to our almost constant movement, the presence of dependents would have been a negative morale factor and an unnecessary distraction from our mission. But while I recognize the necessity of such deployments, I would never again volunteer for such an assignment.

Ships I Have Known and . . . Loved?

Elsewhere in this narrative, I have stated that ships have separate and distinct personalities. That statement is made from the perspective of one who, over a twenty-six-year time span, has sailed in twenty-eight different ships. That does not make me an expert, but it does, I believe, give me the credentials to field an opinion. I do not intend to write of each of those twenty-eight ships individually but will limit my comments to those few that have, for one reason or another, made themselves memorable to me. These comments are not intended to be definitive of any type or class of ship, but indicate only the experience I had in them and their impression on me.

As noted previously, ships are known to be "happy" or "unhappy" for what are often inexplicable reasons. Everything from the personality of the captain, to the mission of the vessel, to her materiel condition, to the morale of her crew has a bearing, but even when those conditions change, she may remain an "unhappy" ship.

A long line of vessels named *Intrepid* for example, have suffered a series of misfortunes, including being sunk by enemy action, while remaining "happy" ships whose crews maintained a high state of morale.

A series of *Saratoga*s, on the other hand, suffered the same misfortunes and, in my experience, carried the "unhappy" reputation of a "bad luck" ship. As I have said, I believe this to be true, although I cannot explain it fully. I characterize them as "happy" or "unhappy," knowing that others who knew them much better than I might apply to them a whole different set of epithets. Perhaps one's characterization depends as much as anything else on the attitudes and expectations with which one comes aboard.

SS *Lurline*

My first ship! My first encounter with the sea! A happy ship. In spite of my negative experiences on her, she taught me about love/hate connections with ships. That grand old lady of the Matson Lines, *Lurline*, along with *Matsonia*, her sister ship, had been taken out of the Far Eastern luxury cruise service at the beginning of WWII and converted to a troop carrier with space for five thousand troops. Evidently anticipating a return to cruise service after the war, the management left most of her amenities intact. The broad promenade decks had temporarily been given bulkheads and pipe bunks to increase berthing space. The opulent staterooms were largely untouched and were occupied by officers and NCOs (non-commissioned officers), leaving the promenade decks for the peons. The great staircase seemed as wide as a city block and made a majestic statement in its descent to the Grand Ballroom and Main Dining Salon. The magnificent crystal chandeliers still graced those social areas; a reminder of the lavish lifestyles once lived out beneath them. In lieu of the usual mess tables, the freestanding four-person tables and chairs were left in place. To a young marine fresh from the hills of West Virginia, it was wonderfully impressive.

SS *Lurline*

Only a week past my eighteenth birthday, I was aboard as a member of the Marine Corps 19th Replacement Battalion. Except for a few brief glimpses of Port Royal Sound during my boot camp training at Parris Island, I had never before seen a ship or the sea. We were given no hint of our destination, except that we were to be replacements for casualties of war. We were told only that our passage would be swift and unescorted, relying on the speed of the ship, and would take a sinuous course, for protection. We would not see land until arrival at our destination.

The troops were aboard as members of many small units, all strangers to one another. There was no unit cohesiveness, no feeling of pride or mutual responsibility for one another. Officers and NCOs did not know the men in their charge and had little interest in maintaining order and discipline. Since we occupied the very bottom of the pecking order, many non-rated people attempted to improve their status by climbing on the backs of their fellow marines. Thievery was common. Gambling, though illegal, was seen everywhere. Turf fights broke out over bunk assignment, places in the heads (toilets), and in the chow lines.

One inconvenience of shipboard life was soon evident to all. There was no place to sit, except at the mess tables. Naturally, many tried to prolong their mealtime seating, though it deprived incoming diners of a place to eat. Turf fights broke out over possession of mess tables. Some attempted to limit traffic through a select area by denying others access, causing more turf fights. The entire voyage was one long testosterone-driven contest for the alpha position in the pack. At the time, it struck me as an oddity of human nature that we who were to serve at the bastions of freedom should be so intent on depriving our fellows of the very freedoms we were supposed to be defending.

Before boarding, I had been assigned mess duty for the duration of the voyage, a situation that would tend to replicate itself with regularity. My work assignment was in the scullery, catching mess trays as they exited the dishwashing machine and transporting them on a handcart back to the head of the serving line, about a mile away. It seemed, and under other conditions might have been, a simple and easy task, but I was to learn that there was nothing simple or easy about it.

Meals were served at staggered hours, and except for a brief closure to switch from breakfast to lunch to dinner, service was nearly continuous from early morning to evening. The decks, due to the action of the ship, were soon littered with various spilled items of food and drink, rendering those surfaces dangerous even to walk upon. The ship's motion, accentuated by her more than 30 knots of speed, was a pitch, or uplifting of the deck, accompanied by a long, lazy roll to port or starboard, where she seemed to lie on her side forever before righting herself and beginning a corresponding pitch and roll in the other direction.

Five thousand trays had to be transported three times daily across the length of the mess deck. Carrying two hundred stainless steel trays per trip, I made that hazardous crossing seventy-five times per day, twenty-five times per meal. The first one or two trips were no problem, for the deck was not yet covered with greasy mealtime debris. But later, as the ship heeled over, the wheels on my hand cart frequently lost their purchase on the slick surface, crashing into tables and diners, wiping out entire rows of angry marines who were not terribly understanding of my predicament. If I had actually received all of the "ass whippings" I was promised on that voyage, I would have been the most pounded on marine since Barney Ross. At the end of my workday, I wanted nothing more than to collapse in my bunk and try to get a few hours of sleep before the torment repeated itself. But even that was to be denied me.

To exacerbate a nearly unbearable situation, at night, unruly gangs of merry-makers created an uproar by jostling the sleepers in their pipe bunks, shouting "Piss call! Piss call! Hit the deck! Piss call!" They were hilarious!

An old tradition of the sea is the initiation of "pollywogs" as they cross the equator for the first time, becoming "shellbacks." Although such celebrations were forbidden due to the numbers of troops aboard, at midnight of that memorable day, those same "piss call" artists decided that they were being deprived of a God-given right.

They broke out hoses and sprayed the promenade decks with sea water—bunks, bedding, marines, and all. I was beginning to wonder what quirk of fate was responsible for my being there.

Ordinarily, I could depend on a few minutes of slack time as the changeover occurred between meals. At such times, I found that I could climb high in the superstructure of the ship, to a point just beneath the signal bridge. This provided a wonderfully unobstructed panoramic view of the ocean with the ship at its center. From that vantage point, the ship seemed to be centered in a huge blue bowl, with the horizon higher than the center. The bow wave foamed and curled as it rolled away from the ship, and the bright sun danced on the sparkling water. A school of porpoise played in and out of the water as they raced alongside, no doubt feeding on the flying fish that launched themselves from the waves at the ship. The water, under the brilliant sun, was a deep blue, almost purple, a color that I had never before seen outside a box of Crayolas. Although I did not learn to like the immediate situation in which I found myself, I was sure that I was in love with ships and the sea.

Once safely past the Hawaiian Islands, the announcement was made that we were bound for American Samoa, with its port city of Pago Pago (pronounced *Pango-Pango*). After ten days at sea, we crowded the rails as we sailed into the small harbor, a collapsed volcanic caldera. Though none of us had ever been there, we were full of erroneous opinions about the place, tending heavily toward grass huts, tall palms, white sand beaches, and passionate dancing girls. Except for the dancing girls, Samoa did not disappoint.

The volcanic mountains, covered by dense jungle growth, plunged precipitously into the sea. A cap of rain clouds covered the mountain's single peak. A narrow ribbon of unpaved road clung precariously to the mountain between the jungle and the sea. Ahead were the open-sided grass huts, or *fales*, interspersed with an occasional rusty tin-roofed house. A few finger-piers and a quay wall could be seen. On the quay wall, several figures wearing sarong-like garments (called *lava-lava*), awaited our arrival. We rubbed our hands in delighted anticipation. In time, we discerned that the sarong-clad figures were burly male stevedores, each weighing at least 250 pounds. "What kind of place is this," we asked ourselves, "where the men wear women's clothing?" A small contingent of the Samoan Marine self-defense force also met us. They were barefoot and, in lieu of trousers, wore khaki lava-lava.

Soon we were formed up in ranks on the quay wall, seabags by our side, where we boarded trucks that would take us to our destinations. I was assigned to the 2nd Defense Battalion. Others went to the 2nd Provisional Brigade or the 2nd Marine Raider Battalion, all part of the 2nd Marine Division. We stood in formation as the Samoan marines sang "The Marines' Hymn" a capella. My last glimpse of the *Lurline* was from the back of a jouncing truck as we made our way northward on the narrow road. She was steaming out of the harbor, delivering her human cargo to other marine units farther west. We watched her go with mixed feelings. After all, she was our home, however temporary, and our final link with our homeland some eight thousand miles away. Much would transpire before we would see that homeland again.

LST 20

(See "The Battle of Tarawa" for other remarks about this series of ships.)

It is my opinion that the early LSTs (Landing Ship, Tank), up to about hull number 575 or so, were unnamed. Perhaps it is indicative of the navy's own lack of appreciation for these workhorse ships that they remained unnamed for so long. There was nothing glamorous about them. They were relatively small, slow, and carried only a reinforced company of troops, but they could deliver their cargo of men and materiel directly to the beach where and when it was needed, off-load in a matter of a few hours, and be off on another mission. This is in contrast to a conventional freighter, which must have port facilities such as piers and quay walls for rapid unloading. In the absence of such facilities on a contested beach, they had to off-load onto small boats and barges, which were then deposited on the beach for distribution as needed.

LSTs, considered expendable, were built to make one voyage and could be abandoned on the beaches of some embattled island with minimum loss. Later, as they became a proven design, and as their immense contribution to the war effort was recognized, the sheer proliferation of numbers demanded that they be given names. Post-war LSTs were much larger and faster, capable of making a flank speed of around 15 knots. They were more spacious and capable of carrying much greater cargo of men and machines. The much maligned waterline exhaust of the earlier design now exited the ship through a topside stack. The basic round-bottomed design, however, remained the same, therefore retaining the same uncomfortable ride. The later series of LSTs are named for the counties, or parishes, of several states.

An LST (Landing, Ship, Tank)

The latest design of which I have knowledge is the Newport class, with hull numbers in the 1190s. These were big ships by anyone's standards. They were 522 feet long, with a beam of almost 70 feet and a draft of nearly 15 feet. Six diesel engines drove her 8450 displacement tons through the water at a speed of 20 knots, enabling her to operate with high-speed amphibious forces. Her bow doors now became a bow ramp. A large stern gate enabled her to launch amphibious vehicles from the after end, while simultaneously dispatching vehicles directly on the beach from her bow.

In the protocols of amphibious warfare, the concept of the LST remains a force to be reckoned with, and I have no doubt that the naval architects are hard at work bringing forth designs and modifications that keep current with the changing demands of modern warfare.

Liberty and Victory Ships

Liberty and Victory ships made an enormous contribution to the war effort in WWII. Both types were cheaply and hastily built as cargo vessels for support of the war effort, but they were manned by merchant crews. Essentially, they were the result of an exercise in how to strip a ship of all civilized amenities. Built to carry cargo, they did that very well.

The Liberty ships were 446' 6" in length, had a beam of nearly 57 feet, and had a draft over 27 feet. They carried 8500 long tons of cargo. Powered by a single steam engine developing 2500 horsepower, driving a single screw at 76 rpm, the top speed was 11 knots. Twenty-seven hundred of these ships were built and twenty-five hundred of them survived the war. It is estimated that two-thirds of all cargo leaving US ports during the war was carried in Liberty ships.

USS *Red Oak Victory*
Each Victory ship was produced in 28 days.
So many were built, the enemy couldn't sink them all.

The Victory ships were slightly larger than the Liberties and were similarly equipped. They were built with the expectation that if they made one voyage, successfully delivering their cargo to the war zone, they would be considered to have paid for themselves. So many were built that the enemy simply could not sink all of them. Each had a US Naval Armed Guard contingent of about forty men aboard to defend the ship against enemy attack, though in late 1943, I was aboard a Liberty ship for several days that had no armed guard and no guns for self-defense.

The Victory ship on which I sailed from the Gilbert Islands to Hawaii in early 1944 had a single screw, a double king-post mast forward, and a single mast aft, to facilitate loading and unloading cargo. No thought had been given to passengers.

To accommodate embarked troops, pipe bunks had been installed in the cargo holds. One level of one cargo hold had been grudgingly designated as a skimpy mess deck with waist-high tables about 24 inches wide. Batter boards were installed to keep mess trays in place. A row of men stood on opposing sides of the table, facing one another as they hastily ate their meals. I do not know how many men were aboard the ship. Some Victories reportedly were able to carry five hundred troops in addition to cargo, but my entire battalion of about twelve hundred men was aboard, though without accompanying cargo. The predominant memory that I retain after almost sixty years is of intolerable heat, and of no place to sit.

There was always a scarcity of places to sit. The berthing spaces were uninsulated and unventilated. In war time, of course, all hatches and doors leading to the decks were shrouded by blackout curtains. It seemed that virtually all hands were seasick, and the smell of sweaty bodies and vomit was rank. Water was rationed, except for seawater. Initially we were forbidden to sleep on deck, but it was so unbearably hot in the holds that, after nightfall, most of us took a blanket and slipped out onto the deck to sleep. We had no pillows; our boots wrapped in our utility jackets served that purpose, while ensuring that they were not stolen in the night.

Since the transport of troops had not been envisioned by the designers, provision of heads, or toilet facilities, was inadequate. A makeshift head had been installed in the bow of the ship to serve the needs of troops. Instead of the usual sinks, toilets, and urinals, troughs had been formed from heavy sheet metal through which seawater ran.

They were oriented fore and aft to minimize spilling over onto the deck. One trough about 12 feet long served as a urinal. Another was fitted with a board, with holes cut in it, for more serious purposes. A drainpipe at the after end of the trough shunted the sewage down to the waterline and into the sea. The drainage pipes were evidently small for their purpose, for they were frequently stopped up. In that case, the backed up sewage often spilled out on the deck. The sight and smell of the place was so bad that such a trip had to be really necessary to cause one to go there.

During one memorable storm, I prepared myself for a hasty trip to the head. As I stepped into the space, I noted that the urinal was plugged with vomit, cigarette butts, paper, and other debris. An inch or more of filth washed back and forth across the deck. A seasick marine was passed out, or so nearly so that he was beyond caring, under the lower end of the urinal trough. As the ship rose to meet each wave, the fluids in the trough ran to the low end and gushed out over the fallen man. For the first time in my life at sea, I became seasick. Running for the lee rail, I fed the fishes what was probably their worst meal in days. Returning to the head to attempt a hasty rescue of my unknown comrade, I was happy to note that someone had dragged him out of the odious overflow.

The picture I have painted is one wherein discomfort was the rule, but as with all rules, there were rare exceptions. In December 1943, Tarawa Atoll was crowded with shipping. A whole flotilla of small utility boats served ship-to-shore traffic. But since there was no small boat facility, the harbormaster had ruled that such boats could tie up to any ship at night and their crew could go aboard for a meal and to sleep. A Liberty ship had arrived laden with beer for the troops ashore. Storage space for that cargo had not yet been made available, so the ship had to wait to unload. Of course, every small boat in the harbor began to tie up to the beer ship. Theft of beer was so bad that the captain appealed to the marines ashore for help, asking for a guard detail to secure his holds and their cargo. I was assigned, along with nine other men, to pull guard duty over the beer. There was no Naval Armed Guard contingent aboard.

We were housed in a twelve-man "dog house" on the after deck. Our bunks were even equipped with sheets, pillows, and mattresses. We took our meals with the civilian crew, who did not know what the term "K-ration" meant. Water was not rationed and showers were unlimited. To a young marine fresh from the grime and grit ashore, this was really high living. We did four-hour shifts on guard and eight hours off-duty around the clock for the next two weeks. We quickly noted that the ship's crew had many cases of beer stashed under their bunks. We pilfered more than our share of beer, claiming it as our right to the spoils of war. That Liberty ship, at that particular time, was certainly a "happy" ship.

Liberty and Victory ships served their elementary purpose very well during WWII. Many survived the war and went into the tramp steamer trade, where I suspect that somewhere in the world some are still sailing. Their longevity and toughness was such that it must be difficult to call any one of them a *really* bad ship. Whenever I think of Liberty or Victory ships today, nearly sixty years later, the scene described in the third preceding paragraph comes immediately to mind, though their service was such that they deserve a much more fitting memorial.

HMS *Aqua Prince*

Constructed and operated as a cargo vessel in the Dutch Maritime Service prior to WWII, when Germany overran The Netherlands early in the war, the *Aqua Prince* sought asylum in the nearest port of a neutral country, the United States. The ship and crew were quarantined for the duration of the hostilities or, in this case, until the US actively entered the war in 1941. Then she was impressed into the US merchant fleet, where she was manned by her original Dutch crew.

I am sure that the crew were happy to be in US service, for in impoundment they were without funds, either for their own upkeep or for that of their ship. Their new American masters were reluctant to expend funds for her maintenance and overhaul, of course, for if she survived the war, she would surely revert to Dutch registry afterward, no matter which side was victorious. As a consequence, her material condition was badly neglected. But the crew was content to be on the US payroll.

Wartime demands for shipping and enemy depredations had stretched the world's merchant fleets perilously thin. Freed from quarantine, the *Aqua Prince* was converted to use as a troop ship by the navy, by the simple and now accustomed stratagem of filling the hold spaces with pipe bunks. Three-inch guns were installed on her decks, and a Naval Armed Guard detachment was placed aboard to operate them.

In December 1944, we of the 2nd AAA Battalion went aboard for the voyage from Kauai, Hawaii, to the newly liberated territory of Guam, a way station to the front. We were immediately set to the task of chipping and painting her rusty decks and bulkheads. This did little to remedy the condition of her exposed hull above the waterline, where her sides blossomed with a spreading cancer of rust. It certainly did nothing to elevate her in the opinion of her unwilling passengers. Provision had once been made to ventilate the smelly berthing spaces, but the pumps, blowers, and ventilator scoops had long since fallen into disrepair and disuse.

When steaming against the prevailing wind, the scoops fed a feeble breath of air into the holds, but without blowers, the duct work was useless and had been stuffed with paper and other debris by countless previous passengers. Again, we resorted to sleeping on the open and exposed deck. Fortunately, this passage was without major storms to chase us back to tormented nights below decks. The ship's crew, marine officers, and NCOs were quartered in the superstructure, where some degree of cross ventilation was possible, but for the non-rated marines in the holds, there was little respite from the heat.

Our own cooks and messmen manned the galley, and contrary to what I had come to expect, I was spared that work detail. Again, as a familiar expedient, a space near the galley had been fitted with stand-up mess tables, 24 inches wide, with batter boards attached. Men stood to eat, facing one another across the narrow tables.

The evening meal was being served as we cleared Nawiliwili

Harbor at Lihue, Kauai. We steamed out of the lee of the island and began to take heavy rolls under the strong trade winds. As the ship heeled over, my across-the-table messmate was suddenly gripped by the pangs of acute seasickness. Heaving and retching uncontrollably, he spewed a projectile of vomit across the table and into my mess gear. For the second time in my seagoing career, seasickness sent me running for the leeward rail, where I gave up my own meal.

The best that I can say for HMS *Aqua Prince* is that she was a minor improvement over the Liberty and Victory ships on which I had sailed, and certainly more seaworthy. In fact, given better conditions and a liberal application of funds to improve her habitability, she might have been a happy and pleasant ship.

USS *Kleinsmith* (APD 134)

Named for a naval hero of the Battle of Midway, USS *Kleinsmith* was originally designated a Destroyer Escort (DE 718) but while still under construction was redesignated as APD 134. This high-speed transport had the communications capability to serve as an amphibious command ship while carrying over one hundred marines.

She was 306' in length, with a beam of 36' 10" and a draft of 13' 6". Her speed (23.6 knots), maneuverability, and shallow draft allowed her to provide close inshore support of amphibious operations and made her an ideal platform for deploying and recovering Underwater Demolition Teams (UDT).

In 1958, while serving as a US Navy

USS *Kleinsmith*
A high-speed transport vessel built to serve as an amphibious command ship

chaplain, I was assigned temporary duty on the *Kleinsmith* for a voyage to Vieques Island, Puerto Rico. This was a whole new seagoing experience for me.

In a storm, her weight, relative to her length and beam, meant that she plowed through the seas rather than riding over them. The weight and bulk of the radar and other electronic gear mounted high on her mast gave her a pronounced tendency to roll in heavy seas. Her sailors frequently commented that they were underwater more than some submarines. In all but the smoothest seas, no meals were served when underway. Instead, platters of sandwiches and urns of hot coffee were kept available for self-service at all hours. Her steel hull was so thin that, from below decks, water could plainly be heard rippling and gurgling along her sides. I came away from that short tour aboard the *Kleinsmith* with renewed respect for the sailors who lived and worked in her.

On May 15, 1960, the *Kleinsmith* arrived in Tsoying, Taiwan, where she was decommissioned. On May 16, she was transferred to the Nationalist Chinese Navy and given the name *Tien Shan* (APD 215). In more recent years, she served the Nationalist Chinese Customs Service Coastal Patrol. Her 5" gun and mount were removed and replaced by a twin 40mm mount. In that capacity, according to one source, she served proudly until she was stricken from the records in 1993.

Landing Ship, Dock (LSD) • Plymouth Rock (LSD 29) • Fort Snelling (LSD 30) • Spiegel Grove (LSD 32) • Hermitage (LSD 34)

All of the above ships are similar (except the *Hermitage*) in design and capabilities (the *Hermitage* was 10" longer, 4" wider, and capable of making 23 knots versus 21.) They carried a full crew of about three hundred, with four hundred troops aboard. The *Hermitage* was air-conditioned and had space for a flotilla commander with staff. During my time aboard these ships as squadron chaplain, with the *Boxer* (LPH 2) as flagship, we operated as a fast helicopter amphibious assault force, giving marines experience in the vertical envelopment concept.

Each of this type has a huge well deck, large stern doors, or flood gates that open, permitting the well deck to fill with seawater. The ship, ballasted down, can then receive Tank Landing Craft by floating them into the well. The doors are then closed, ballast water pumped out, and the ship then continues to its destination where the process is repeated, allowing the LCT to disembark.

Hurricane bows gave them increased speed (over the LST) and seaworthiness. They were fitted with a small helicopter landing pad and could carry and launch a small landing force. Their design made them an ideal vehicle for recovering astronauts and their space capsules after a water landing, and they were used as such during Project Mercury in the early sixties. They were very comfortable and versatile ships, and I remember them with fondness.

All of the above ships have now been decommissioned and are out of service, except for the *Hermitage*, which was transferred to the Brazilian Navy in 1980. They have since been replaced by newer and even better designs. The concept makes a valuable addition to the nation's defense establishment.

USS *Boxer* (LPH 2)

The *Boxer* is the fifth ship of the US Navy to bear that name. A sixth *Boxer* was built by the British Navy as HMS *Boxer* (14) in 1812. She was captured off Maine by USS *Enterprise*, but was not taken into the US Navy.

The last *Boxer* (CV/CVA/CVS 21) was launched in December 1944, too late to see action in WWII. She displaced 27,100 tons, was 888 feet long, with a beam of 147 feet and a draft of nearly 29 feet. Her speed was 33 knots and she carried a crew of 3448. With the outbreak of hostilities in Korea in 1950, she made a record crossing of the Pacific in eight-and-a-half days, carrying 150 planes and 1000 troops to the war zone. Her return trip was even faster, made in 7 days, 10 hours, 36 minutes.

USS *Boxer* (CV-21) An aircraft carrier that served in both the Pacific and Atlantic fleets

The *Boxer* was in her third tour of wartime duty off Korea when, in 1952, a fire swept her hanger deck, causing 11 casualties and seriously damaging the ship. She was repaired in Yokosuka, Japan, and returned to a fourth tour of fighting in Korea, during which time she received her eighth battle star for her service in the Korean conflict.

She operated off the West Coast until 1960, when she was transferred to the Atlantic Fleet, redesignated an Amphibious (Helicopter) Landing Ship, and made flagship of Amphibious Squadron 10, operating out of Norfolk, Virginia.

If there is any validity to the concept that ships have personalities, then we must say that her transfer and redesignation as an LPH left the *Boxer* seriously depressed and dispirited. The use of modern jet aircraft required an angled flight deck and hurricane bow, and she was not deemed worthy of the cost of conversion. She had outlived her usefulness as an aircraft carrier, and her demotion to the proletarian duty of carrying troops and helicopters was a heavy blow.

To add insult to injury, 1000 marines were integrated into nearly all departments, the first ship of the navy to integrate her crew to that extent. It was an unfortunate mix, for neither the marines nor the navy personnel were happy with the arrangement. It was as though a grand old lady, Grand Dame of the Fleet, after an illustrious career as an aircraft carrier, had been demoted to service as charwoman or bag lady. All hands, from seaman recruit to commodore, seemed to regret her conversion and took little pride in their assignment. As far as I know, the helicopters made no complaint. The only people who were content with the arrangement were at Headquarters, Marine Corps, which badly needed the ship to test their use of helicopters as assault aircraft in the new concept of vertical envelopment.

I was assigned to the staff of Amphibious Squadron 10, the parent command, but since the *Boxer* had her own chaplain aboard, I tried to spend as much time as possible circuit riding the other four ships of the squadron. For nearly the next two years, we were underway most of the time, ferrying marines to Vieques, Puerto Rico, for practice landing exercises, returning them to their home base of Camp Lejeune, North Carolina, and completing the circuit in Norfolk. We were seldom in home port more than two or three weeks before repeating our shuttle duty with the marines for another two months or more.

The *Boxer* is now happily out of commission, replaced by more modern ships designed for duty as helicopter and troop carriers. I do not know her ultimate fate, but I believe that she may have been broken up for scrap.

APA (Amphibious, Personnel, Assault) • USS Bexar (APA 237) • USS Okanogan (APA 220) • USS Talladega (APA 208)

Each of the above ships of the Haskell Class were virtually identical in design and improvements. They were 455 feet in length, with a beam of 62 feet and a draft of 24 feet, fully loaded. They displaced up to 14,837 tons and carried 1600 troops at a speed of 18 knots. The *Okanogan* and *Talladega* were launched in 1944, the *Bexar* in 1945. The design was intended to discharge troops over the side via cargo nets and into waiting LCVPs (Landing Craft, Vehicle and Personnel) for the assault phase of an amphibious landing. There were a few refinements, but each could carry a reinforced Battalion Landing Team intact.

In total, I spent about three weeks on the *Bexar*, two months on the *Talladega*, and five months on the *Okanogan*. At that time, none were air-conditioned, except that midway through the cruise, while alongside the pier in Subic Bay, Philippines, the *Okanogan* did get a jury-rigged air conditioning system operating intermittently. These ships were not terribly hot when at sea, but in port under the tropical sun, they were unbearable. At one point, at Subic Bay, we temporarily moved troops ashore into barracks because of the comfort factor.

Cowed by the acid personality of her captain, the *Bexar* was one of the unhappiest ships I have known. (See "North to Alaska."). He appeared to bitterly resent having marines aboard, although that was his primary mission, expecting them to remain below decks and out of sight at all times. His treatment of the crew, officers, and men alike was simply outrageous. Since he desired to keep a close and controlling hand on everything, he did not delegate responsibility. Mistakes or requests for information about procedures sent him into a towering rage. Fortunately for the ship, such seagoing command assignments are of short duration, usually for one year, so all hands were eagerly looking forward to a change of leadership. When I think of him, I am reminded of a famous WWII admiral whose daughter wrote of him, "He was the most even-tempered man in the Navy. He was *always* in a rage."

The *Bexar* was potentially a good ship and deserved much better of her captain than she got. He was an excellent seaman and an expert ship handler, but his unfortunate personality was a combination of captains Queeg and Bligh, both of whose crews mutinied under their leadership.

In late summer of 1963, my battalion of marines moved aboard the *Talladega* for a trip to the Philippine Islands. We staged a practice landing on the beaches of Lingayen Gulf and operated ashore for two days before re-embarking aboard the same ship. It was the first time since WWII that I had navigated (climbed) a cargo net hanging loosely over the side of a rolling troop ship. I learned that it does not get easier with age and practice.

While aboard the *Talladega*, we made port in Kaohsiung, Formosa and in Subic Bay, Philippines. Returning to Okinawa briefly, we moved aboard the *Okanogan* for our tour of duty as the Ready Battalion for the afloat phase of our deployment. For the next five months, we operated off the coast of South Vietnam, with port visits to Kaohsiung and Hong Kong. It was during that phase that the *Okanogan*'s air-conditioning was made operational. Needless to say, the second half of our tour was much more comfortable than the first.

We arrived at the end of our "afloat" phase and were returning to Okinawa when President Kennedy was assassinated. It is said that everyone has a clear recollection of where they were and what they were doing when they heard the news. I have an indelible memory of the event. Breakfast was just over and I had stepped out of the wardroom onto the deck for a breath of fresh air. A chief petty officer, a black man, came running out of the galley to where I stood at the rail. He was sobbing uncontrollably. Startled, I asked him what was wrong. He replied, "They killed him, chaplain. They killed him!" He was so distraught that he could tell me nothing more.

I went to the communications section, where I was told who had been killed. I knew, of course, that Kennedy was an immensely popular president, but it was only then that I began to understand the particularly deep degree of affection in which he was held by the black people of our country. The *Okanogan* immediately reversed course and we were back on station, steaming off South Vietnam for another six weeks.

It was an unforgettable 13-month tour of duty, which I was happy to conclude with my return to California and to my family in May 1964.

USS *Estes* (AGC 12)

The specifications of this ship were as follows: Displacement, 7240 tons. Length 459' 2". Beam, 63'. Draft, 24'. Speed, 16 knots. Complement, 633. Troops, 1600.

The *Estes* was launched on November 1, 1943, by the North Carolina Shipbuilding Co. of Wilmington, North Carolina, as the freighter SS *Morning Star*. Before her fitting out was completed, in February 1944, she was acquired by the US Navy and was commissioned USS *Estes* (AGC 12) on October 9, 1944. Her mission would be to serve as a communications and control ship, and as flagship for Amphibious Forces, Pacific Fleet. She sailed in January 1945 for rehearsal landings in the Marianas Islands, and continued on to serve as a command-and-control center for the landings at Iwo Jima. On March 24, 1945, she was performing the same function for the landings at Okinawa.

After the war, she performed occupation duty in China and the Philippine Islands. She returned to the United States in 1948 and was decommissioned in 1949. Her retirement was short-lived, however, for she was returned to service in January 1951, operating off Korea and in Japanese waters. She participated in two series of atomic tests in the Enewetak Atoll and the Marshall Islands, and one cruise to supply government activities in the Arctic. In 1954, she was control ship for the operation "Passage to Freedom," the evacuation of refugees from North Vietnam, and later in evacuating the Tachen Islands.

USS *Estes*
A communications and control ship, and flagship
for amphibious forces, Pacific Fleet

In May 1966, I received orders to report to USS *Estes* in San Diego on July 1. Upon doing so, I learned that we were shipping out on July 5 for a nine-month cruise to the Western Pacific and South Vietnam. Hastily moving my family into a new house, I was ready to join the ship and we departed as scheduled.

After a three-day stop at Pearl Harbor for conferences with the Commander, US Pacific Fleet, we proceeded to Guam for a brief stop and then directly to Subic Bay, Philippine Islands. At that point, the *Estes* had not been retrofitted with air conditioning, and Subic Bay was fully as hot as expected. It was a blessed relief to be back at sea and enroute to Kaohsiung, Formosa for conferences with the commander of the Nationalist Chinese forces. We had a marine Battalion Landing Team aboard, and our immediate task was to land them in the Mekong Delta, south of Saigon.

After waiting on station for about ten days, we took the marines back on board. They had encountered no Viet Cong forces, so we transported them north to join other US Forces in the Da Nang area. A five-day visit to Hong Kong provided a brief respite from the seemingly endless patrolling the length of Vietnam. In February 1967, we left Vietnamese waters and returned to home port in San Diego, only to learn that, after three weeks in port we were scheduled for a major overhaul in the Puget Sound Naval Shipyard in Bremerton, Washington, where we remained until August.

We returned to San Diego, and after three weeks of shakedown and retraining, again headed for Vietnam. This cruise was busier than the first. We landed our marine battalion landing team again in the Mekong Delta, where the marines were united with other US forces in the Da Nang area, while we headed for Subic Bay, Kaohsiung, Hong Kong, Bangkok, Singapore, and back to Vietnam.

One morning I had a message from John Bontrager, chaplain of USS *Iwo Jima*, inviting me to consult with him at our earliest opportunity. I learned that the *Iwo Jima* was then about 60 miles north of our position. I was informed by our helicopter pilot that he would be flying to the *Iwo Jima* later that day, so I secured a place in the helicopter and was able to have a pleasant reunion with Chaplain

Bontrager and a conference about chaplain corps rotation and other personnel matters.

Taking off again, we headed for the US airport at Da Nang. Coming in low over the city, we began to take heavy small arms fire from the enemy forces hiding in homes around the airport. We were able to land with no apparent damage, and I left the helicopter planning to later take a boat back to the ship, thankful that we were uninjured. On taking off again, the helicopter suddenly crashed in the tidal swamps about three miles from the airport, downed by a bullet-severed hydraulic line. Neither pilot nor copilot was injured, but the helicopter was a total loss.

The South China Sea is a shallow body of water, which makes for giant waves during storms. While in transit to Bangkok and Singapore, we encountered such a storm with immense waves and suffered some minor damage, which was successfully repaired by the ship's crew. At the end of the storm, we had eight feet of water in the forward chain lockers, and the captain's gig, secured high above the main deck, was carried away. The *Estes* had also struck some underwater object and suffered damage to her propeller and shaft. An eventual trip to Yokosuka Naval Base in Japan was necessary to make repairs. After two weeks in dry dock, we returned to Vietnam and Subic Bay.

While we were cruising off Vietnam, I received orders for transfer to the naval station at Charleston, South Carolina. A few days later, the ship was in Subic Bay. I flew out of Clark Air Base to Travis Air Force Base in the San Francisco area, where Peggy met me and we flew back to San Diego together.

The *Estes* was a good ship and her crew a happy one. It was the busiest two-year period of my naval career, but I left her feeling the satisfaction of a job well done.

USS *Nevada* (BB-36)

One of the older battleships to serve in WWII, USS *Nevada* was commissioned in March 1916 and saw service during WWI. I have no details as to her record of service in that earlier conflict.

The *Nevada* was at Pearl Harbor when the Japanese surprise attack came on December 7, 1941. She was struck in the port bow by a torpedo, forward of her armor plating, but was able to get underway. She made for the open sea, but the Japanese, seeing that she was the only battleship moving in the harbor, concentrated their attack on her in an attempt to sink her and block the channel. She was hit by five bombs, one cutting off ventilation to the machinery spaces and forcing evacuation. A large fire near the forward magazine caused that space to be flooded.

During the attack, 50 men were killed and 100 more were wounded. She was deliberately grounded near East Loch in Pearl Harbor, from which place she was hastily refloated and sent to Puget Sound Navy Yard for repairs. In December 1942, she rejoined the war effort, participating in the capture of Attu Island, Alaska. Sent to the Atlantic Fleet, she supported the landing at Utah Beach, the bombardment of the Normandy coast, and the capture of Cherbourg. A few weeks later she participated in the landings at Toulon, in Southern France.

Again transferred to the Pacific Fleet, she provided preinvasion bombardment of Iwo Jima in February and early March 1945. She arrived at Okinawa on March 24, 1945 where, three days later, she was hit by a Japanese *kamikaze* plane, killing eleven men and damaging one of her main battery turrets. A week later, two men were killed by a hit from a shore battery. At the end of June, she steamed to operations off the Japanese home islands, in preparation for that imminent invasion. Fortunately, the war ended on August 15, 1945.

She was present for the formal surrender in Tokyo Bay and returned to Okinawa in September 1945. There, in the company of several other marines, I was happy to be assigned to her for my passage back to the United States.

In 1946, the *Nevada* became a target ship for the atomic tests at Bikini Atoll, surviving two atomic explosions. On July 31, 1948, she was targeted and deliberately sunk by naval gunfire and aerial torpedoes during a naval exercise, thus ending her distinguished career. She was awarded seven battle stars in recognition of her participation in seven major battles of WWII.

Massive by anyone's standards when launched, by WWII the *Nevada* was dwarfed by her more modern counterparts, such as USS *Iowa*. With her overall length of 583 feet, her beam of nearly 108 feet, and her draft of over 28 feet, her design speed was only 21 knots. A 14"-thick armor belt extended from over 7 feet below the water line to 3 feet above it, completely enclosing the machinery and magazine spaces. The superstructure was similarly protected. Her displacement of 35,400 tons gave her enough weight to make her impervious to all but the greatest waves, and riding her was as smooth as a canoe in a duck pond. She plowed into heavy seas and powered through them with only the slightest shudder or roll, taking waves over her decks and turrets and shouldering them aside.

USS *Nevada* (BB-36)
Served in WWI and WWII. She was hit by five bombs
at Pearl Harbor and was my ride home in 1945.

For me, life aboard such a ship was a luxury cruise. Although I was officially aboard as a member of the marine detachment, in reality, I was just a passenger being transported home. I had all the privileges of a crew member but none of the duties and watches. Water was plentiful.

Laundry was washed, starched, and ironed by the ship's supply department, a luxury I had not enjoyed in nearly three years. The food was wonderful and in unlimited quantities. As a supernumerary, I had no assigned bunk, so I slept on a conveyor belt running from the main magazine to the 14" gun turrets on the main deck—but it was the best bed I had known in months. As usual, there was no place to sit except on the deck, but I was on my way home. It could hardly have gotten any better.

We spent an entire month leisurely running all of the qualifying drills and exercises required of a capital ship, which are so difficult to find time for while fighting a war. We spent one day on liberty in Honolulu while replenishing our supply of food, water, and fuel. A week later we entered San Pedro harbor in California. All things considered, it was the best shipboard experience I had ever had, and I must believe that the *Nevada* was the happiest ship I was ever aboard. Or perhaps I was just the happiest person aboard.

Even then, however, it was widely recognized that the reign of the battleship as the Queen of the Fleet was over. They were just too big, expensive, and vulnerable to command a place in a modern navy, and in a few short years all were gone, displaced by aircraft carriers and guided missile cruisers. I am delighted to have had the opportunity of sailing in one, even for such a brief time.

Transition: Hills to Sea to Desert

While cruising off Vietnam in July, 1968, I received orders to repost to the US naval station in Charleston, South Carolina, for a tour as base chaplain. Peggy sold the house in San Diego while I was en route home, and she was waiting in a San Diego motel with Allen and Rebecca when I arrived. She had also purchased a new car for the trip east. She was becoming so independent that I wondered if I were really necessary to the family. Actually, she always managed extremely well without me and I cannot praise her enough, for I know the burden was often heavy.

Peggy, San Diego, 1968

As we assumed our duties at Charleston, it became apparent that my active service in the navy was drawing to a close. The Chaplain Corps found itself with more chaplains than its mission required, and massive cuts in our numbers were necessary. I was a navy reservist, never having integrated into the regular component. Within a few months, all of my year group of reservists were discharged. I loved the active naval service and would have gladly stayed on, for I was then within five years of retirement.

I felt fortunate to be able to secure immediate employment as a chaplain at the VA hospital in Albuquerque, New Mexico. I joined the US Navy Reserve unit there and was able to complete my retirement eligibility in the grade of commander, though actual retirement with pay would have to await my sixtieth birthday.

A major conflict with my supervisor at the Albuquerque VA Hospital resulted in my seeking and receiving a transfer to Chillicothe, Ohio, in 1980. I will pass over the unpleasant episode without comment, except to say that it involved my refusal to participate in what I regarded as unethical and possibly illegal behavior. In Chillicothe, we were living within a hundred miles of Roane County for the first time in twenty-seven years and were able to frequently visit friends and relatives there and in Nicholas County.

A hospitalization in Chillicothe with a diagnosis of congestive heart failure was instrumental in my decision to retire on my sixtieth birthday, March 28, 1985. Selling our home there, we returned to Albuquerque. Since retirement, I have had numerous examinations and a cardiac catheterization by local cardiologists who have found no evidence of heart disease.

Here in the "land of enchantment" we intend to remain, near our daughters and grandchildren, until we too are "gathered to our fathers." Both Peggy and I have type 2 diabetes and hypertension. As we have shared our lives together, we are now able to share another bonus—the same medications! Life is sweet and good!

The Wedding Fee

I had known J.D. Lampe for several years through my position as chaplain in the Veterans Administration Hospital in Albuquerque. J.D. was a heavy smoker with a long-standing habit, who suffered from advanced emphysema and heart disease. He was divorced from his wife. In fact, he was thrice divorced from the same wife, and each had been married briefly to someone else. Together they had a large family of children and were hardworking and decent people. They just didn't like each other very well.

Now J.D.'s health was failing rapidly, and he was eager to get his familial and marital affairs in order. He had recently been talking to his ex-wife, the mother of his children, and they had agreed to one more attempt at the wedded state. He requested that I perform the ceremony for them in the hospital chapel. After counseling with both and finding them to be serious in their intent to fulfill their vows, I agreed to officiate.

Leaving no stone unturned in their effort to "do this right," they planned a full formal wedding ceremony with a complete retinue of attendants, formal dress, catered flowers, and a lavish reception. As a patient, there was no charge for the use of the chapel or reception room, nor was there a fee for my services. But even so, the whole affair must have set J.D. back many hundreds of dollars.

He bought a new engagement ring. The matching wedding bands were entrusted to the care of the best man, a longtime friend but an alcoholic with a reputation for "scamming" his acquaintances. I wondered about the wisdom of this, but after all, he was not *my* best man.

A full rehearsal was scheduled, and everything proceeded without a hitch. J.D. had persuaded his doctors to discharge him long enough for a quick honeymoon trip to Las Vegas, after which he promised to return to the hospital. All was in readiness.

On Monday morning, J.D. was back in his hospital bed. I greeted him heartily, "How was Las Vegas?" I inquired.

"Don't know. I never got there," he responded. "Hell, we were fighting before we got to Gallup, and she left me in Flagstaff and caught a bus back home. We didn't even spend the night together."

What could I say? I expressed my disappointment and prepared to go on my way.

Suddenly J.D. asked, "Did my best man give you anything?" "No," I said, "but nothing was expected. I don't charge a fee for my services."

"Why that ****** rascal!" J.D. exploded. I gave him fifty dollars for you."

I was reminded of an old bit of doggerel by an unknown author:

> The knot was tied; the two were wed
> And then the smiling bridegroom said
> Unto the preacher, "Shall I pay
> To you the usual fee today?
> Or would you have me wait a year
> And give you then a hundred clear,
> If I should find the married state
> As happy as I estimate?"
> The preacher lost no time in thought,
> To his reply no study brought.
> There were no wrinkles on his brow.
> He said, "I'll take three dollars now."

The Honeymoon That Wasn't

Bing Ware was admitted to the detoxification unit in Albuquerque's Veterans Administration Hospital suffering from a mild case of the DTs. He was delivered to the detoxification unit by his girlfriend, Dee, who by all accounts might have been admitted herself had she been a veteran.

Within a few days, Bing was feeling much better; however, a thorough examination revealed that he was also suffering from a severe heart condition. In the course of my daily visits with him in the Cardiac Intensive Care Unit, I came to know both Dee and him quite well. They were in their early to mid-fifties and appeared to be devoted to one another. Each had been married before and was divorced. They were a friendly and congenial couple, very attractive, and quite well-liked by patients and staff personnel. Dee joined a local AA chapter and rented an apartment nearby so that she could remain close to Bing.

Bing's recovery period was not uneventful, marked by several recurrences of the cardiac symptoms. Both he and Dee testified to a radical change in their personal habits. They were sure that, each having the help and loving support of the other, they would never again have an alcohol problem. Eventually, after several weeks of treatment, the doctors began to discuss discharging him to his home in Portales, New Mexico, a four- or five-hour drive to the east of Albuquerque.

Bing and Dee began to plan for their future life together and soon announced their intent to marry. The wedding would be held on Friday in a local wedding chapel, following Bing's release from the hospital. On the designated day, they were off to be married, to the accompaniment of many fervent good wishes on the part of their friends. Some were skeptical, but most had "good vibes" about the couple. They would make it if anyone could.

On the following Monday morning, I saw Bing walking into his old room. He wore hospital pajamas and sat in a chair beside his bed. I paused and said, "I thought you were discharged."

"I was," he snarled as he bolted into the bathroom. Obviously, he did not want to discuss it. His nurse motioned me aside. "He's pretty upset by what happened," she said, and began to tell me the story.

Following the wedding, Bing and Dee started driving east toward Portales. After a few blocks, they decided to stop at Cervantes Bar for a celebratory drink. A second drink was taken to bolster them for the long hot drive across the eastern plains of New Mexico. Soon three hours had passed and they had barely made their way to the city limits of Albuquerque. A stop was made at Tijeras to relieve themselves and renew their flagging spirits. Another stop at Clines Corner, and they were hardly 45 miles into their journey. After leaving Clines Corner, their route took them south toward Vaughn. Here they faced a long stretch of desolate highway with no refreshment stations and no restrooms.

Feeling the call of nature coming rather urgently, they decided to risk a quick stop to relieve their misery "country style." Dee, who was driving, pulled onto the shoulder of the road. Bing faced the weeds of the roadside, while Dee squatted briefly behind the car. She quickly finished her business, absentmindedly got back in the car, and drove off to the east, leaving Bing to irrigate his weed patch.

Bing was stranded with only a few dollars and still nearly 150 miles from home. He was hungover, and his anger was building by the minute. After about an hour, a Greyhound bus picked him up and brought him back to Albuquerque. He hailed a cab and returned to the VA, where he was readmitted as a precautionary measure.

Dee, meanwhile, had driven on to Portales where, upon pulling into Bing's driveway, she discovered that her new husband was no longer with her. She immediately began to retrace her route but could not even remember where they had made their ill-fated pit stop. Several hours later, she returned to the VA Hospital, where she found Bing, who by now was refusing to even speak to her.

They came to the mutual decision that, given their common

problems, they were ill-equipped to help one another and would do better fighting their battles alone. Soon, each went his own way, and I never saw either of them again.

I was sorry that they didn't make it together, for they were both personable and likable people. But it seemed that they fed off each other's weaknesses, and in unity, failed to find the strength to survive.

I suppose it was a case of "Divided we stand, united we fall."

Stroke!

On September 21, 2002, my world—and life as I had known it—was changed beyond my wildest imaginings. Actually, I should say "our" instead of "my" because in descending into my own pit of despair, I took Peggy and the family with me and changed their lives as well.

Although I had been treated for hypertension for forty years, and had developed diabetes after retirement seventeen years earlier, I considered myself fairly active. We did our own lawn and garden work, took the dog, Babe, for her daily walks, and considered ourselves to be in fairly good health.

Sometime in the wee, small hours of the morning of September 21, 2002, I was awakened from a sound sleep for the usual reason. Peggy uncharacteristically did not awaken, so I was spared her usual cautionary warning not to leave the lid up. As I made my way into the bathroom, I noticed that my feet were balky and unresponsive. I charged it to sleepiness and soon made my way back to bed and returned to sleep. We had planned some early chores and attendance at an estate sale at a nearby home, so Babe and I dispensed with our morning walk. After a trip into the grocery store and post office, we drove up the hill to the estate sale. That visit to the post office would prove to be my last unassisted walk.

Arriving at the site of the sale, I remarked that I was feeling a little tired and asked Peggy if she would go in alone, leaving me to rest in the car. I may have dozed a bit while waiting, but after about twenty minutes I saw her approaching on the sidewalk. As she got in the passenger seat, I experienced some confusion in responding verbally to her. In attempting to start the car, I found that my fingers would not turn the ignition key. Recognizing the difficulty, I asked her to drive home, and after arriving there, became alarmed only when I could not get out of the car without help. With Peggy's assistance, we made it inside the house and she called the paramedics. As we waited, I thought of the many times I had watched ambulances respond to similar calls in our neighborhood of mostly older residents, without ever thinking that they might one day be coming for me.

Within a short time, we were on our way to a large downtown hospital, where I was quickly diagnosed with a probable stroke. We were soon shunted off into a quiet corner of the emergency room where we were "out of sight, out of mind." I was largely ignored until about 5:00 p.m. My daughter Becky was with us, and she had called her friend, Debbie Wisenhunt. Bless Debbie, who would demonstrate a positive genius for appearing when needed. I developed severe chills, followed by convulsions. The ER nurse looked at me, covered me with a heated blanket, and suggested to my family that they lie across my legs to keep me from falling off the gurney.

When the convulsions subsided, I felt the need to relieve myself. Becky went to find a nurse and a urinal. After a lengthy and increasingly desperate wait, Debbie picked up a blanket and thrust it into my arms saying, "Here, use this." I did, gratefully. When the nurse discovered how I had misused her blanket, she was not pleased. Finally, I was admitted to one of the medical wards and put to bed. At that point I was able to eat dinner and walk to the bathroom with an assistant alongside.

The next morning, I was examined, given numerous tests, including an MRI, and was told that while I had experienced a mild stroke, with therapy I could look forward to virtually a complete recovery. I happily settled in for a routine hospitalization, grateful that it was not worse. Within a day or so, however, I developed pneumonia and was given a nasogastric feeding tube and a urinary catheter.

Within 48 hours of the onset of the stroke, daughter Linda had come from Kentucky and son Butch (Allen) from Oregon. From this point forward, the family was assembled and formed a united support system for Peggy and me.

I remember little of the next several days, except that I lost what little mobility I had retained. Somewhere along the way, I began to hallucinate horribly. Although the sequence of events is fuzzy, the delusions themselves remain in my mind with unmistakable clarity. An entire scenario was created in my mind in which I participated in the desperate withdrawal of the US Marines from the Chosin Reservoir in the Korean War, despite the fact that I have never set foot in Korea. Another involved an early WWII British Hurricane torpedo bomber pilot who crashed and was killed in northwestern Canada, and whose fate was kept secret from his family for the next fifty years.

I can still see the final scene of my mental movie: a fade-away shot of an old wreck of an airplane, with the bitter winds blowing over the frozen grasses as arctic foxes romped and played in the ruins. For a span of several days, my mind accepted these events as actual happenings, though I slowly began to recognize that it was all a part of my delirium. It became obvious that my confidence in a quick and unremarkable recovery was misplaced.

A fortuitous move to the medical intensive care unit put me into more expert treatment hands and, as a bonus, gave me one of my most unforgettable views of the city of Albuquerque, especially at night. From one of the upper floors, high above the Rio Grande valley, the lights of the city sparkled and glowed in the cold, clear night air, and I never tired of the magical quality of it.

As I began to improve and was returned to my regular medical ward, I was scheduled for an MRI to monitor my stroke. Becky accompanied me to the site. The nurse in charge had been instructed to give a series of four injections at half-hour intervals prior to the MRI. I arrived at about 8:00 p.m. and waited until close to ten before the shots were given. The MRI technician was pressing for an abbreviated preparation, so the nurse opted to administer all four shots as a single dose. As I was assisted to a standing position beside the gurney, we watched as she lined up the four vials and loaded them into a single large syringe. Becky questioned her, "Aren't those supposed to be given a half-hour apart?"

"No," replied the nurse, "it will be all right. Besides, we are running very late."

"Please check the doctor's order," Becky insisted. "I'm sure the doctor wanted them given separately, at intervals."

"Look," the nurse flared, "I've been doing this for a long time, and I know what I'm doing." With that, she stuck the needle into my abdomen and pushed the plunger, beginning the most frightening experience of my entire life. I felt as though I had been blindsided by a hammer to the head. As I collapsed on the floor, my last conscious thought was, *Oh God, she just punched my ticket!*

According to Becky, the doctor was called and confronted the nurse, accusing her of ignoring the order to space the injections at thirty-minute intervals.

"You didn't enter that into the chart," she said, defensively.

"I most certainly did," the doctor replied and opened the chart to display the written order.

I had terrible hallucinations while I was out. When I finally came to the next morning, I found myself in restraints. I called out, pleading for someone to remove them. I was told that I had been restrained "for my own protection" and that only a nurse could remove them. I demanded to see the hospital administrator. An assistant administrator eventually showed up and introduced himself. When he began to explain what had happened, I cut him off, saying, "This is my room and I have the floor. I have something to say to you. I am a retired hospital chaplain, and while I cannot speak expertly about appropriate treatment procedures, I am an expert in inappropriate treatment. I know when my rights as a human being have been violated. I can understand the necessity of a patient being restrained on occasion, but I do not accept a patient who is paralyzed being put in a straightjacket. To whom could I have been a threat? I protest in the strongest of terms being ignored for hours and being denied an explanation for my being in restraints when I requested it. Please be assured that I fully intend to sue this hospital for abuse and violation of my rights as a patient. When my attorney calls on me, I expect that he will be extended every courtesy. This interview is ended."

In retrospect, I suspect that I should not have been so forthright with my stated intent to sue, for by the time my attorney subpoenaed my records, they had been changed to reflect an inaccurate and untrue picture of what had happened. The doctor's order had been removed and a new page inserted bearing no instructive notation as to the manner of administering the injection. I was stupid, for I knew that doctors regularly rewrite charts for purposes of clarity; if they do it to clarify, why not to conceal?

Without the formal evidence of official malfeasance, we had no recourse, and the court action was eventually dropped. But with the threat of legal action impending, word must have spread rapidly, for from that time onward, I was a pariah, and my dealings with the hospital were to be badly compromised. The issue of patient abuse and violation of rights would never be legally addressed.

In light of the apparent negligence of the staff, I became very apprehensive when my family went home at night, and they accommodated my fears by setting up a shift system for babysitting me. The stated goal of my treatment was to enable me to enter therapy at Health South Rehabilitation Hospital, and now it became a race with time. About the middle of October, all was in readiness for the transfer, and ambulance transport was arranged. I was delighted to be back on track toward recovery, and I am sure that the hospital management was equally happy to see me leave.

An ambulance was arranged to transfer me to Health South Rehabilitation Hospital. Peggy rode up front with the driver, and an attendant was in the back with me. We drove into the Health South loading zone and prepared to unload. Peggy stood on the curb by the ambulance door. The driver pulled the transport gurney foot forward toward the door as my attendant assisted at the head. As my head cleared the door, the gurney legs collapsed and I was thrown violently onto the asphalt, still strapped to the gurney, which was now upside down on top of me. The right side of my face and temple took the full force of the fall. Of course, I could not be moved until photos were taken and the accident had been fully documented. It seemed to take forever. A huge bump was raised in my temple area, with a gross discoloration of my face and right eye.

It was determined that the attendant had failed to ensure that the gurney legs were fully extended and locked, so that they collapsed under my weight. I was rushed back to the hospital and thoroughly scoped, MRI'd, poked, prodded, and x-rayed. It was shown that I had sustained a concussion with bleeding in the brain, and I came to understand that my injuries were life-threatening, especially when a doctor kept showing up to insist that Peggy sign a "do not resuscitate" order to be placed in my chart. I was reassured and relieved when she declined to comply, though I did take steps to assign certain clean-up chores in case I did not survive to do them myself.

Results showed that my injuries were much more serious than I had initially thought. I would gradually lose the ability to move my arms, hands, and legs, to speak intelligibly, to cough on command, and to swallow. I was now effectively paralyzed from the neck down, with oxygen being administered, an IV needle in my arm, and a feeding tube up my nose. In this instance, a suit was filed, resulting in an eventual settlement.

The doctor informed me of the possible need for surgery to relieve pressure on my brain, and I signed the consent form, though we agreed to a plan of "watchful waiting." I recall asking him about my chances of survival and being told they were fifty-fifty, depending to a great extent on my own will to live.

The family shift work of daddy-sitting was reinstituted and, though I cannot be sure of course, I credit their faithful attendance and assistance with my continued existence. My nephews, Bill and Greg Kopp, came to keep me company and to lend a hand. Debbie Wisenhunt continued to visit frequently. My niece, Carol Chinchello, and my sister-in-law, Lorene Goff, came from West Virginia and spent a few days. I must say "a hearty God bless you" to each of them. I found their presence made a positive difference in my comfort level, for through it all I remained unaccountably fearful and paranoid about hospital personnel.

Being alone without family present seemed a much greater threat than dying. Several prayer circles were busily engaged on my behalf, and I am grateful for them all. Cousins Bill Bailey and Don Lowe sent almost daily messages of encouragement and good humor, for which I am most appreciative. I do believe in laughter as good medicine.

The family gathered to give support.

Soon after the ambulance accident, I revisited the nasogastric feeding apparatus, with scheduled feedings every six hours. At that point I had not "eaten" for about eight hours, so the feeding paraphernalia was rolled in, including a portable scope device that would enable the progress of the procedure to be graphically monitored. As a nurse filled a big syringe with liquefied nutrition and forced it into the end of the tube leading down the esophagus into my stomach, I was reminded of how the French used to force-feed geese in the production of *pâté foi gras*. The practice has now been discontinued for geese, I am told, though evidently not for humans. I watched the screen as my stomach filled up with fluid. The technician continued the force feeding, and as the monitor showed the liquid rising into my chest level, I knew, up close and personal, just how that goose must have felt.

"Hey," I gurgled, "I'm running over."

"That can't be," replied the nurse, consulting the graduations on the side of her syringe, "I still have six more ounces to go."

She continued to force the plunger. At that point, Linda burst forth and started yelling "Stop, he's aspirating!"

Her warning came too late, as the fluid had spilled over into my lungs. I have no recollection of how my "drowning" was resolved, but when I regained awareness, it was pneumonia time again, and I deduced that in a moment of delirium I had pulled the nasal tubes out of my stomach and nose. I was being scheduled for surgery to insert a permanent feeding tube directly through the stomach wall.

Some difficulty was encountered in locating a surgeon to do the procedure, but one was finally found and surgery was scheduled immediately.

When the doctors arrived, there was a great flurry of activity. The scene was reminiscent of a formal changing of the guard. Situation reports were crisply given and crew number one evaporated. A whole new gang took over with a great deal more solemnity and seriousness of purpose than the first. The chief surgeon lifted the draping sheet from my face and said, "I'll be doing your surgery now, and we'll be using a local anesthesia." With that he dropped the drape back in place and an injection was given at the site of the incision. The surgical team proceeded efficiently, as the quiet babble of background voices diminished to near silence.

Soon I was aware that the event was in the final inning. The surgeon described for the listening ear of his public, and for posterity, that the tube was now fully inserted through the stomach wall and was being stitched to the skin of the abdomen as insurance against being accidentally pulled out. He was using a suture of organic material, which would remain in place for one month, at which time it would deteriorate and permit removal of the tube. I would have occasion to remember his remarks a few weeks later when the tube came out unintentionally.

Normal and satisfactory progress was evidently made, for I was soon again scheduled for discharge to Health South. Some negotiation was required to persuade Health South to accept my transfer with an indwelling catheter and feeding tube, and I was very happy when they relented and allowed the move to take place. Now I would finally be able to get on with my rehabilitation through intensive therapy.

The relocation took place late in the day and, this time, was without mishap. I settled gratefully into my bed at Health South, where I was attended by a battery of medical personnel who saw to my admission. I was surprised to be awakened at 5:00 a.m. by the Chief of Respiratory Therapy, who showed evidence of concern. My doctor was summoned, and it was determined that I had been discharged the day before with the pneumonia issue unresolved. I would have to return to the hospital for a resumption of medical treatment.

It was family conference time. We quickly decided that it was time to try another hospital, and there was agreement that although we were running out of choices, this time we would try St. Joseph's Hospital, one of Albuquerque's large medical establishments of good reputation. Inquiry was made and agreement was reached that I would be permitted to have a family member in attendance at all times. We proceeded with the uneventful transfer to St. Joe's.

It would seem that all hospitals would be so alike as to be almost indistinguishable from one another. But the atmosphere in each is so different as to be quickly recognizable. There is a subtle atmosphere about each and a distinct attitude among the staff distinguishing each from the other, a phenomenon I had long since discovered sets US Navy ships apart from one another. For the most part, St. Joe's was a peaceful island in the turbulent ocean of sickness and recovery.

Becky was really quite awesome. She had grown into a very knowledgeable, firm, and effective ombudsman for me. She informed herself about procedures and staff responsibilities, was unfailingly polite and pleasant, but was never hesitant to point out instances of dereliction or neglect. For example, she came into my room one Monday morning and asked, "Did you get your bath today?" I suspect that she smelled me.

"No," I replied, "and not yesterday or the day before."

"Let me find someone," she said. She went to the chart desk and, finding the nurse absent, requested that she come to my room when she returned. Upon her arrival, Becky quoted from the guidelines for patient care that patients were to be bathed at least every second day with a sponge bath on alternate days.

"Well, a bath was charted," the nurse responded. She immediately called the responsible aides and asked them to explain. They stated that when I had an "accident" they always wiped me off with a washcloth and charted it as a bath.

"That is totally unacceptable," Becky stated firmly. "I expect that my father will be fully bathed now and that the rules for bathing will be followed in the future."

She was never unpleasant but she did get results, and the staff never showed any open sign of resentment, though I suspect that some may have had some secret dark thoughts when they saw her arriving. I was grateful to have her loyal watch care, and am sure that the certainty of her intervention corrected many problems and prevented numerous others.

My physical state at this point was that although I felt relatively little discomfort, I remained virtually paralyzed from the neck down, including my vocal chords. I had slowly regained most of my vocal usage, but had little or no control over my limbs or bodily functions. It had been most frustrating to have my spoken words bear little or no resemblance to the idea I was trying to express, but eventually, I had become able, for the most part, to make my words and thoughts match. At one point, we communicated by means of a visual alphabet, someone pointing to a letter on a chart and my giving a thumbs up or down for yes or no, laboriously spelling out words, letter by letter. For a time I became fixated on the fear that I would lose my vocabulary and be unable to communicate meaningfully, so found myself using the longest, most complicated words I could remember. I reasoned that if I could recall the big words, the little ones would come on their own.

The right side of my body had been most seriously affected by the stroke, and it was an occasion for rejoicing when I found that my right thumb would move on demand. I spent hours mentally typing on an imaginary keyboard, trying to will my fingers to make the correct responses, but with limited success. I found that while the nerve pathways remained open, the sinews permitting muscular movement relaxed and contracted so slowly that meaningful, directed motion was functionally often insignificant. My right hand would grasp an object, but turning loose was a whole different problem. Reaching out was accomplished easily enough, but withdrawing, which required a different set of muscles and tendons, was a difficulty of another degree of magnitude, a difficulty that remains more than two years later.

Health South was a very good place from the first day. The staff was well-trained and motivated, and they were able to transfer their constructive and optimistic attitude to patients. At this point, we decided that we could safely dispense with the round-the-clock family watch. After a few days of bed exercises, I was delighted when told that I was ready for the physical therapy room and was introduced to my two primary therapists, Suzie and Sally. From the beginning, I was given to understand that while they stood by to help, I would have to do the hard labor. They were friendly and likeable but adopted a no-nonsense attitude toward their work.

The next morning, Suzie, the occupational therapist, showed up at 6:00 with a grasping device about two feet long. She helped me to sit on the edge of my bed, showed me how to use the "reacher" to dress myself, and then stood by while I struggled with the task at hand. I soon learned to do everything except put on my shoes and pull up and fasten my pants, things I still labor unsuccessfully to accomplish. She was soon joined by Sally, her partner physical therapist. Sally asked me, "What is the one thing you most want to do in therapy?"

"To stand on my own two feet," I replied quickly.

I suspect that she already knew what my answer would be, for she promptly responded, "OK. Today we will stand."

We proceeded immediately to the therapy room, a large gymnasium-like affair filled with a bewildering array of equipment and an assortment of physical, occupational, and speech therapists. My two female therapists were joined by three large muscular males before a pile of specially pre-cut lumber. "This is a standing frame," Sally explained. "We are going to help you stand on your feet while we construct the frame around you."

Two of the men stood me upright and supported me, while the other therapists built up the enclosure around me, stick by pre-cut stick. Then, inserting bracing members under my elbows and others to block my knees, I was made to stand. It took the best efforts of five people and was not something that I was willing to settle for permanently, but it was a start. After all, the longest journey begins with a single step. I had stood on my own two feet and believed that I might do so again. It was only 9:00 a.m., and already it was one of the best days of my life.

Gwen, my physical therapist

The physical therapy progressed very quickly. Nearly every day, activity advanced to a new level. There were no huge breakthroughs, but there was a steady succession of small steps forward that gave constant encouragement and motivation. My right side remained largely unresponsive, but soon I was standing in the parallel bars and could move the left foot forward and drag the right up to the same level. The feeding tube remained in my stomach wall, and I still could not swallow. That was a big unknown and therefore a problem, for I could not even be considered for discharge until both were resolved. A new goal was set for discharge to day therapy on December 20.

Gwen, the speech therapist, broke out her big guns. "How would you like a nice big dish of ice cream," she asked.

"But I can't swallow," I said.

"We are going to start working on that right now," she answered, as she produced a cup of ice and a stainless steel dental tool. "This is called 'thermal stimulation,'" she said. "We chill the dental tool in the ice and touch it to a point near your tonsils. Usually it triggers an automatic swallowing response. I will show you how and then let you try."

She touched the back of my throat near the tonsils and I swallowed. Neat! "Now you try," she said, as she returned the tool to the ice. Looking in a mirror, I did as suggested. Again I swallowed. "Practice," she suggested, "and count. When you have dry-swallowed a hundred times, you can have ice cream." By Monday morning I had swallowed five hundred times and could usually do it without thermal stimulation.

Within a day or so, I was taking meals in the dining room and, except for a few minor episodes of choking when something did not go down just right, I had no real problems. Liquids were difficult and for a time had to be mixed with a thickening powder. There is something lacking in hot coffee thickened to the consistency of cream of tomato soup. Water is not only the most difficult of liquids because it is the thinnest; it is also the most unappetizing when thickened. And after two months of taking nothing by mouth, the ice cream, which I had so looked forward to, was so sweet initially as to be almost sickening.

The feeding tube had been left in place until there was reasonable confidence that I could take solid foods without choking. I was scheduled for a computerized swallowing study at the hospital. A long wait ensued in the waiting room. Of course, since I had not yet gained full control of my bodily functions, I was wearing a plastic and paper diaper with adhesive pull-tabs. I could wait, but not very long, and I had learned that a felt need must be attended promptly if disaster was to be averted. I felt the need and informed my attendant, "Hey, I gotta' go!"

I had long ago discovered that a need on my part did not necessarily induce a positive and timely response in others who felt no corresponding sense of urgency. The nurse began a leisurely search for an orderly to assist me, but help came too late. We hastened to the bathroom, a skimpy affair consisting of a toilet and wash basin located in a converted broom closet. There was not sufficient room for myself and my attendant, leaving little room to maneuver onto the commode. In the turmoil of getting in position, neither of us thought to check the feeding tube which, in keeping with the attending chaos, had become stuck to one of the diaper's plastic pull-tabs.

It was reminiscent of a Charlie Brown moment. The feeding tube pulled out of my stomach and plopped wetly onto the filthy floor of

Coming home, with Peggy and Butch

the restroom. A surgeon would be needed to insert a new tube, but the practitioner who had initially placed it was unavailable. A substitute was summoned and he clearly was not pleased to have been tapped for the job, but it was eventually accomplished with a predictable amount of grumbling and discontent. Much of his unhappiness was directed toward the original surgeon, who apparently should have anchored the tube with an inflatable bulb on the end, preventing accidental dislodgement. Hours later, we were on our way back to Health South, and I was feeling hungry and very well-used.

My new discharge date was set to coincide with the expiration of my inpatient Medicare contract, December 20, 2002. It was understood that I would continue with home therapy on an outpatient basis. As the countdown continued toward discharge, it was evident that giant steps toward recovery were a thing of the past. Future progress, if any, would be measured in tiny increments.

December 20 came and with it came a huge surprise. Eager as I was to go home, I was not happy to learn the course my outpatient therapy would take. It seemed that in order to provide staff with an extended Christmas holiday, the decision had been made to discontinue therapy for all patients and to virtually close up the shop for the three weeks until January 12, 2003. Though I protested vigorously, as I am sure other patients did also, on the basis that virtually all gains would be lost during so long a hiatus, the decision would not be reversed and, at least in my case, my prediction proved to be true. By the time outpatient treatment resumed, I had lost function to such an extent that I was never to regain the performance level of December 20.

The Health South van picked me up at home each morning after eight o'clock and dropped me off in the afternoon about 4:00. During that period, Health South made the national network news regularly. The organization had come under critical scrutiny for the excessive salaries and profligate spending by the CEO and his staff, and the corporation faced imminent bankruptcy proceedings. Impact on the therapy room was almost immediate and negative. Staff-to-patient ratios plummeted. The Medicare-mandated requirement of forty minutes of active therapy per hour diminished to twelve to fifteen minutes of real-time treatment. I am sure that Medicare continued to be charged the full hourly rate, but now each therapist worked simultaneously with three or four patients, moving from one to the other in turn, and patients spent much of their time waiting for the availability of therapists or equipment.

It was during this period that my doctor, who was busily engaged in setting up her own private practice and dissociating herself from Health South, began a series of experiments with muscle relaxant medications to combat severe leg cramps and spasms. The problem was that they worked too well. Even the minimum dosage made me so weak that I could not function at any level. By the time a dose was administered and recovery from its ill effects was accomplished, a week or more had passed with a corresponding loss of performance. It became very frustrating and irritating. I looked forward to dropping back from day-patient status to home-based therapy, in which a team of therapists and aides would work with me two or three days per week in the home. At least I would be spared the 14-mile long commute by van to the hospital each day.

At that time my doctors and the family had arrived at the conclusion that Peggy and I should not continue to attempt to live independently. She had suffered several episodes of phlebitis and cardiac symptoms and was physically unable to provide the assistance I needed. Reluctantly, the decision was made to sell our home in Albuquerque and move to Kentucky to be near Linda and her family. Butch lived in Oregon, and Becky's own state of health was such that she could not give the necessary level of care and attention. Within days, the house was sold and we were deep into packing and planning for the transfer.

My state of strength and mobility demanded air transport, and arrangements were made with Great Plains Airline for a flight to Nashville, where Willem, my son-in-law, would meet us for the two-hour trip by car to their home in Hanson, Kentucky. The transfer was accomplished without incident. Instead of buying an existing house, which would have to be extensively remodeled to make it wheelchair friendly, we decided to take up Linda and Willem's generous offer to permit a separate wing to be added to their home.

It is a lovely site, with a peaceful rural atmosphere and a superb view of Otter Lake. There we could maintain a separate residence conveniently located for Linda's access because the burden of supervision of our care would necessarily fall on her. It would become necessary to hire a housekeeper one day per week and a personal aide for four hours daily to assist with bathing, dressing, exercise, etc. In the interim, until our quarters could be built, we would store our household goods in their garage and occupy their bedroom, becoming a part of their family unit.

Addition under construction

No one dreamed that settling on a design and the actual construction of our apartment would be so time-consuming. Although we were all conscious of the passage of time, the approach of winter made it mandatory to postpone the commencement of construction until more favorable weather returned in the spring.

Meanwhile, Peggy was experiencing increased forgetfulness, decreased attention span, and a lack of energy and alertness that was uncharacteristic and alarming. She was found to have an abnormally low heart rate of 23 beats per minute, and a pacemaker was prescribed. At this time, almost a year later, we are very pleased with the pacemaker, for it has helped to restore much of her old personality, vigor, and alertness.

Once underway in late April 2004, given the expected delays and interruptions occasioned by weather and scheduling, the building has moved ahead much as scheduled and is now, in early November, nearly completed. It is a two-story plan with large porches upstairs and down, two bedrooms, two baths, kitchen, great room, and multipurpose room. It is the largest home we have ever owned, much of which is devoted to the accommodation of my handicap and my wheelchair. We feel very fortunate.

Peggy and Sidney Lowe
65th Wedding Anniversary • March 30, 2006, Hanson, KY

AFTERWORD
Homeward Bound

by Linda Lowe

Most of the previous pages were written by Sidney, my father, beginning in 1993. This was a time when he was collecting old photographs and writing family histories and stories. He and Mother were living in Albuquerque, New Mexico. My sister Rebecca and her two sons lived in NW Albuquerque, about 20 minutes from Mother and Dad. I lived with my family in NE Albuquerque, less than ten minutes from them. Except for my brother and his family, who were fifteen hundred miles away in Eugene, Oregon, we saw a lot of each other and often had family dinners and celebrations. Dad came to my house most mornings, where we worked together in my little backyard office on various writing and ancestry projects. As he left about noon, he would always say, "Well, that was a good day's work."

In 2002, my husband, Willem, was transferred by his employer to Madisonville, Kentucky. Willem and our two college-age children went ahead to the new house while I stayed behind in Albuquerque to sell the old one and supervise the packing and moving. When my work was completed on the evening of September 18, I went to spend the night with Mother and Dad. On Thursday the 19th, they took me to the airport so I could join my family in Kentucky.

I was just getting settled in when the call came that fateful Saturday, September 21, 2002, when Dad was taken to the hospital having a major stroke. It had started slowly so that he didn't fully realize what was happening. Close to noon, when he was out running errands with Mother, the symptoms could no longer be denied. Mother somehow got him back home and called an ambulance. She alerted Becky, but Becky waited until Sunday to call me to come home urgently.

I repacked my bags and went straight back to Albuquerque. There I was joined by my brother and the rest of the family for an eight-month odyssey of navigating a major family crisis. During those eight months, none of us left the scene except for four days around Christmas, when Butch and I attempted a short visit to our own families in Oregon and Kentucky. But Becky called, asking us to return to Albuquerque immediately.

My brother took a leave of absence from his work, and together, he and I coordinated and organized to make sure Mother's needs were met at home and a round-the-clock care schedule was maintained for Dad. Becky worked hard at finding local support, especially with the health-care facilities and medical details. Dad later said that he would never have survived the stroke without the love, support, and encouragement of so many friends and family. His stroke was extreme and had many complications, and I do believe he was right: "Getting Daddy Well" was a total love effort. The severity of his situation was underlined for us by several doctors who attempted to persuade the family to approve DNR (Do Not Resuscitate) orders. Our guiding light was Dad himself, who categorically refused to consider any such option and who exhibited an indomitable will to live. We, of course, voiced our own selfish desires to keep him among us, and we formed an impenetrable wall of defiance!

Of course, there were months of hospitals, rehab facilities, and constant discussions about what was going to come next: how they would manage. No facility would accept them living jointly because their care needs were so different. Months of visits with Dad at various facilities passed, and eventually he was released to outpatient care.

Once home, the dynamic changed from survival to making decisions about long-term care. None of us could bear the idea of them being maintained in separate facilities, away from the sustaining support they had come to depend on. As an added complication, it had become very apparent that Mother was undergoing significant mental decline. She was simply incapable of caring for Dad or for herself beyond her personal grooming. She could no longer cook, pay bills, make appointments, or manage daily maintenance decisions, and she no longer drove. Their health-care needs were not even in the same realm.

After agonizing over the decision of what to do and where to go, Dad and Mother finally accepted our offer to come to Kentucky, where they would build a house attached to ours and where we could oversee their care. The team, headed by Dad, focused on the many goals that needed to be achieved by May 2, as I wanted to be home in Kentucky for my wedding anniversary on May 4. We intuitively transformed into a unified unit with a sole purpose. Without any discussion that I can remember, Becky continued to get Dad back and forth to rehab every day and to see to his medical care, while Butch and I tackled cleaning out and organizing the accumulation of fifty-seven years of household goods and memorabilia. They had a large house with three bedrooms, a full attic, an underground structure, a 2½-car garage full of workshop tools, etc. By May 2, the team had the house sold, the furniture and personal items were either packed or given away, and the three of us—Mother, Dad, and I—boarded a plane out of Albuquerque.

There was only one plane that would accommodate our needs—a Great Plains Airlines flight from Albuquerque, to Denver, to Nashville that would not require us to change planes; changing planes was NOT an option. The airline was a godsend and made every effort to arrange the details of both boarding in Albuquerque and deboarding in Nashville. This was a major undertaking for all of us.

After his stroke, I became adept at the maneuvers essential to manhandling him from one place to another. Getting all of us from Albuquerque to Nashville gave even me a challenge as I moved him from one conveyance to another. Dad had to be loaded on the plane before all other passengers using a special freight elevator. Once on the plane, he had to be transferred to an armless rolling chair that could squeeze down the aisle and moved to the first seat in his row. While the crew held him securely in place, I stood on the seat behind him and lifted his entire weight to slide him over and situate him into the safer middle seat. It was definitely a group effort, and the crew was very supportive throughout. I don't think they had been asked to do anything similar before. Once we arrived in Nashville and all the other passengers had disembarked, we reversed the procedure.

My husband had brought my very roomy 1978 Lincoln Continental (which the kids nicknamed the USS *Nimitz* due to its size and tendency to wallow) to Nashville to collect us. First, however, we had to find a place for Dad to empty his bladder. True, I had fitted him with a catheter before leaving Albuquerque, but it had been a very long day and a collection bag can only hold so much. We decided our best bet was a nearby park that had a picnic table on a knoll. We wheeled him to the top, held blankets up high and encircled him for the best privacy we could manage while he held on to the table and we emptied his collection bag. We were prepared for the two-hour drive home.

My Lincoln Continental

I tell this story in detail only to illustrate the challenges Dad faced every time he left the comforts of home. Gas station bathrooms often had the access aisles filled with cartons stacked five-high. Most incredible to me, hospital toilets were often too small to accommodate wheelchairs! The barriers to people with special needs were endless. And this was 2003, well after the Americans with Disabilities Act of 1990!

Otter Lake house with the new addition on the left

In any case, we finally got him and Mother to their new home on Otter Lake Loop in Hanson, Kentucky. This was the house Willem and I had bought just months before Dad had his stroke, and it was decidedly handicap unfriendly. We got an electric stair chair so he could go upstairs to the primary bedroom he and Mother shared, but we had to cut the bathroom door out so he could get to the toilet. There was no solution for showering until we built a cube out of PVC pipe and hung shower curtains around it. We hooked up a hose to the hot water faucet in the laundry room and set up the whole contraption on the back deck overlooking the lake. Dad loved this!

Though the houses on the lake were on multi-acre lots and we could not actually see the other houses clearly, Dad thought it was hilarious to pull himself upright by the handrail, naked except for a towel wrapped around his waist, and call out to all the neighbors, "Good morning, ladies!" He put his all into the performance and would call out in his loudest little tiny voice, still profoundly affected by the stroke. He was sure this was the greatest joke possible on the dignity of this well-heeled community, and he was delighted. He repeated it daily until the cold weather forced him indoors, where we had managed to make changes to yet another bathroom where he could bathe properly.

View of the neighborhood from the back deck where Dad did his exercises.

My son, Chris, helping Dad with morning standing exercises.

We were all well aware that Dad was 100% quadriplegic, totally paralyzed except for minimal use of his left forearm, hand, and his head. Fortunately, he had regained total mastery of his mind and speech faculties. At his most incapacitated, when the strokes were still attacking him relentlessly, he could only communicate with us by blinking his eyes or doing thumbs-up when we held up a spelling board and pointed to various letters. Even then, he would insist on spelling out the whole sentence and using the longest word he could think of for the purpose. I asked him once why he didn't just say "cold" when he wanted a blanket. He replied that he was exercising his vocabulary, and he made us spell out that whole sentence, too!

He could read, carry on interesting conversations, and participate in instructing us in his care. He even kept close track of when the gas gauge on the car would be down to the last quarter tank, and would admonish us to fill up with gas. With great difficulty and much concentration, he could eventually sign his name, but he usually allowed me to write and sign his checks. He insisted on having a desktop computer, a laptop, and an iPad. Only the telephone remained beyond his abilities to manipulate, as he could not dial the numbers reliably or hold it up to his ear. He dreamt until the last couple of years of his life of regaining enough control of his body to drive his handicap van with a left-hand steering control. He always had goals!

Pookie

Cassie "harassing" Dad

Sometimes his adventures on the computer provided for moments of levity. He loved to push the buttons—any buttons. Every now and then his screen would be inundated by porn sites and he would call to me: "Get Chris (my son) over here. There are a bunch of naked women on my computer."

He also managed to sign up for "lifetime" French lessons. One day, a large and heavy box was delivered in his name. I wasn't expecting anything, and when I opened it, I found a huge array of CDs for learning French. When I asked him if he had ordered a lifetime course of French lessons he said no, but he might have signed up for a sample. I said I didn't know he was interested in learning French. "No, not particularly," he said. "But I do like to get things in the mail." Of course, I immediately called the "lifetime lessons" company to ask if I could return the kit. I explained that my dad was in his eighties and was exploring new things on his computer. The lady on the other end responded very sweetly, "No problem. Just send everything back. We get a lot of that."

He had a motorized wheelchair and loved demonstrating in the driveway that it could go six miles an hour. Sometimes we attached a flag to the chair and walked alongside him as he drove the two miles around the lake. He loved pointing out the different kinds of birds' nests and identifying the bird calls. Mockingbirds were among his favorites because they could sound like so many of their neighbors, but they were no match for Dad.

Dad on a "walk"

We lived happily side by side for 11½ years, until Mother passed away on June 23, 2012. Mother died of complications of diabetes, having had a blood clot behind her right knee followed by an amputation of the lower leg. She also had congestive heart failure, kidney failure, sepsis (an infection of the blood), an infection of her stump wound, an infection of her stomach lining, a second blood clot behind the left knee, and finally, a probable embolism in the lung. Her illness was long and painful, but she never complained or expressed any regret. Her most common comment was to say how much she loved Daddy or to ask how Daddy was doing. She was at her sparkly best when we would see she was awake and would call everyone in to crowd around her bed. Even on days when she could no longer speak intelligibly (because of the sepsis), she would try to lead all of us in singing "Amazing Grace." It was her favorite hymn and even when the tune wasn't quite there, we knew what it was and would join in. She was the star of the show and was so pleased with herself, laughing and clapping her hands. Her joy was such a gift to us, and we cherish our memories of her kindness, her bravery, and her remarkable resolve to give the best of herself.

Side by side, but too old to race

In the last year or so of her life, she lived half in our world and half in the world beyond. In those dreamy times, she would often be with the family members who had already crossed over. I would go to her room to check on her and she would be laughing.

"Hi, Mommy. You visiting with the sisters?"

"Oh, yes. They are all here." And she would start naming them off.

"Are you picnicking by the brook?" (It was their favorite place on the family farm when they were children.)

"Yes. Rose brought the pintos. She always brings beans. Peanut brought potato salad. She makes the best potato salad." And she would go on to detail all the cousins and aunts who were there and how cool the brook was on their hot feet. They were a very close family and knew no joy in life greater than being together, no less in death than in life.

One of the things that amazed me most was that she resolutely refused to acknowledge that she had lost her leg. We told her several times it was gone, but she would just go on as if we had never said a thing. She saw that it was gone. We took great care of her dressings and her medications. Of course, we expected her to have the normal phantom feelings of her leg being there, but in the eight months she lived as an amputee, her only awareness seemed to be when she would ask us to be careful of her leg when we adjusted her in the bed.

I was with her 24 hours a day and never saw her cry with pain or show any other emotion. The people of her generation were brought up to be stoic, but Mother carried it to an extreme. She equated crying with bringing embarrassment to my father, and that, she would not countenance. When the pain became too severe, she would chant, like a Native American chant. In the hospital, the nurses occasionally asked about her tribe. I could only explain that she refused to cry and the chant was the only indication of her pain level. She simply refused to groan or cry out. As the pain increased, she would chant louder, but she would not cry. I never expect to see the likes of that again.

Dad was also very stoic. When Mother died, I did not see him weep, but he did go off by himself to spend time with her memory. He was torn about having her second leg amputated, but finally agreed that he did not want her to suffer another operation. He also knew that mother was by then blind and deaf as a result of her diabetes, and that sepsis had robbed her of her mental abilities. He knew she would not have wanted to live in that state for the sake of staying alive, and he did not want her to suffer any more. Finally, we all agreed that we would deny the second amputation, confident that would also have been her choice. She lived four months beyond that decision.

We often talked about her, telling funny stories or remarking on how much we missed her sweetness and her naivete. About 1978, we joined all our families and met in Hawaii for a vacation. Mother had always been blind in her left eye due to lazy eye, and she didn't see all that well with the other eye.

Hawaii 1978, second honeymoon

One day we took her on a pedicab tour in Honolulu. Our driver was a handsome young surfer type with blonde hair and a colorful T-shirt that read, "I'm a Virgin!" Mother climbed in the cab, took note of his T-shirt and exclaimed, "Oh, I'm from Virginia, too!" Needless to say, our driver was thereafter enchanted with Mom.

Mother did have a driver's license for a one-eyed driver. We were never quite sure how the DMV decided that was a good idea, but she never had an accident until she was in her seventies, and then it was with a parked car! After that, she refused to ever drive again. But up until then, she drove in our neighborhoods wherever we lived.

One day she drove to a nearby shopping center and as she passed Sears, there was a man wearing a raincoat at a crosswalk. As she passed him, he flashed her. She got a few feet away and slammed on the brakes. Then she backed up. Not sure she could trust her eye, she stopped, leaned forward, took a good long look, and satisfied that she had indeed seen a man flash her—TWICE—she drove off. When she got home, she was thrilled to tell us about her adventure, but what really astonished her was that he had so little to be so proud of. "If that's all I had, I don't think I'd be showing it off," she said. That was so Mom.

Dad's overriding wish was that he would outlive Mother. He had promised her that he would always take care of her and as long as he was alive, she would have all the resources she needed. And her greatest desire was that she would never have to live without him. As it happened, they lived almost the same number of days on this earth (Dad, 32,074 and Mother, 32,038). He lived about seven months after she died (to tie up all the loose ends), but she was six months older than he was. How remarkable was that? They spent their whole married life in perfect tune like that.

He was able to take care of her until the end. He sat beside her in his wheelchair and held her hand until she breathed her last. I started to feel for a heartbeat, but he said, "NO! No! Don't do that! Just let her be." She had been through so much and she deserved the peace that was finally hers.

That was June 23, 2012. A few days later Mother's cremains were returned to us in a beautiful blue cloisonne urn. Dad had begun searching stones and markers for their grave many months before, but after Mother passed, he started making decisions. He gave careful consideration to the design and color of the stone. We had to go visit an actual monument store to see the "real" colors. He liked the rose, the black, and the mahogany stones best. We finally decided that the rose didn't look much like him, the black didn't look much like Mother, but the mahogany was just the perfect color for them together. He liked that the stone came from Mount Rushmore.

He had written a poem for the stone many years before:

A Single Rose

Bring me a single rose of crimson hue,
To catch and hold the sparkling dew,
To represent the tears by loved ones shed,
Above my resting place when I am dead.
Its fallen petals kiss the earthen mound,
And lie in blessing on my burial ground.
A single rose, in loving memory brought,
Shall wed us to the earth, and thus to God.

Once the script for the names and dates was decided, he realized there was no room for the poem. "Let's put it on the back," I said. Dad and Mother both liked to get full value for their money, so when I pointed out that there would be no extra charge to have it engraved on the back as long as we did it when the stone was ordered, he loved the idea!

I searched the Bible for a verse to put on the front of the stone and found Proverbs 3:24:

"When thou liest down, Thou shalt not be afraid:
Yea, thou shalt lie down, and thy sleep shall be sweet."

We chose it with Mother in mind, but it was perfect for both of them.

So the stone was ordered, engraved, and set in place at Rocky Branch Cemetery, across the valley from the farm where Dad had grown up and amongst the valleys he and George Boatwright roamed as boys. By the time the stone was engraved and set, it was October, and Dad insisted on going to see for himself that everything was as it should be. I was reluctant to take him on such an arduous trip so late in the year, so I tried to persuade him to wait until spring when the weather might be more stable. "No problem," he said. "If you can't take me, I'll find someone else." Well, that sealed the deal, and I started packing the van.

Dad's health was so precarious, and even at home we lived with a mini-hospital. We had the only motorized ceiling-lift in a private home in Hopkins County—it was for transporting him by sling from one room to another. He had a pneumatic mattress with cylinders that inflated and deflated in sequence to prevent bed sores. He wore a CPAP mask that blew air into his lungs all night because he had complete apnea, and it was hooked up to an oxygen concentrator that sounded like a semi with a jake brake. Mother, of course, had her share of machines, but they were greatly diminished by Dad's hospital array. Being in the bedroom sounded a bit like being in an iron lung of the 1950s.

Getting the van packed for a four- or five-day trip was no small feat. I preplanned with a four-page list that included a case full of medicines, a nebulizer, painkillers, a CPAP machine and oxygen concentrator, emergency pneumonia kits, two wheelchairs (motor and manual), a porta potty, a walker, etc. And the Airport Radisson Inn in Charleston was the only place where we found accommodations with adjoining rooms and bathrooms big enough to hold our traveling circus. Loading took two days.

The momentous weekend arrived, and Dad's fortunes were good—on the same day we made our trek, Dad discovered that his boyhood friend George Boatwright was also going to be at Johnson Creek. He had been living in Florida with his wife, Georgia, but Georgia and her sister had both passed and George was being taken by his sons to New York to live with them. He was stopping briefly in the old neighborhood to bury the ashes of two family members at their family cemetery. This was a bittersweet meeting of two lifelong friends who were afforded a few inadequate moments to meet and say a last goodbye.

George's sons didn't have much time to linger, and the weather was turning bitter cold. A storm was brewing. These were not at all the circumstances I would have wanted for them, for they had no shelter from the weather and no private time to say their farewells. After a few hugs and pats on the backs, a few glances that held a lifetime of love, George climbed in the car with his sons and left for his new home and we headed up the hill to our own cemetery. There, Dad inspected the stone, the color, and the inscriptions and pronounced it a beautiful memorial. He was well-pleased with his and Mother's final resting place, though no remains would be put in place until after Dad had passed.

Dad and George Boatwright, last farewell of old friends

We returned to our home on Otter Lake pleased with how the trip had gone. We agreed this was the easiest trip we had made, and Dad showed no adverse effects from the four days away, though exposed to cold, windy weather, germs from public restaurants, and lots of kisses and handshakes. We even discussed organizing a family reunion in the spring since he had done so well.

October passed and so did November. But in the second week of December, he had to go to the Emergency Room with a bout of low blood pressure. He was admitted and stayed a week while the doctors worked on his heart—atrial fibrillation. He was released and went home. But after 24 hours, he returned to the ER. This pattern repeated, except for a two-day respite for Christmas, with admissions for congestive heart failure (CHF), irregular heartbeat, more atrial fibrillation, pneumonia, a bowel obstruction, sepsis, and a second bout of pneumonia—in all, six week-long stays at the hospital.

Finally, the doctors had no more to offer. There were simply no more medical miracles for organs damaged by thirty years of diabetes and its complications. I had always promised to be honest with him and hide nothing. I went to his bedside and gave him the doctor's report frankly and calmly, then simply asked if he wanted to go home. His doctor made every effort to stabilize him enough to allow that to happen. On Friday, at 4:30 in the afternoon, the ambulance took us home. Characteristically, as he was getting settled in the back of the ambulance, he said, "Where is Linda? Don't forget Linda!" He needn't have worried.

On arriving home, we got him settled in his recliner in the living room. After a bit, the nurse's aide who was helping with his care suggested he might want to start getting ready for bed. "Yes," he said, "but I want to sleep in my bed, in my room." It took four of us to make that happen, as he had been sleeping in his reclining chair in the living room since his series of illnesses. The aide and I stayed up all night, checking on him, turning him, making sure of his comfort.

As morning came, he looked rested and well, and he insisted on getting up in his motorized wheelchair, as was his habit. Chris always attended to his morning routine of going to the bathroom for his grooming and then to his place at the breakfast bar—everything as usual. Almost. Though Chris had prepared his coffee and oatmeal as he had for the last eight years, we discovered Dad had lost his ability to swallow. Still, he sat up in his wheelchair for a while longer, then agreed about 10:00 to be put in his recliner to rest for a while. There, he napped and said something occasionally. I leaned into his ear and said, "Daddy, I'm going to miss you so much."

"I know," he whispered back. A little later he said, "I don't want to die."

"I know, Daddy, but it's not a choice we have."

"I know," he replied.

Several times, it was quite clear Daddy was trying to tell me something, but I couldn't make the sounds into words. Each attempt took his total effort whether it was successful or not. Finally, we talked to him but he no longer tried to talk to us. We told him we loved him and would miss him. I told him how proud I was that he was my father. I promised I would finish putting his writings into books and that I would make sure the estate would be settled fairly and lovingly, just as he had always said he wanted it. I promised I would take care of all the details.

Sometime in the late afternoon, I climbed onto the recliner with him and held his hand. We took a little nap. I knew the time was growing short. The house was stark and quiet. I asked my daughter, Emily, to play some music on Pandora. I thought Dad would like that. The song that was playing was "Claire de Lune." Then we all stood around him in astonished wonderment as "It's Time to Say Goodbye" came on. The song ended and he softly breathed his last. It was January 19, 2013.

Dad and Mother had their cremains buried on May 26, 2013, the Sunday of Memorial Day weekend. There was one day, one service, one grave. His urn, touching hers, will stay for eternity as they were in life—side by side, always touching. There were three songs: "Amazing Grace" for Mother, "Homeward Bound" for Dad, and "Be Still My Soul" for those of us left to mourn. We said whatever poor words we could find to honor them and placed the ashes of their last two dogs in with them. The Marines gave a final salute and the long mournful sound of "Taps" filled the mountain air. Chris and Emily refused the kind offers of other mourners to fill in the grave; that was their final offering of love to their Grandma and Granddad—there on the top of a wind-swept hill, close to where Dad lived his youth, at the end of a long row of grandparents, parents, brothers, and sisters gone before.

Homeward Bound

In the quiet misty morning,
When the moon has gone to bed,
When the sparrows stop their singing,
And the sky is clear and red,

When the summer's ceased its gleaming,
When the corn is past its prime,
When adventure's lost its meaning—
I'll be homeward bound in time.

Bind me not to the pasture,
Chain me not to the plow,
Set me free to find my calling,
And I'll return to you somehow.

If you find it's me you're missing,
If you're hoping I'll return,
To your thoughts I'll soon be list'ning,
And in the road I'll stop and turn;

Then the wind will set me racing,
As my journey nears its end,
And the path I'll be retracing,
When I'm homeward bound again.

Bind me not to the pasture,
Chain me not to the plow,
Set me free to find my calling,
And I'll return to you somehow.

In the quiet misty morning,
When the moon has gone to bed,
When the sparrows stop their singing,
And the sky's clear and red,
When the summer's ceased its gleaming,
When adventure's lost its meaning
I'll be homeward bound in time.

—Folk song, lyrics by Marta Keen Thompson

Acknowledgments

Before he died, I promised my father I would make sure his stories were published. The thought of such a project overwhelmed me, but eventually I started culling through his prolific writings—selecting, organizing, and editing—and ten years later, I sought professional help to bring the project to fruition.

First, I wish to express my gratitude to my friend of fifty years, Jennifer Read Hawthorne, who fell in love with my dad's stories and came out of retirement to edit the book. Jennifer's expertise as an author and editor brought understanding and polish to the manuscript and the process of publishing. I couldn't have done it without her.

I would also like to acknowledge Gary Rosenberg, the book's graphic designer, for the beautiful cover and layout of the book, which capture the essence of the story told here.

A special word of thanks is owed to David Lowe and Keith O'Dell for contributing to the historical richness of these stories by guiding me through the countryside of West Virginia in a quest for pictures to bring my father's stories to life. Their intimate knowledge of Nettie and Spencer, West Virginia, provided photographs and details otherwise not available to me.

A huge thank-you to my daughter, Emily Dave, and her husband, Svarit Dave, for helping me with technical issues, photo sources, and moral support. And my precious grandchildren, Saheli and Yash, for always making me laugh.

Mother and Dad valued family above all else. Sidney and Peggy are pictured on the next page in Albuquerque in 1998 along with their three children, Rebecca, Allen, and me. Rebecca and Allen, always devoted children, showed up to join me full-time for the eight months of stroke recovery with love, emotional support, and physical labor when we all needed each other the most.

The family, Albuquerque, 1998

My children, Emily and Christian, dedicated themselves to the care of their grandparents. Emily was their on-call nurse, and Chris put his career on hold for eight years to be their full-time caregiver. No mother could ask more of her children nor grandparents of their grandchildren.

Emily, Dad, Chris, and Mom

Photo Credits

Editor's Note: Most of the photos in this book are from the personal collection of Sidney D. Lowe and family. I gratefully acknowledge the following people and organizations for additional photos, many of which are in the public domain, and which add substantially to the author's stories. In rare instances where attribution is unspecified, every effort has been made to contact the relevant owners or publishers.

"One-room Schoolhouse" (inside). Courtesy of Mayor Terry A. Williams, City of Spencer, West Virginia.

Marion Post Wolcott. "Abandoned oil well derrick near Charleston, West Virginia," September 1938. Library of Congress, Prints & Photographs Division, Farm Security Administration/Office of War Information Black-and-White Negatives Collection, public domain.

CigarettesPedia. "Wings short pack."

Carolyn M. Highsmith. "Downtown block that includes the Robey Theatre in Spencer, West Virginia." *Wikipedia Commons,* public domain.

Gibson Girl Dress. "Edwardian Victorian riding habit" (Typical Victoria riding habit, similar to my mother's). *Etsy.*

US Department of the Interior. "Looneyville, West Virginia US Topo Map." (The route we took from our farm to Looneyville). Map image courtesy of *MyTopo.*

"1930 Dodge Fire Truck." Courtesy of R.M. Sotheby's.

Tim Kiser. "The Nicholas County Courthouse, Summersville, West Virginia," July 2007. *Wikimedia Commons (CC BY-SA 2.5).*

US Marine Corps. US Marine Corps Emblem, used by permission.*

Wikipedia contributors, "USS *LST-20.*" *Wikipedia, The Free Encyclopedia,* public domain.

The World Factbook. "South Side of the Tarawa Atoll" (Aerial view of Tarawa with Betio island in the foreground). Public domain.

Wikipedia contributors. "Operation Cottage" (Bow door compartment: my improvised bedroom). *Wikipedia, The Free Encyclopedia,* public domain.

Sergeant Tom Lovell, USMC. "Tarawa, South Pacific," 1943 painting (Hundreds died in the chest-deep water.). *Wikimedia Commons,* public domain.

US Marine Corps. "Landing Strip on Betio islet, Tarawa atoll" (Red Beach 1). *Wikimedia Commons,* public domain.

Wikipedia contributors. "Battle of Tarawa" (Laying down a covering fire). *Wikipedia, the Free Encyclopedia,* public domain.

US Marine Corps. "Flamethrower in Tarawa Jungle" (Marine with a flamethrower). *Wikimedia Commons,* public domain.

National Park Service (National Archives, USMC #99547). "Cemetery at Tarawa" (The largest of thirty-seven cemeteries on Tarawa). *Wikipedia, the Free Encyclopedia,* public domain.

Naval History & Heritage Command Photo Section, Photo #NH -95704, "Northwest end of Betio Island, Tarawa" (Aerial view of Betio peninsula, Tarawa atoll), November 1943. Public domain.

Grant. "Betio, Tarawa Atoll, Gilbert Islands" (Map showing Red Beach, where I conducted my nighttime patrol), November 2017. *The Players' Aid.*

Shubham Chatterjee. "Tachypleus gigas" (Horseshoe crab), June 2012. *Wikimedia Commons (CC BY-SA 3.0).*

Paul Asman and Jill Lenoble. "Samoan Flying Fox" (Fruit or fox bat located on Samoa). *Wikimedia Commons (CC BY-2.0).*

Wikipedia contributors, "*Fala Tele* in a Village" (Samonan fale exterior). *Wikipedia, the Free Encyclopedia,* public domain.

University of Otago, "Interior of Samoan House" (Samoan fale interior). Hocken Collections, Uare Taoka o Hākena, University of Otago Pacific Islands Collection » P98-073. Used by permission.

Frederick O'Brien. "White Shadows in the South Seas" (Traditional lavalava dress), circa 1909. *Wikimedia Commons (Gutenberg.org file: 14384),* public domain.

US National Archives. "90mm gun crew." Public domain.

Wikipedia contributors. "A View of Yontan Airfield, Ryukyu Islands, Japan." *Wikipedia, The Free Encyclopedia,* public domain.

Wikipedia contributors. "USMC Corsairs of VMF-311 at Yontan Airfield during Battle of Okinawa" (Dazzling fingers of searchlights). *Wikipedia, the Free Encyclopedia,* public domain.

US Navy. Insignia of the United States Navy Chaplain Corps. Wikimedia Commons, public domain.**

Donald Pearman. "Chevy Straight-8." Pinterest.

Lars-Göran Lindgren Sweden. "REO Speed Wagon Truck," 1939. *Wikimedia Commons (CC BY-SA 3.0).*

Steve Newbauer. "Highlining Between Ships at Sea" (The proper baptism of the padre). *Navysight.*

Marine Corps Association. "Adak Island Base." Public domain.

Naval Facilities Engineering Systems Command (NAVFAC). "Two Soldiers at the Adak Entrance Sign" (Testament to the local sense of humor). Public domain.

US National Park Service Gallery WAPA 2505 photo. "The Matson Line passenger liner SS *Lurline* approaching Pier 10 at Honolulu," 1930s. *Wikimedia Commons,* public domain.

"Canadian LST offloading a Sherman tank, circa 1943" (An LST, Landing, Ship, Tank) *Wikimedia Commons,* public domain.

Leonard G. "SS Red Oak Victory in 2013." *Wikimedia Commons,* CC BY-CC0 1.0, public domain.

US Navy. "USS *Kleinsmith*." Public domain.**

US Navy photo 80-G-418776. "The *USS Boxer* (CV-21)." *Wikimedia Commons,* public domain.**

US Navy. "USS *Estes* (AGC-12)," August 1955. *Wikimedia Commons,* public domain.**

Division of Naval Intelligence, "USS *Nevada* (BB-36)," September 1943. *Wikimedia Commons,* public domain.

---

*Neither the United States Marine Corps nor any other component of the Department of Defense has approved, endorsed, or authorized this book.

** Use of released US Navy imagery does not constitute product or organizational endorsement of any kind by the US Navy.

Made in the USA
Middletown, DE
04 December 2025

24008639R00175